Personality Disorders

Personality Disorders

A Short History of Narcissistic, Borderline, Antisocial, and Other Types

Allan V. Horwitz

Johns Hopkins University Press

Baltimore

© 2023 Johns Hopkins University Press
All rights reserved. Published 2023
Printed in the United States of America on acid-free paper

2 4 6 8 9 7 5 3 1

Johns Hopkins University Press
2715 North Charles Street
Baltimore, Maryland 21218
www.press.jhu.edu

Library of Congress Cataloging-in-Publication Data

Names: Horwitz, Allan V., author.
Title: Personality disorders : a short history of narcissistic, borderline,
antisocial, and other types / Allan V. Horwitz.
Description: Baltimore : Johns Hopkins University Press, 2023. |
Includes bibliographical references and index.
Identifiers: LCCN 2022030974 | ISBN 9781421446103 (hardcover) |
ISBN 9781421446110 (ebook)
Subjects: LCSH: Personality disorders—History. | Personality
disorders—Treatment—History. | Personality disorders—Social aspects.
Classification: LCC RC554 .H675 2023 | DDC 616.85/81—dc23/eng/20220708
LC record available at https://lccn.loc.gov/2022030974

A catalog record for this book is available from the British Library.

*Special discounts are available for bulk purchases of this book. For more information,
please contact Special Sales at specialsales@jh.edu.*

CONTENTS

Most histories of mental illness focus on psychoses such as schizophrenia or bipolar disorder and neuroses including hysteria, anxiety, and depression. Few pay much attention to the personality disorders: maladaptive patterns of behavior, thinking, and feeling that arise in childhood and persist throughout the life course. Yet, for the past century, these conditions have been of central concern to the mental health professions. From the 1930s to the present, patients with personality disorders have made up a considerable proportion of those who receive mental health treatment. Some types—for instance, narcissistic, borderline, or antisocial—are well known in the general culture. Nevertheless, no volume provides a broad, historical, and multidisciplinary overview of the personality disorders and their rise to prominence. This book strives to fill this gap.

Personality disorders raise many challenging questions for students of mental disorders. Perhaps the most perplexing is what a personality disorder is a disorder *of*. For the past two centuries, a core aspect of views about medical disorders is that they are entities that exist outside their unique manifestations in particular men and women. Diseases are unwanted and harmful intrusions on normal functioning with causes, trajectories, and outcomes that do not depend on the characteristics of the people who have them. In contrast, a personality disorder does not interfere with someone's typical way of being because it *is* their typical way of being. They cannot be extracted from the types of people who have them because they are closely entangled with the essential qualities of who someone is. Moreover, both mental and physical disorders are usually seen as objective, value-free entities. Personality disorders, in contrast, intrinsically involve value judgments about desirable and undesirable personality traits. They are, therefore, inseparable from socioculturally and historically shaped evaluations.

Another striking aspect of the personality disorders is the variety of disciplines that have dealt with them. Since the concept of personality arose in the nineteenth century, studies of its disorders have been marked by the rise, fall, and resurgence of a variety of perspectives. At various points in time, psychology, psychoanalysis, the social sciences, and psychiatry—each grounded in different disciplinary assumptions—have brought their particular approaches to bear on the causes of and responses to the personality disorders. The resulting variety of views is intensified by the distinct outlooks of researchers who study and clinicians who treat these conditions. Unsurprisingly, controversies about virtually every aspect of personality disorders have perennially marked their investigation. Sharp disagreements, including whether they are viewed as medical diseases or problems in living, as distinct entities or extreme variants of normal personalities, or as conditions to be studied through scientific or intuitive methods, have recurred from the beginning.

Any study of personality disorders inevitably involves consideration of personality in general. "Disorder" implies that something has gone wrong with some process or structure so that all conceptions of personality disorder unavoidably have to account for what constitutes a "normal" personality. Some insist that what are called "personality disorders" are more intense versions of normal personality traits, others that relatively clear boundaries exist between disordered and normal personalities, yet others contend the very notion of a "personality disorder" is misguided. This book necessarily examines not just personality disorders but also views of personality more generally.

A final word regards terminology. The terms "character" and "personality" are often employed distinctly but are sometimes used interchangeably. Before the twentieth century "character" was by far the more common usage. "Personality" emerged in the early twentieth century as the preferred term among American psychologists, who considered the notion of character too value laden. In contrast, personality was presumably a descriptive appraisal that carried no judgmental connotations. To the present, psychologists rarely mention "character" in their works. Psychiatrists, too, have generally referred to the phenomenon they study as "personality," not character. The *Diagnostic and Statistical Manual of Mental Disorders* (DSM), for example, contains elaborate discussions of personality disorders, but the word "character" does not appear in its index. In contrast, psychoanalysts, neo-Freudians, social scientists, and many clinicians use the two terms interchangeably. I have similarly taken liberties in employing these two terms.

✳

This book has greatly profited from the work of many specialists in the field. I am particularly indebted to two anonymous reviewers whose detailed critiques made many invaluable suggestions. While the references and bibliography indicate the sources I have relied on, I have especially benefited from the writings of Roger Blashfield, Marjorie Garber, Elizabeth Lunbeck, George Makari, the late Theodore Millan, Joel Paris, and Thomas Widiger. I am also grateful to Christopher Lane for generously sharing his files on the *DSM-III* deliberations and to Deena Gorland, the librarian at the Melvin Sabshin Library and Archive of the American Psychiatric Association, for granting me permission to use this material here. This collection is referred to as "DSM Coll." in the notes to the chapters. Other friends and colleagues including Marta Elliott, David Mechanic, Jane Miller, and Peter Zachar have been sources of support for this project. At Johns Hopkins University Press, Matt McAdam, Kait Howard, and Adriahna Conway have provided invaluable assistance. Carrie Watterson has once again been an incredibly astute and helpful copyeditor.

Personality Disorders

CHAPTER ONE

Issues

Since the early part of the nineteenth century, psychiatrists and other mental health professionals have striven to describe mental disorders through the same disease models that apply to physical ailments. Diseases are entities with common trajectories, causes, and treatments that are independent of particular individual characteristics. Arguably, the disease model fits mental states such as panic attacks, melancholic depressions, invasive thoughts, or posttraumatic flashbacks that are unwanted intrusions on people's senses of self and can be studied and treated without regard to their personal features. The same, however, cannot be said about the personality disorders, which definitionally involve basic aspects of who a person is. The modern history of these conditions is marked by recurring efforts to shape them into medical entities. In addition to their holistic qualities, personality disorders intrinsically feature values that stem from cultural norms rather than universal standards of physical or mental functioning. This means that accounts of personality disorders often contain judgments of disliked behaviors that are far removed from objective descriptions of natural processes. From their earliest formulations through their current definitions in the *Diagnostic and Statistical Manual of Mental Disorders*, fifth edition (*DSM-5*), criteria for the personality disorders have combined accusatory judgments with clinical assessments.

What Is Character?

Around 320 BCE the philosopher Theophrastus, a student of Aristotle, created early portrayals of individuals and their defects in his work *Characters*. Theophrastus sketched vivid single-paragraph portraits of thirty diverse types

such as the Dissembler, the Flatterer, the Talker, and the Sycophant. The Bab-
bler "is the sort who says to anyone he meets, regardless of what that man says
to him, that he's talking nonsense and that he himself understands the whole
thing and that the man will learn something about it if he listens to him." The
Shameless Man "after shortchanging someone, goes back to ask him for a
loan." The Obnoxious Man "in the theatre applauds when everyone else has
stopped, and hisses actors whom the rest of the audience take pleasure in
watching and when the audience is silent, he throws back his head and belches
to make the spectators turn around."[1]

Theophrastus's characters have several notable qualities. One is that they
anticipate what is now called the "prototype" approach to diagnosing mental
disorders.[2] It does not depict specific individuals but portrays stereotypical
models that others can easily recognize. A second is that his types represent
inner dynamics that remain constant regardless of what goes on in the external world. They "go about their routines, undisturbed by, or even unaware of,
the events swirling around them."[3] None of his characters adapts to circumstances, but, instead, all maintain their basic features even when they are
clearly situationally inappropriate. Third, Theophrastus's descriptions provide uniformly negative evaluations. Indeed, the subtitle of my edition of
Characters is *An Ancient Take on Bad Behavior*. The characters Theophrastus
described served as the model for such studies for two subsequent millennia.[4]
Even today, the *DSM-5* criteria for various types of personality disorders such
as the paranoid, narcissist, or histrionic types contain Theophrastian echoes.

Theophrastus's teacher, Aristotle, also wrote extensively about character.
Yet Aristotle's account, which emphasized how people could learn to become
virtuous, thoroughly differed from his pupil's. The title of the second book
of *Nicomachean Ethics* is *Moral Virtue, How It Is Acquired*. Here, Aristotle
rejects the idea that people are born virtuous because "none of the moral
virtues arises in us by nature." Nature provides everyone with the capacity to
act in virtuous or shameful ways, but habit leads to the kinds of character we
develop: "We become just by doing just acts, temperate by doing temperate
acts, brave by doing brave acts."[5] Because the cultivation of habit, not any
innate quality, leads to particular character types, virtues can be taught and
learned. It was especially important that training begin at an early age: "It
makes no small difference, then, whether we form habits of one kind or another from our very youth; it makes a very great difference, or rather *all* the
difference."[6]

Unlike Theophrastus, Aristotle was concerned with virtue. He first distinguished two types of character traits: some are intrinsically good or bad, while in others virtue resides between the extremes of excess or deficiency. Aristotle used the passions of spite, shamelessness, and envy and actions such as adultery, theft, and murder as examples of the first type: "They are themselves bad, and not the excesses or deficiencies of them. It is not possible, then, ever to be right with regard to them; one must always be wrong."[7] Aristotle thus makes clear that virtue is not a statistical quality: "Goodness is both rare and laudable and noble."[8]

In contrast, other passions and actions are most virtuous when they fall between the extremes of excess and deficiency: "Fear and confidence and appetite and anger and pity and in general pleasure and pain may be felt both too much and too little . . . but to feel them at the right times, with reference to the right objects, towards the right people, with the right motive, and in the right way, is what is both intermediate and best, and this is characteristic of virtue." For this broad category, "virtue is a kind of mean, since, as we have seen, it aims at what is intermediate."[9] Thus, someone who is friendly falls between the excesses of the obsequious person on one extreme and the surly individual on the other. Likewise, the way a brave person faces danger is midway between one who is rash and fearless and the coward.[10]

Aristotle's writings on character differ from Theophrastus's in another way. The latter looked at character as an individual quality that remains constant regardless of the social context. Unlike Theophrastus, Aristotle situated character in the circumstances of birth, wealth, and power. He noted the disparity between the arrogance found among the wealthy and powerful and the humility of the poor and powerless. Each major stage of the life course—youth, the prime years, and old age—also featured characteristic traits. The intense emotions, optimism, and arrogance of youth contrasted with the caution, pessimism, and moderation of the elderly, while the middle aged fell between these extremes. For Aristotle, character was rooted in factors such as age, resources, and social standing as much as in inner qualities.[11]

Finally, Aristotle distinguished between *ethos*, which refers to individuals' inherent character, and *pathos*, which involves the emotions they express in given situations. This provided him with a contextual method to distinguish various temperaments from mental disorders. People's dispositions lead them to respond to circumstances in predictably variable ways: "The man who is by nature apt to fear everything, even the squeak of a mouse, is cowardly . . . , while the man who feared a weasel did so in consequence of disease."[12] A fearful personality predisposes one to experience constant states of anxiousness.

Although Aristotle considered such temperaments undesirable, they were not disordered. In contrast, fears of particular objects that were not rational sources of fear, such as weasels, likely resulted from some disease. Aristotle's writings on personality, which distinguish appropriate fears that arise in dangerous contexts from disordered fears of safe objects and situations, remained influential for many subsequent centuries.

A century before Theophrastus and Aristotle, the Hippocratics understood health and sickness in naturalistic terms: "Men ought to know that from the brain, and from the brain only, arise our pleasures, joys, laughter, and jests, as well as our sorrows, pains, griefs and tears."[13] What would much later be called "personality" resulted from the balance among four kinds of bodily fluids, or "humors." The choleric, melancholic, sanguine, and phlegmatic temperaments corresponded to dominant amounts of yellow bile, black bile, blood, and phlegm, respectively.

The Hippocratic corpus developed holistic portrayals of personality that linked psychology to physiology. Its lasting legacy was to equate mental and physical illnesses alike to disruptions in the overall relationship between individuals and their surroundings. Personality was the key to understanding disease: "It is more important to know what sort of person has a disease than to know what sort of disease a person has," Hippocrates reputedly said.[14]

Six centuries later, Galen, the most prominent physician in the Roman Empire, linked excessive quantities of each humor to four distinctive character types. Healthy dispositions arose when the four humors were in proper balance. Conversely, just as some physical defect led to organic disease, disproportions among the humors resulted in mental disease.[15] Irritable choleric personalities stemmed from an abundance of yellow bile, lethargic melancholics had too much black bile, optimistic sanguine types were dominated by blood, and timid phlegmatics were associated with excessive phlegm. Modern notions of "temperament" continue to refer to relatively unchangeable constitutional dispositions to behave and feel in characteristic ways.

In the fourth century BCE, Herodotus, often called "the father of history," traveled widely through the ancient world, visiting Egypt, Phoenicia, Mesopotamia, and Crimea, as well as the entire Greek world. He emphasized how culture shaped virtually all human activities.[16] Unlike the Hippocratics, Herodotus considered what is commonly regarded as "human nature" as variable from culture to culture. Individual behavior does not derive from innate traits but from the customs of particular groups. Anticipating the cultural relativism that would develop in twentieth-century anthropology, character traits that one culture valued, another culture would denigrate and vice versa. Modal personality styles across cultures were neither inferior nor superior but simply different from each other.

The questions Theophrastus, Aristotle, the Hippocratics, and Herodotus raised about personality and its disorders persist through the present. To what extent do they refer to inner qualities of individuals or to aspects of situations and social circumstances? What is the relative influence of innate or learned forces on personality? Do judgments of personality primarily reflect objective characteristics or social values? Are personality disorders extremes of continuous traits that are present in everyone, or do they stem from inherently dysfunctional conditions? To what degree can personality traits be viewed in isolation or as holistic adaptations to environment?

From Character to Personality

Ancient Greek writings served as the exemplars for Western writings about character types through the nineteenth century. For more than two millennia, "character" was the dominant way to describe (or "characterize") personal qualities.[17] By the nineteenth century, however, Theophrastus's negative approach to character had inverted. No longer associated with babblers, buffoons, and busybodies, discourses on character were concerned with ideals of duty, moral principles, and gallantry. People with character embodied Aristotle's virtues. Samuel Smiles, the Scottish author of a book he titled *Character* (1871), captured the essence of the concept at the time: "Character is human nature in its best form. It is moral order embodied in the individual."[18]

Throughout the nineteenth century, following Aristotle, individuals were assumed to have control over their behavior so that character traits could be taught and learned. Therefore, character was not only desirable but also achievable. Many efforts aimed at "character education" or "character building" arose as numerous self-help manuals, schools, and educational reformers strove to instill this quality into a wide swath of the population.[19] The terms most associated with the concept of character included "citizenship," "duty," "work," "honor," "reputation," "morals," "integrity," and "manhood."[20]

In contrast to the long history of character, personality is a relatively new way of describing the basic qualities of individuals. People of strong character subordinated their own interests to those of the community. In contrast, by the eighteenth century some writers started to use the term "personality" to indicate a person's individuality and distinctiveness.[21] In the following century it was often applied to those, especially women, with lively and spirited traits. It was not, however, until the end of the nineteenth and beginning of the twentieth century that a culture of personality began to supplant the culture of character. If character was evaluated as good or bad, personality was appraised according to appeal or lack thereof. Character had a moral essence; personality referred to psychological qualities, especially those that made people stand out from others. It was someone's unique manner of feeling, thinking, and relating to others.[22] Although not everyone has character, everyone does have a personality.

The emergence of personality resulted from dramatic social changes. Personality was unlikely to be a central social focus when life was organized around groups, not individuals. "Man was conscious of himself only as a member of a race, people, party, family, or corporation—only through some general category," famed historian Jacob Burkhardt wrote of the Middle Ages.[23] Before the nineteenth century, daily life in the mostly agrarian Western world was organized around families, not individuals. Inhabitants of its small communities had "an automatic sense of identity" that stemmed from their family ties.[24] Institutions sorted people into suitable social roles mainly according to inherited status rather than individual qualities. Personality had a limited place in such societies.

Over the course of the nineteenth century, the Industrial Revolution, the rise of heterogeneous urban centers, migration, social mobility, and immigration led previously integrated and homogeneous social structures to break down. Many interactions came to take place among strangers rather than well-known family and community members. Identity no longer stemmed from inherited status but from the personal experiences of individuals. In contrast to character, personality became a more suitable emphasis as societies came to value individuality, achievement, consumption, abundance, and self-expressiveness. It now seemed possible for people to escape the constraints of social obligations and forge distinctive selves. Entrepreneurs, bohemians, and artists, among many other identities, arose to replace rigidly stratified social roles. Society became a collection of individuals who were no longer assured of the certainty, security, and permanence of their familial identities.

By the end of the nineteenth century, personality was a major source of interest in both Europe and the United States. It referred to the typical ways that people behaved, thought, felt, and related to others. Qualities related to charm, the ability to form friendships, likeability, and projecting personal energy replaced the earlier emphasis on duty, moral courage, and personal integrity.[25] "As traditional and local bonds unraveled, social solidarity itself came to rest on the ability of these newly free individuals to integrate personally their diverse social roles. An affiliative society depended much more heavily on the integration of the personality than did a traditional one," sociologist Andrew Abbott observes.[26] While studies of personality thrive in many contemporary disciplines including psychology, psychiatry, and neuroscience, the notion of character is virtually invisible in all fields.

Disciplines

The rise of personality as a topic of interest in the latter part of the nineteenth century occurred in a period when many new disciplines including psychology, psychoanalysis, and the social sciences were emerging. The major intellectual context was German philosopher Immanuel Kant's sharp division between the natural and the cultural approaches.[27] The former were subject to universal laws. Physics provided the model for the natural sciences. It reduced processes to their elemental components and used empirical methods to develop law-like propositions that hold across all times and places. In contrast, Kant proclaimed that the study of inner human experience was inherently resistant to scientific approaches that develop general laws and instead required intuitive understandings of particular individuals, events, and cultures. Natural forces did not dictate human behavior because people had the power to construct their own characters.

When personality began to replace character as the dominant way of picturing individuals at the end of the nineteenth century, psychiatry, along with its sister field of neurology, dominated the study of mental diseases. At the time, the field clearly fell on the natural sciences side of the Kantian divide: psychiatry only respected descriptions and explanations that involved anatomical, physical, and chemical factors.[28] In addition, almost all psychiatrists worked in mental institutions where they oversaw the housing and treatment of the most severely ill patients. Because personality disorders were rarely severe enough to require inpatient treatment, psychiatrists seldom encountered them. The sole exception was psychopathic personalities (now called those with antisocial personality disorder), who were usually found in prisons and jails but sometimes entered mental hospitals. The types of patients they encountered ensured that most psychiatrists had little interest in the new phenomenon of personality.

Sigmund Freud founded psychoanalysis around the turn of the twentieth century. At the time, analysis had virtually nothing in common with psychiatry. It fell on the cultural side of the Kantian dichotomy, blending intuitive clinical studies with philosophical concerns. Its object was "the idiosyncratic, meaning-saturated, morally inflected psychical life of the human being."[29] While psychiatry studied manifest and visible traits, psychoanalysts strove to understand how the meaning of symptoms arose from intrapsychic processes such as repression, ambivalence, and conflict.[30] For analysts no clear line divided the healthy and the sick. Personality "disorders" generally occurred when defense mechanisms, which should be flexible and adaptive to situations, became rigid and maladaptive. Its central concepts did not easily lend themselves to traditional scientific methods, and its theories were squarely on the intuitive side of the Kantian divide. Freud, for example, doubted the validity of experimental tests of analytic ideas because "the wealth of dependable observations on which these assertions rest make them independent of experimental verification. Still, they can do no harm."[31]

The neglect of personality and its disorders in psychiatry and the intuitive approach of psychoanalysis left an opening for other nascent disciplines to gain jurisdiction over the systematic study of these conditions.[32] Psychologists were the first to aggressively pursue the study of personality. When the field emerged in Germany toward the end of the nineteenth century, psychologists were especially concerned with combating the Kantian assignment of the study of human experiences to the cultural sciences, so they rejected the study of character as overly value laden and unscientific. Instead, they viewed personality as an object of value-neutral investigations. Their initial efforts strove to show that human experiences could be explained through the same kinds of carefully controlled laboratory studies and observable sensations that marked the natural sciences. From the start, psychologists employed rigorous scientific methods grounded in empiricism and experimentation. To accomplish this, they measured statistically defined behavioral traits abstracted from situations, cultures, or historical circumstances. However, because they studied untreated rather than clinical groups, psychologists were generally uninterested in studying personality *disorders*.

Sociology and anthropology, too, emerged as coherent fields of study toward the end of the nineteenth century. Before the 1930s, however, neither field showed much interest in issues concerning personality. The scant attention to the social and cultural aspects of personality among psychiatrists, psychologists, and psychoanalysts, however, left an opening for the study of the societal determinants of personality and personality disorders. At this time, an immensely popular culture and personality school emerged from the work of anthropologists Ruth Benedict and Margaret Mead. "Culture," Mead wrote, is "personality writ large."[33] Their work centered on two major themes. The first was that personality styles were cultural products: the same individuals would have different personal characteristics if they lived in different societies. The second was that definitions of both normal and disordered personalities stemmed from culturally relative value systems. The personality styles one culture emphasized would be alien in others and vice versa. Likewise, what some groups might call a "personality disorder," others would consider healthy and desirable. Anthropologists did not work with individual patients or in institutions, but their close observational studies of behavior in diverse groups attracted the attention of society at large.

In the 1930s the culture and personality school was joined by a new generation of psychoanalysts, who developed what came to be called the "neo-Freudian" school. The neo-Freudians focused on how the social, political, and historical conditions of a country shaped resulting personality structures. Personality took a distinctive national character. For example, in late nineteenth-century Vienna, parents strove to exert strict control over premarital sex, especially among daughters; several decades later, such prohibitions were much weaker.[34] The role of guilt and the superego in the personalities that developed in the two eras differed accordingly. After the socially oriented neo-Freudians immigrated to the United States, they aligned with the culture and personality school to pursue their joint interests.

The study of personality thus emerged at a time when no single discipline—whether psychiatry, psychoanalysis, psychology, or social science—could claim sole jurisdiction over the field. The lack of a single dominant disciplinary paradigm meant that no consensus developed of personality or its disorders, a situation that persists at present.

What Is Personality?

Ever since personality became a focus of study in the nineteenth century, basic recurring questions have arisen about its nature. Many of the issues raised by the ancient Greeks remain entangled in intense disagreements.

Isolated Traits or Holistic Organization?

One central question has been whether personality is best portrayed as a collection of separate traits or as an interconnected whole. The four Hippocratic humors—yellow bile, black bile, blood, and phlegm—were believed to vary independently of each other. Likewise, many current researchers depict personality as a collection of distinct qualities. The most common schema of this type is the "Big Five" traits of openness through closedness to experience, conscientiousness through negligence, extraversion through introversion, agreeableness through antagonism, and neuroticism through emotional stability. All individuals receive separate scores that range from low to high on each quality.[35]

Other observers view personality much like Theophrastus, as the totality of an individual's characteristic pattern of emotions, feelings, and interactional styles. The definition of one of the founders of American personality psychology, Gordon Allport, is representative: "Personality is the dynamic organization within the individual of those psychophysical systems that determine his unique adjustments to his environment."[36] In this formulation, personality does not consist in isolatable traits but involves the interrelationships between the parts and the properties of the system as a whole. In the words of neurologist Oliver Sacks, "The miracle is how [cerebral regions] all cooperate, are integrated together, in the creation of a self."[37]

Sacks also provided a compelling picture of the unique nature of each personality: "If we wish to know about a man, we ask 'what is his story—his real, inmost story?'—for each of us *is* a biography, a story. Each of us *is* a singular narrative, which is constructed, continually, unconsciously, by, through, and in us—through our perceptions, our feelings, our thoughts, our actions; and, not least, our discourse, our spoken narrations. Biologically, physiologically, we are not so different from each other; historically, as narratives—we are each of us unique."[38] Such holistic views do not abstract personality traits from specific people but strive to uncover the particularities of singular individuals. Far from being decided, the question of whether personality consists in separable or unified qualities was one of the major unresolved issues in the last revision of psychiatry's *Diagnostic and Statistical Manual of Mental Disorders* in 2013.

Inner Quality or Interactional Process?

Another recurring issue has been the extent to which personality refers to qualities that reside within individuals, such as Theophrastian characters or Hippocratic temperaments, or in interactions with the external world, as Aristotle conceived. Is personality the result of internal processes detached from relationships and situations that people bring to their engagements in social practices such as negotiating status hierarchies, forming friendships, obtaining resources, or resolving conflicts?[39]

Or is personality an aspect of how individuals relate to their circumstances? Allport contended it cannot be present among people who have no social relationships; although Robinson Crusoe had intelligence that could be measured alone on his desert island, his personality only became significant once Friday arrived.[40] That is, meaningful definitions of personality cannot be isolated from particular situations, roles, and relationships. For example, introversion and extraversion are expressed differently from a subordinate or a superior position. Sigmund Freud explained of military hierarchies, "the behaviour of a non-commissioned officer who accepts a reprimand from his superior in silence but vents his anger on the first innocent private he comes across."[41] Its social aspect differentiates personality disorders from other sorts of mental disorders such as schizophrenia, depression, or anxiety, which can arise among totally isolated individuals.

Psychiatrist Carl Jung believed personality features both internal and adaptive sides. The "anima," or "soul," refers to the inner qualities of personality, while the "persona" concerns the ways people display themselves to the social world.[42] Allport, too, posited that "personality 'is' something and personality 'does' something."[43] More recently, personality psychologist Walter Mischel developed the "if . . . then . . ." approach: People don't act in consistent ways across different situations but alter their behaviors to respond to various circumstances. The stability of personality results from the characteristic ways people act: if they are in certain states, then they respond in consistent ways.[44]

Part of the Natural or the Cultural World?

The degree to which personality traits are innate, biologically based qualities that are essentially similar worldwide or result from particular kinds of cultural socialization has always divided students of personality. One view echoes the Hippocratic trope that all aspects of personality stem "from the brain, and from the brain only." In the early nineteenth century, phrenologist Franz Joseph Gall located specific personality traits in distinct brain regions. At the end of that century, Francis Galton proposed that his half cousin Charles Darwin's theory of natural selection applied to temperament and character with as much force as it did to physical characteristics.[45]

Neuroscientists resurrected this view at the end of the twentieth century. One prominent theory roots particular aspects of personality such as novelty seeking, harm avoidance, and reward dependence in distinct neurochemical systems of dopamine, serotonin, and norepinephrine, respectively.[46] Because these neurobiological properties are universal, it follows that essential aspects of personalities must also be found worldwide. Another brain-based approach roots personality in the synapses that interconnect neurons rather than in various neurochemicals. "You are," neuroscientist Joseph LeDoux proclaims, "your synapses. They are who you are." Ultimately, all biological, psychological, cultural, and social impacts on personality can be realized only through their embodiment in synaptic connections. "Life's experiences leave lasting effects on us only by being stored as memories in synaptic circuits."[47]

Personality disorders can sometimes result from organic disturbances in particular brain regions. The best-known case of this type, featured in neuroscientist Antonio Damasio's *Descartes' Error* (1994), concerns Phineas Gage, a railroad foreman in Vermont. In 1848 an explosion drove an iron rod completely through Gage's brain. While his intellect and language seemed unaffected, Gage's personality underwent a total transformation. "His disposition, his likes and dislikes, his dreams and aspirations are all to change. Gage's body may be alive and well, but there is a new spirit animating it," Damasio reports.[48] His examination of Gage's skull confirmed that the damage occurred in the frontal lobes of the prefrontal region of the brain while other cerebral areas were unaffected. Many of Oliver Sacks's case studies also demonstrate how injuries in particular brain regions produce upheavals in personalities while other functions remain intact.[49] Such cases do not show that a large number of personality disorders result from brain damage, but they do indicate that the normal functioning of personality requires that specific areas of the brain are intact.

One implication of the natural view, dating back to the writings of Theophrastus and the Hippocratics, is that personality does not come and go but is generally apparent in early childhood or even at birth and endures throughout a lifetime. Personality is thus deeply embedded, pervasive, and long standing. From this point of view, personality cannot be taught or easily changed.[50]

A different view, which Herodotus propounded, emphasizes the social, cultural, and historical influences that lead each culture to impart group-specific personality styles to its members. Personality types are quintessentially social products that owe their meanings and contents to unique cultural traditions. From this perspective, humans select the identities they embrace from the narratives their cultures provide them. Selves arise from learning social expectations about what kinds of personalities are valued in particular groups and historical periods. The result is that typical personality styles vary considerably both across time and from culture to culture. "If we had been born somewhere else and reared somewhere else, we would be different kinds of people," anthropologist Margaret Mead would come to conclude.[51]

From the relativist perspective, the current Western view that anchors self-hood within unique individuals is a social creation. Anthropologist Clifford Geertz's observation about modern personalities is representative: in the West each individual is seen as "a bounded, unique, more or less integrated, motivational and cognitive universe, a dynamic center of awareness, emotion, judgment, and action organized into a distinctive whole and set contrastively both against other such wholes and against its social and natural background."[52] Geertz contrasts this view with societies that have no comparable concept of a single unified self or of distinctive individuals, where identities stem from kinship, clan, and social roles. Before the twentieth century selves were largely shaped by social roles and obligations; since that time they mainly consist in internal thoughts and feelings.

An implication of the cultural approach, echoing Aristotle, is that training, education, and social environments, not inborn temperaments, form habitual modes of behavior that become automatic responses to the individual's surroundings. Different personality styles are not fixed in childhood but evolve over successive stages of the life course. The recklessness commonly found among youth typically changes to more risk-averse strategies after they become parents. This caution among the middle aged in turn transforms to the contentment that prevails among the elderly, who rarely display aggressive or impulsive behaviors. Numerous therapies and self-help strategies assume that people can overcome childhood personality patterns to achieve fulfillment and self-actualization as they age.[53]

Another implication of the social view is that personality styles—"relatively enduring personality characteristics and patterns that are modal among the adult members of a society"—can characterize groups as well as individuals.[54] English prime minister Benjamin Disraeli provided the most succinct description: "Nations have characters, as well as individuals."[55] The notion that nations have distinctive characters has ancient roots. An early example is Roman historian Tacitus's characterization of the psychology of Germanic tribes in the first century AD as having an unusual ability to endure hard work, little capacity for peace, and no self-control when they drank.[56] Nineteenth-century sociologist Herbert Spencer also presented capsule descriptions of the emotional characters of various societies that resemble Theophrastus's sketches of individuals. His portrayal of Samoans is illustrative: "Not so lively as Tahitians. Good humored, social in disposition, very desirous of pleasing, and fond of amusement and traveling. Indolent, fickle, and deceitful."[57] More recently, family therapist Monica McGoldrick described the typical Irish personality as outwardly cheerful but inwardly isolated.[58]

Notions of individuality that are at the heart of Western views of personality also stem from particular group expectations: "When our culture provides us with life narratives couched in psychological terms, our lives really do become psychological in their form," sociologist Nikolas Rose writes.[59] Historical events, too, can shape personality, as seen in the lifelong risk aversion common among the generation that came of age during the Great Depression.[60]

What Is a Personality Disorder?

The difficulties of defining personality are matched or even surpassed by questions about what a personality *disorder* is. Psychologists historically ignored the topic, assuming that the tails of statistical distributions adequately indicated disorders. Psychoanalysts typically viewed the borders between normality and pathology as so porous that attempts to demarcate a clear boundary were likely to be fruitless. Social scientists saw culturally relative values as creating disordered and normal personality traits alike. In contrast, psychiatrists have often attempted to distinguish disordered from normal personalities. The recalcitrance of personality disorders to medical models, however, has perennially stymied their efforts.

Medical disorders are typically defined as defects in the structure or function of some organic system that are associated with pain or a reduction of well-being.[61] One of their central characteristics is that they exist "outside the unique manifestations in particular men and women."[62] The symptoms, courses, and outcomes of, say, cancer, tuberculosis, or asthma are independent of the individuals that these diseases afflict. Therefore, medical diagnoses strive to isolate patients' extraneous personal qualities from their symptoms to identify what disease they have. At the end of the nineteenth century, German psychiatrist Emil Kraepelin imported this conception into psychiatric classifications when he defined dementia praecox (schizophrenia) and manic depression through typical features and prognoses that were independent of the particular qualities of the individuals who had them.[63]

Arguably, medical models are suitable for many classes of mental disorders. Both the psychoses and neuroses feature symptoms that seem inconsistent with the fundamental nature of their bearers. Intrusive thoughts, compulsions, intense agitation, extreme anxiety, somatic preoccupations, panic attacks, hallucinations, deep depressions, and the like seem to interfere with the sense of self. They are conditions that people *have*, not ones that define who they *are*.

Personality disorders, however, resist definitions involving symptoms that happen to people. The personal qualities of the individual are intrinsic aspects of a personality disorder, not irrelevant features that need to be set aside to understand the condition. Narcissistic, obsessive-compulsive, or dependent personalities neither involve strange departures from reality, as the psychoses do, nor unwanted symptoms, as in the neuroses, but are fundamental aspects of identity.[64] Their characteristics seem to be natural parts of their bearers' lives and so are inextricably related to "manifestations in particular men and women."[65] Therefore, it is inherently more difficult to specify the disordered aspect of a personality disorder than it is with other classes of mental illnesses. The value-laden terms used to describe sufferers of the personality disorders also pose obstacles to casting them as medical entities. Nineteenth-century efforts relied on terms such as "depraved," "perverted," and "decency" that are far afield from typical conceptions of disease. Kraepelin incorporated personality disorders into his medical classification only as deviant and criminal behaviors.[66]

Current efforts to define personality disorders remain resistant to disease models. The *DSM-5* uses "dysfunction" to define mental disorder: "A mental disorder is a syndrome characterized by clinically significant disturbance in an individual's cognition, emotion regulation, or behavior that reflects a dysfunction in the psychological, biological, or developmental processes underlying mental functioning."[67] The presence of a dysfunction indicates the failure of some organic or psychological mechanism: depression involves the malfunction of loss response mechanisms, anxiety disorders arise from the faulty operation of fear detection mechanisms, or bipolar conditions result from impaired emotional regulation mechanisms.

Unlike most other kinds of mental disorders, the question of what a personality disorder is a dysfunction *of* is much harder to answer. The *DSM*'s general definition reads, "A *personality disorder* is an enduring pattern of inner experience and behavior that deviates markedly from the expectations of the individual's culture, is pervasive and inflexible, has an onset in adolescence or early adulthood, is stable over time, and leads to distress or impairment."[68] The manual then defines nine specific personality disorders divided into three clusters. Cluster A contains the "odd" paranoid, schizoid, and schizotypal types; Cluster B includes the more "dramatic" antisocial, histrionic, and borderline conditions; and Cluster C comprises the "anxious" avoidant, dependent, and obsessive-compulsive personality disorders.[69]

This definition has five major aspects. The first is temporal. Personality disorders arise early in life and then are stable and "enduring." Second, they typify who a person is and so are "pervasive." The third component is overtly evaluative: personality disorders deviate "markedly from the expectations of the individual's culture." Fourth, they are "inflexible" and so do not readily adapt to changing situations. Finally, they lead to "distress or impairment" or both.

Personality disorders thus involve the characteristic ways that individuals behave, feel, think, and relate to others as opposed to exhibiting symptoms that come and go. They are not ego-alien but refer to the totality of someone's essential nature. In addition, personality disorders do not arise because of some external precipitant but remain more or less unchanging regardless of the environment. The holistic, fixed, and lasting aspects of the personality disorders distinguish them from the other eighteen specific classes of mental disorders.

While the *DSM* definition indicates how personality disorders differ from other types of mental disorders, it leaves many questions unanswered about what separates personality disorders from *normal* personalities.[70] Many of their components—"enduring pattern of inner experience," "onset in adolescence or early adulthood," "stable over time"—apply equally to normal and disordered personalities. Likewise, "behavior that deviates markedly from the expectations of the individual's culture" does not necessarily involve having a disorder. Immigrants, nonconformists, criminals, geniuses, sexual minorities, or those who hold exotic religious beliefs can deviate markedly from cultural expectations without having mental disorders.

The *DSM* criterion that any mental disorder must be "associated with significant distress or disability in social, occupational, or other important activities" for the personality disorders is also problematic.[71] Because many, or even most, personality disorders are consistent with people's self-conceptions, they are often not distressing. Nor do they necessarily entail disability. Narcissists can prosper in consumer-oriented market cultures (and can even ascend to the US presidency), antisocial personalities can amass great wealth, and avoidants can thrive in certain settings and occupations that do not require social interaction. The distress or disability criteria are often inapplicable to the personality disorders.

"Inflexibility" has been the most useful way to differentiate disordered from non-disordered personalities. Those with personality disorders have chronic dysfunctions that make them incapable of altering their responses to the demands of different situations or the needs of other people. Although inflexibility need not be pathological, someone's inability to adjust their responses to external conditions and relationships seems to be the central quality that distinguishes disordered from normal personalities.

Conclusion

Three interrelated aspects—individual constitutions; particular life histories; and historical, cultural, and social influences—to a greater or lesser extent shape personality. Each facet primarily falls under the authority of different disciplines so that no field can claim exclusive jurisdiction over the study of personality and its disorders. When personality emerged as a major field of study at the beginning of the twentieth century, a number of distinct disciplines competed to legitimize their definition.

It has been particularly difficult to fit personality disorders into the traditional medical model of disease as independent of individual characteristics. Yet scientific legitimacy requires that mental illnesses of all sorts are seen as objective entities that can be isolated from the qualities of individual personalities. The history of personality disorders is largely a tale of recurrent, yet unsuccessful, attempts to mold them into entities that fit as value-free medical entities.

Over the course of the twentieth century, a particularly sharp division arose between researchers who study and clinicians who treat personality conditions. Researchers value rationality, logic, and the scientific method above all other considerations. Clinicians, however, place the greatest significance on practical efficacy in dealing with particular clients. Because researchers strive to develop general laws and clinicians to understand the specific problems of individuals, their values, methods, and goals intrinsically conflict. This could account for why, in the third decade of the twenty-first century, it is hard to discern much progress since ancient Greek formulations defining, explaining, and treating disturbed personalities.

CHAPTER TWO

Personality Disorders Emerge

Before the twentieth century neither personality nor personality disorder was of much concern to any clinical or academic field. Asylum-based psychiatrists had little interest in people with personality disorders, who were rarely found among their mostly psychotic populations. Informal networks of family and friends, sometimes with assistance from clergy or general physicians, generally responded to the sorts of interpersonal difficulties that various personality types might create. Although Freud developed some early speculations about how various personality styles arose, his initial focus was more oriented toward understanding the genesis of neurotic symptoms than toward understanding holistic character structures.

Psychologists took advantage of this gap and initiated the first academic studies of personality. World War I and its aftermath then produced a growing interest in identifying specific personality types and placing them into appropriate roles in military, corporate, and educational institutions. This war also led Freud and some of his circle, who had showed scant interest in the subject over previous decades, to turn to examining personality and its disorders.

Psychiatry's Limited Concern with Personality Disorders

Most studies of mental disorders in the nineteenth century searched for their organic grounding. The field of phrenology, which emerged early in the century, was the first organized effort to measure character traits. Its founder, German neuroanatomist Franz Joseph Gall (1758–1828), was probably the best-known scientist in any field at the time.[1] Gall and his associates replaced ear-

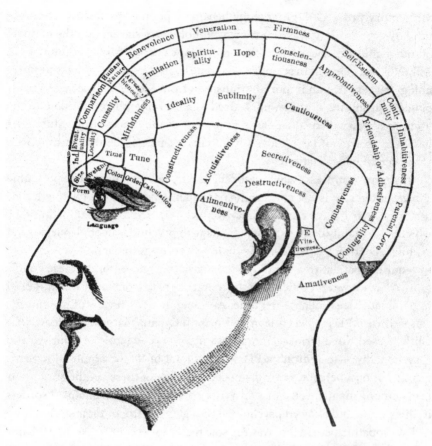

Figure 1. Diagram of phrenologists' conception of the embodiment of personality traits in the brain. Wellcome Library, London. Creative Commons, http://creative commons.org/licenses/by/4.0/.

lier concepts of a unitary, nonmaterial soul with the notion of an organic brain composed of many different units. They strove to locate the origin of particular character qualities in specific brain regions (figure 1).

Phrenologists believed that appropriate examinations of the pattern of bumps on a person's skull could disclose an individual's character and temperament. Gall associated twenty-seven diverse character traits (e.g., courage, destructive urges, friendliness) with specific areas of the brain. These qualities were basically fixed at birth by the size of the pertinent part of the skull. For example, combativeness was located behind the ear, self-esteem at the top of the head, and cautiousness nearly in the middle of the parietal bones.[2] As the century proceeded, phrenology became a popular pseudoscience practiced by laypersons. It was also used by upholders of slavery and the removal of Indigenous Americans from their native lands to justify white domination. Although the field was in scientific disrepute by mid-century, at the time phrenology represented an important transition from the metaphysical to the biological grounding of the mind. Indeed, the movement from the soul to the brain has been called "the defining moment of the nineteenth century."[3] Its basic tenets are not far removed from current neuroscientific assumptions about cerebral localization.[4]

In sharp contrast to Gall's preoccupations, few psychiatrists at the time showed interest in issues concerning personality. Well into the twentieth century, psychiatric theory and practice were closely tied to mental institutions, which were mainly composed of patients with psychotic, alcohol-related, and syphilitic conditions. Because personality disorders were rarely severe enough to require inpatient treatment, the field gave scant attention to these conditions, so we know very little about the frequency of personality disorders (PDs) in psychiatric treatment at the time. An exception is a review of patients diagnosed with PDs between 1879 and 1929 in Croatia's largest psychiatric facility. It used three terms—"moral insanity," "psychopathic inferiority," and "psychopathy"—to indicate a PD. From a total of 18,960 admitted patients just 141, or 0.74 percent, were diagnosed with one of these conditions.[5] Their rarity among inpatients led most psychiatrists to ignore personality disorders in this period and allowed psychologists to gain control of their study.

Psychopathic personality was the sole major exception to psychiatry's initial neglect of personality disorders. Early in the nineteenth century, a concept of "moral insanity" emerged that opened a space for the later appearance of personality disorders.[6] In his 1835 monograph, *A Treatise on Insanity and Other Disorders Affecting the Mind*, British physician James Prichard observed

> a form of mental derangement in which the intellectual faculties appear to have sustained little or no injury, while the disorder is manifested principally or alone in the state of the feelings, temper or habits. In cases of this nature the moral or active principles of the mind are strangely perverted and depraved; the power of self-government is lost or greatly impaired and the individual is found to be incapable . . . of conducting himself with decency and propriety in the business of life.[7]

Prichard's association of moral insanity with "strangely perverted and depraved" mental properties that rendered sufferers unable to act "with decency and propriety" anticipated the future development of psychopathic and, later, antisocial personalities. His definition launched a tradition where character defects that deserved social condemnation were viewed as forms of mental disorder.[8]

Psychopathic personality was the first personality disorder. German psychiatrist J. L. A. Koch coined the term "psychopath" in 1888 to describe individuals with impaired moral capacity. Three years later he developed the concept of "psychopathic inferiority" that assumed psychopaths were born with a constitutional flaw that made them prone to lifelong patterns of antisocial behavior.[9] The imprecision of the term mostly served to blur the lines between mental disorder and criminality.

The personality disorders also lacked prominence in the classifications of Emil Kraepelin (1856–1926), the major diagnostician of mental disorders at the time. Kraepelin paid little heed to them until the sixth edition (1904) of his famous textbook, where he noted four categories of psychopathic personality: born criminals, pathological liars, querulous persons, and people such as vagabonds, spendthrifts, and dipsomaniacs who were driven by some basic compulsion.[10] He proposed that such personalities were consequences of inborn constitutional defects and so were part of lifelong patterns. As Kraepelin's work indicated, "psychopathic personality" and its successor term "antisocial personality disorder" were inseparable from value-laden concepts such as "perverted," "depraved," "decency," and "propriety."

Toward the end of his career, Kraepelin gave greater prominence to the association of various personality types with their propensity to develop particular types of mental disorder. He did not view these as independent entities but linked them to various kinds of mood disorders. In the eighth edition of his text, he singled out depressive, manic, irritable, and cyclothymic temperaments, which he called "fundamental states."[11] These were permanent moods that began in youth, were predisposing factors to manic-depressive insanity, and were present during the intervals of manic and depressive disorders. For example, the depressive temperament "is characterized by a *permanent gloomy emotional stress in all the experiences of life.*"[12] The irritable temperament, which was marked by suicidality, frequent mood changes, and outbursts of rage, resembles current criteria for borderline personality.[13] In this volume Kraepelin also described the persecution, distrust, and discontent experienced by paranoid personalities in terms very similar to current definitions: "The patient feels himself on every occasion unjustly treated, the object of hostility, interfered with, oppressed. . . . The patient is difficult to get along with, is fault-finding, makes difficulties everywhere, perpetually lives at variance with his fellow-workers, on trivial occasions falls into measureless excitement, scolds, blusters, and swears."[14]

Around the same time, German psychiatrist Ernst Kretschmer (1888–1964), reverting to nineteenth-century conceptions, linked four distinct body types—thin, muscular, fat, and disproportionate—to distinct character types. Kretschmer associated thinness with introversion and, in extreme cases, schizophrenia and fatness with extraversion that sometimes developed into manic depression. He also described schizothymic and schizoid temperaments that resemble current notions of schizotypal, schizoid, and avoidant personality disorder.[15]

If Kretschmer's physiological thrust looked backward to the previous century, his German contemporary Kurt Schneider (1887–1967) anticipated future conceptions of personality disorders. Schneider's first major innovation was to disengage personality disorders from biological views, instead grounding them in experiences involving a mix of individual and social suffering: "Those with personality disorders suffer because of their disorders and also cause society to suffer."[16] His *Psychopathic Personalities* (1923) also pioneered a view of personality disorders as a distinct group that is remarkably similar to the current *DSM-5* categories. Nine of his ten types—emotionally unstable, explosive, callous, self-assertive, asthenic, weak willed, affectless, insecure-sensitive, insecure-anankastic, and abnormal mood and activity are recognizable predecessors to the extant categories of borderline, antisocial, narcissistic, avoidant, dependent, schizoid, paranoid, obsessive-compulsive, and cyclothymic, respectively.[17] Schneider's fanatic type is the only one not found in the current manual; conversely, the schizotypal and histrionic types are the only *DSM-5* categories that have no counterparts in his typology.

Schneider viewed personality disorders more as clinically relevant problems in living than as disease-like states.[18] For example, his category of weak willed referred to those who were gullible, immature, and easily exploited by others. He also noted that personality disorders could not be derived from exaggerations of normal personality types.[19] Psychiatric attention to psychotic conditions and neurotic symptoms, though, clearly overshadowed interest in personality problems at the time.

American Psychiatry

In general, American psychiatrists in the early twentieth century were less concerned with developing taxonomies than were their European counterparts. The initial US diagnostic manual emerged from the highly practical management needs of asylums rather than from any theoretical interest in classification. In 1918 the American Medico-Psychological Association (renamed the American Psychiatric Association in 1921) issued the first standardized psychiatric handbook, the *Statistical Manual for the Use of Institutions for the Insane*. This manual guided psychiatric diagnosis in the United States through the end of World War II. It contained twenty-one principal groups (and an additional group of "not insane"). Twenty of these were psychoses and just one—psychoneuroses—was nonpsychotic.

Among the psychotic conditions was psychosis with psychopathic personality: "Psychopathic personalities are characterized largely by emotional immaturity of childishness with marked defects of judgment and without evidence of learning by experience. They are prone to impulsive reactions without consideration of others and to emotional instability with rapid swings from elation to depression, often apparently for trivial causes. Special features in individual psychopaths are prominent criminal traits, moral deficiency, vagabondage and sexual perversions."[20] Psychopathic personality, however, would not be recorded when manic depression or schizophrenia was present. Although no evidence indicates how common this diagnosis was, it was unlikely to be high. Most persons who displayed its traits would enter jails and prisons, not mental hospitals.[21]

The mental hygiene movement was the major exception to American psychiatry's asylum-based practices. Originally launched by former mental patient Clifford Beers in 1908, the movement changed its thrust changed after World War I, from that of reforming mental institutions to that of implementing more sweeping efforts to alter the ways individuals adjusted to their environments.[22] Hygienists' general approach foregrounded the totality of individual personality rather than any specific personality disorder. From the 1920s onward they posited that mental difficulties were at the root of a huge variety of social problems ranging from crime and delinquency to marital strife to industrial unrest, among others. Mental hygienists assumed that facilitating individual adjustment to the social environment could prevent more serious issues from arising. To this end, they developed numerous sorts of intervention programs, mostly with children and adolescents, that strove to alter the personalities of maladjusted youth.[23]

One of the founders of the mental hygiene movement, Adolf Meyer (1866–1950) was the most prominent American psychiatrist during the first half of the twentieth century. His approach, which he called "psychobiology," contrasted with the dominant anatomical thrust of European psychiatry. It emphasized the need to study the totality of individuals' life histories and how they interacted with their organic endowments and psychosocial environments. Meyer's belief that each individual combined an idiosyncratic mix of biological predispositions, psychological conditioning, and social experiences prevented him from developing any systematic theory: "We are all 'individuals' and we are alike only in one fact, in the fact that we are all different."[24] Although he never developed specific concepts of personality or personality disorder, Meyer's influential work opened a space within US psychiatry for studying the relationship of personality types and mental disorder. For the most part, however, before World War II, US psychiatrists were not major players in defining, understanding, or treating personality disorders.

Freud's Initial Studies of Personality

A concern with personality was also slow to emerge as a central emphasis in psychoanalysis. Freud's main interest during the early development of the field lay in explaining the reasons why people developed specific kinds of symptoms, rather than their general forms of personality functioning. His initial studies examined forces such as the unconscious, repression, and libido that produced ego-alien neurotic symptoms that did *not* fit the patient's typical character. Freud's best-known early patients were hysterics (e.g., Dora), phobics (e.g., Little Hans), and obsessives (e.g., Rat Man).

The basic principles of psychoanalysis amplify the complexities of studying personality and its disorders. Freud did not conduct experiments, use statistics, or rely on any sort of objective measurements. Instead, he emphasized hidden, unconscious psychological processes that are not easily discernible. This led to his initial focus on methods such as interpreting dreams and slips of the tongue that provide windows into the true meanings of symptoms.

Psychoanalysis also rejected unitary views of personality because of the omnipresence of mental conflicts and ambivalence. It viewed personality traits as defense mechanisms that people employ against discomforting but unrecognized instincts and memories. Indeed, when Freud saw what seemed to be an excessive personality trait, he often suspected that an opposite trait was secretly responsible. In his analysis of a delusional German judge, Daniel Schreber, Freud attributed Schreber's hatred of another man to repressed homosexual love: "The obsessive thought 'I should like to murder you,' means . . . nothing else but 'I should like to enjoy love of you.'"[25]

This initial thrust meant that, with some exceptions, Freud mostly neglected issues concerning personality (which he called "character") for much of his career. However, his thesis that diverse aspects of sexuality arose at different stages of childhood led him to focus on various body organs—the mouth, the anus, and the genitals—that provided an analytic framework for examining character structures. Oral, anal, and phallic personality types represented fixations on particular early developmental stages with long-term effects on a person's character.

Freud elaborated this thesis in his short essay "Character and Anal Eroticism" (1908). "Such people," Freud observed, "are born with a sexual constitution in which the erotogenicity of the anal zone is exceptionally strong."[26] They displayed the three interrelated traits of orderliness, parsimony, and obstinacy: " 'Orderly' covers the notion of bodily cleanliness as well as of conscientiousness in carrying out small duties and trustworthiness. Its opposite would be 'untidy' and 'neglectful.' Parsimony may appear in the exaggerated from of avarice; and obstinacy can go over into defiance, to which rage and revengefulness are easily joined."[27] It was "incontestable that somehow all three belong together" so that anal eroticism was more than just a constellation of symptoms but instead was a holistic character type closely resembling what is now called an "obsessive-compulsive" personality disorder.

Anal character styles, Freud explained, developed from a combination of biological predispositions and experiences with toilet training when children are about two or three years old. They were often defense mechanisms people mobilized to deal with unwanted, and usually repressed, erotic instincts that originated in this period. While innate sexual drives often accounted for why some people had unusually strong anal urges, the resulting erotic feelings became manifest in different ways. Some people developed permanently fixated anal characters marked by traits such as orderliness, stinginess, stubbornness, rigidity, control, and frugality.[28] A second group, however, sublimated their original anal erotic instincts into socially acceptable resolutions of internal conflicts, for example, channeling one's preoccupation with money into accumulating a substantial fortune. A third group developed reaction formations against anal erotic instincts and displayed overly rigid moral systems. Freud did not attempt to explain what types of people were likely to respond with anal characters, sublimations, or reaction formations. He also briefly raised the question of whether different erotic zones were connected to distinct character types: "One ought to consider whether other types of character do not also show a connection with the excitability of particular erotogenic zones."[29] This essay formed the basis for future psychoanalytic studies of character types.

Freud's "On Narcissism" (1914) is the second of his lasting contributions to the study of personality. In 1889 Havelock Ellis, a British expert on sexuality, described a pathological form of self-love, autoeroticism, and self-absorption "Narcissus-like" after the figure from Greek myth who fell in love with his own reflection in a pool of water, could not stop staring at it, and withered away and died.[30] At the time narcissism was defined as "the attitude of a person who treats his own body in the same way in which the body of a sexual object is ordinarily treated."[31]

Freud's innovation was to show how narcissism was a normal, rather than deviant, stage of human development. Before they made their first connection to any other person, all infants naturally took themselves as their first love object; self-love preceded the love of others. Most people ultimately transformed their initial narcissistic energy into their interpersonal relationships. Some individuals, however, never overcame their original orientation and remained stuck in an infantile stage of development. Narcissistic personalities displayed traits from a phase that most people had transcended. Freud singled out homosexuality as particularly intertwined with narcissism because its love objects were based on sameness rather than difference: "In their later choice of love objects they have taken as a model not their mother but their own selves."[32] In general, though, Freud wrote little about issues directly connected to personality before the latter stages of his career.

Freud Turns to the Study of Personality

Freud's initial theories developed in a culture marked by repressive attitudes toward sexuality. Men and, especially, women were forbidden to have sexual relations before marrying.[33] After marriage, women were often confined to unsatisfying sex, having "only the choice between unappeased desire, infidelity, or neurosis."[34] Men had more choices, but those who went to prostitutes risked developing gonorrhea or syphilis while masturbators were thought to be at risk of impotence and neurasthenia. "Society seems doomed to fall a victim to incurable neuroses which reduce the enjoyment of life to a minimum, destroy the marriage relation, and bring hereditary ruin on the whole coming generation," Freud miserably concluded in 1893.[35]

The events surrounding World War I and its aftermath led Freud to radically transform psychoanalytic theory in a direction more congenial to the study of personality. The war itself made apparent that contemporaneous, rather than childhood, events could account for psychic traumas. It also destroyed respect for the old social order so that "the only redoubt of integrity became the individual personality."[36] By the early 1920s, sexual attitudes and behaviors were dramatically changing for women and men alike. A new generation emerged that valued very different personal traits from those their parents had embraced. The war's impact led Freud to pay more attention to how total personalities responded to their present environments.

The publication of *The Ego and the Id* in 1923 launched a new theoretical era in psychoanalysis that focused on the study of character structures. This book, which Freud's biographer Peter Gay calls "the cardinal text of his last decades," shifted analytic attention to the conscious self in what came to be called "ego psychology."[37] In it, Freud observed of his previous efforts, "We land in endless obscurities and difficulties if we keep to our habitual forms of expression and try, for instance, to derive neuroses from a conflict between the conscious and the unconscious."[38] His portrayal of the basic psychological processes changed from a focus on unconscious repressions to the tripartite division of selves into ego, id, and superego.[39] By the end of the 1920s, Freud and his circle had developed a new theory of the mind centered on how individuals related these three processes to their interactions with the external world.

The id was the "dark, inaccessible part of our personality," home of primitive sexual and aggressive instincts.[40] The oldest component of the psyche, it "contains everything that is inherited, that is present at birth, that is laid down in the constitution."[41] It had no morality but only instincts that seek discharge. Reason could not tame the id, which has the sole goal of satisfying sexual and destructive needs. The laws of time, too, did not apply to the id: "After the passage of decades [repressed infantile impulses] behave as though they had just occurred," Freud observed.[42] Indeed, the id had no contact with the external world at all and so was beyond the influence of cultural factors. The id's insatiable demands created tremendous intrapsychic conflicts.[43]

The superego was the second source of personality struggles. Unlike the amoral id, the superego produced judgment and punishment with resulting guilt. The origin of the superego lay in the Oedipus complex that was a product of the confrontation between unconscious libidinous desires for the parent of the opposite sex and the fear of parental retaliation for having these desires. It initially arose from the exercise of parental authority in early childhood but then took over the power, function, and methods of parental agency. "It observes the ego, gives it orders, judges it and threatens it with punishments, exactly like the parents whose place it has taken," Freud contended.[44] He assumed that although the superego's content could vary across societies, its relentlessness was universal.

Once it became autonomous the superego "seems to have made a one-sided choice and to have picked out only the parents' strictness and severity, their prohibiting and punitive function, whereas their loving care seems not to have been taken over and maintained."[45] Later interactions with teachers and other role models had little influence over the superego, which remained fixed in the earliest stages of childhood. "To Freud," sociologist Dennis Wrong observes, "it is precisely the man with the strictest superego, he who has most thoroughly internalized and conformed to the norms of his society, who is most wracked with guilt and anxiety."[46]

The move to a structural theory of personality placed special emphasis on the self's third agency, the ego. It not only must attempt to control the relentless instincts of the id and the demands of the moralistic superego but also carry out the "decisive factor" of another force: the person's relationship to the outer world.[47] If the id embodied the pressures of the biologically inherited past and the superego the recurrent weight of the cultural past, the outside environment represented the power of the present. The ego must try to come to terms with and, with more difficulty, resolve the intense desires of the id and the powerful exhortations of the superego, all the while dealing with the demands of external reality. "The ego," Freud summarized, "driven by the id, confined by the super-ego, repulsed by reality, struggles to master its economic task of bringing about harmony among the forces and influences working in and upon it." The result was "realistic anxiety regarding the external world, moral anxiety regarding the super-ego and neurotic anxiety regarding the strength of passions in the id."[48]

In his *New Introductory Lectures on Psychoanalysis* (1933), Freud expressed sympathy for the intrinsically difficult position of the ego: "We are warned by a proverb against serving two masters at the same time. The poor ego has things even worse: it serves three severe masters and does what it can to bring their claims and demands in harmony with one another. These claims are always divergent and often seem incompatible. No wonder that the ego so often fails in its task. Its three tyrannical masters are the external world, the super-ego and the id."[49] Each of the three aspects of the personality has its own aims, which often conflict with the aims of the other two.

If Karl Marx foregrounded conflicts between social classes, Freud emphasized those within each individual. The ego must resolve the contradictory demands of the id, superego, and external reality and at the same time pre-serve its own autonomy.[50] These internal structural antagonisms threaten the unity of the self. The conscious commands of the superego and the repressed demands of the id are not just independent of one another but are usually contradictory as well. The attempts of the ego to reconcile these forces are "never complete and unqualified."[51] The conflictual aspect of internal life explains why many people develop neurotic character structures. Analytic practice shifted from focusing on unconscious forces to strengthening the ego's capacity to control the joint pressures of the id's drives and the super-ego's demands and at the same time to make adequate adjustments to the environment.

This tripartite theory suggests three major character types, although Freud never elaborated them in detail. He proposed that those with especially pow-erful ids developed erotic characters focused on loving and being loved. Peo-ple with particularly strict superegos were likely to become obsessional. Fi-nally, narcissistic personalities arose among those with weak superegos and limited erotic needs. Freud also observed that various mixtures of these three types were far more common than pure types.[52]

The structural theory of character did not alter Freud's focus on the study of inner processes that were distinct from positions in historical or social formations.[53] The internal worlds of his individuals were largely separable from any concrete time or place. Indeed, Freud postulated a fundamental opposition between individuals and social processes: "Every culture must be built up on coercion and instinctual renunciation."[54] In *Civilization and Its Discontents* (1930), he maintained that neuroses could not be culturally shaped because, by definition, neurotic symptoms "distinguish the patient from his environment."[55] Personality, or character, structures arose through inner dy-namics that shaped behavior. Yet, because the ego faced outward toward the environment as well as inward, battling with the id and superego, Freud's struc-tural theory paved the way for later analysts, as well as anthropologists and sociologists, to develop social theories of personality (see chapter 3).

Normal and Abnormal Character Types

Freud did not sharply distinguish disordered from normal character types. All people were "subject to the laws that govern normal and pathological activity with equal severity."[56] Everyone, not just those with personality dis-orders, inherently suffered much psychic tension because of the intense, con-flicting demands of the id, superego, and external world. Consequently, they employed defenses such as projection, reaction formation, or repression to deal with inner conflicts. Erotic, obsessional, and narcissistic characters, as well as their various mixtures, were all "part of the normal course of mental life."[57] Each person must deal with continuous struggles to resolve the conflicting demands that impinge on the neurotic and normal alike.

For Freud, all people faced the same issues of managing instinctual urges, internal conflicts, regressions, and repressions. What distinguished the normal from the disordered was that "a normal train of thought, however intense, can be managed in the end."[58] For example, Freud wrote of the anal character, "We expect normal people to keep their relations to money wholly free from libidinous influences and to regulate them in accord with realistic considerations."[59] In contrast, anal character disorders were marked by "excessive" or "compulsive" pursuit of activities that others were better able to control. The disordered never overcame their infantile libidinous attachment to defecation. Such feelings were held with more vehemence and obsessiveness and so were more distinct from normal personalities in degree rather than in kind.

From its inception in Freud's thought, narcissism also blurred the distinction between normal and abnormal personalities. It could be pathological when it was not supplanted by object love at later stages. When it appeared at the right developmental stage, however, it could even be beneficial. Among adults, narcissism often had positive aspects: "People of this type impress others as being 'personalities'; it is on them that their fellow men are specially likely to lean; they readily assume the role of leader, give a fresh stimulus to cultural development or break down existing conditions."[60]

The new structural theory turned analytic practice from curing specific symptoms to changing character structures. While neuroses typically developed because of experiences that arose in the oedipal period from four to six years old, personality disorders emerged in the earlier pre-oedipal time. The basic nature of the personality—for normal and disordered people alike—was basically fixed by the age of five or six and often earlier. One result was that analysts came to believe that character problems were more difficult to treat than classic neurotic conditions marked by particular symptoms. In particular, neurotics generally welcomed attempts to rid them of their distress, but patients firmly resisted efforts to alter their basic characters.[61] Analysts found that their treatments were "threatened by resistances set up against him by the patient, and these resistances he may justly attribute to the latter's character, which now acquires the first claim on his interest."[62] Another result was that those with character disorders needed to stay in therapy for considerably extended periods of time. It was left to Freud's heirs to elaborate the relatively brief considerations he gave to various character types.

A Note on Jung

Swiss psychiatrist Carl Jung (1875–1961) developed a lasting typology of personality. In contrast to Freud's medical training, Jung's background was steeped in religion, philosophy, and literature. His earliest work was an unusual bridge between quantitative styles of psychological research and psychoanalytic theory. Jung used Freud's method of free association as a touchstone, developing word association tests that connected people's responses to stimuli words that he thought could be linked to unconscious processes of repression. He conducted empirical studies that presented subjects, usually psychiatric patients, with lists of one hundred words and asked them to respond to each with the first word that came to mind. He then assessed how much time they took to respond and the nature of their replies. Although Jung's later work did not pursue this line of research, it provided a unique blend of scientific experimentation and analytic theory.

Originally designated as Freud's heir apparent, Jung's apostasy in replacing the sexual and instinctual aspects of the psyche with the sovereignty of the spiritual and mental led Freud to expel him from the analytic movement in 1913. Jung then pursued an ambitious study of the historical, mythological, religious, and philosophical conceptions of personality that he published in his massive *Psychological Types* (1921). This comprehensive survey led Jung to posit two basic personality types. Introverts focused on their own situations in the world and had little concern with the expectations of other people: "The individual occupies the centre of his own interest and becomes in his own eyes the only person worthy of consideration." In contrast, extraverts were oriented to outside conditions and defined themselves in relationship to what was happening in the external world: "We speak of extraversion when he gives his whole interest to the outer world, to the object, and attributes an extraordinary importance and value to it."[63] Jung did not regard these types as mutually exclusive but instead insisted that the same person could have both introverted and extraverted qualities. Jung further divided the psyche into the rational functions of thinking and feeling and the irrational pair of sensation and intuition. From this schema Jung derived eight basic psychological character types. He did not, though, rigidly place people into a single category but insisted that everyone embodied a mix of types. Freud dismissed

Jung's tome, calling it "the work of a snob and a mystic, no new idea in it. . . . No great harm to be expected from this quarter."[64]

Jung became even more spiritually oriented in the last decades of his career when he focused on the religious aspects of the soul. Behaviorist John Watson was one of his sharpest critics, considering Jung a "religious mystic" who made no contribution to empirical psychology.[65] Jung himself considered the basis of psychology to lie in "certain historical and moral premises laid down by Christian education during the last two thousand years."[66] If he began his career as the best hope for integrating quantitative psychology and psychoanalytic theory, Jung ended it immersed in a fully spiritualized and mythologized notion of personality.

Jung's current impact largely stems from his influence on the Myers-Briggs Type Indicator (MBTI), which assumes that extraversion (E), introversion (I), sensing (S), intuition (N), thinking (T), feeling (F), judging (J), and perceiving (P) are the key aspects of personality. The MBTI then derives sixteen personality styles—for example, INFJ, ENFD—that characterize the entire population. Unlike Jung, however, it assumes that each person embodies an unchanging personality type that is fixed at birth. All types are viewed as normal and have special advantages relative to other possible styles. The goal of the MBTI is to maximize the fit between these invariant personality styles and the social niches that are most suitable to them. While professional psychologists deride the MBTI as thoroughly unscientific, it has attracted many devoted followers among laypeople and corporate managers.[67]

Psychology Discovers Personality

Psychologists developed the initial scholarly concern with personality. The discipline of psychology arose around the same time as psychoanalysis. Apart from their nearly simultaneous appearance, however, the two fields had virtually nothing in common. When psychology emerged during the last part of the nineteenth century, it had to distinguish itself from philosophy, on the one hand, and psychiatry, on the other hand. Before this period, a sharp divide existed between the empirical and objective natural sciences and the nonquantifiable and subjective cultural studies. Kant's influential distinction posited that while inner experiences could be understood, they were not subject to general laws. He considered psychology to be a cultural approach that relied on intuition to study the nature of the inner self.[68]

The prodigious research program of German psychologist Wilhelm Wundt (1832–1920) was a landmark in transforming psychology's identification with cultural methods to a firm alliance with the natural sciences. The latter made stupendous progress in the second half of the nineteenth century with discoveries including the germ theory of disease, evolutionary theory, and X-rays. Much like the physical sciences, which were increasingly making previously invisible factors such as electricity, atoms, and germs visible and measurable, Wundt's efforts showed that private, individual consciousness could also be the object of experiments that uncovered lawlike regularities. Although Wundt did not study personality, his investigations into wide-ranging topics including memory, cognition, and emotion clearly linked the new field of psychology to the experimental methods found in the natural sciences. "The laboratory assumed an almost religious significance in this period," historian James Capshew observes.[69]

The work of German psychologist Gustav Fechner (1801–1887) was another milestone in the creation of a field grounded in observable measures. Fechner's psychology had no use for Kant's intuitive cultural interpretations. He insisted that psychologists should use inductive methods grounded in observation to develop objective laws. The major goal of what he called "psychophysics" was to "set up the proper operations by which numerical values could be assigned to psychological variables."[70] To this end, Fechner developed propositions that stated quantitative relationships between external stimuli and internal responses.

While psychology initially emerged in Europe, the United States quickly became the center of the field's research. William James, the most notable US psychologist at the turn of the century, observed, "The assumption that the mind is a real being, which can be acted on by the brain, and which can act on the body through the brain, is the only one compatible with all the facts of experience."[71] Psychology was objective, detached, and quantitative, not subjective, empathetic, or speculative. Its subjects were tied to observable phenomena: "The subconscious mental facts are either not mental but physiological, or mental but not subconscious," influential Harvard psychologist Hugo Münsterberg pronounced in 1909.[72] By the 1920s, US psychology had thoroughly shed any connection to the humanistic enterprise and was fully identified with the natural sciences and mathematics.[73]

Most famously, John Watson's (1878–1958) behaviorism banished all references to consciousness and insisted that psychology's purview was limited to visible behaviors. The taboo on examining internal mental processes was meant to establish the field as "a purely objective experimental branch of natural science."[74] In addition, Watson rejected all views of human behavior that relied on biological inheritance, instead emphasizing the power of environmental reinforcement. "There is no such thing as an inheritance of capacity, talent, temperament, mental constitution and characteristics," Watson boldly proclaimed.[75] Anticipating later developments, "the order of the day was technical specialized research published for technically competent audiences in technical journals, with popularizations in all areas of speculation frequently relegated to hacks, incompetents, and has-beens."[76]

From its inception, then, American psychology was identified with quantitative studies that relied on data collection, statistical analysis, and experimentation.[77] In a similar vein, psychologists rejected the notion of "character," which they associated with unscientific moral and ethical judgments. One textbook noted of character traits, "All these predicates are appraisals rather than statements of fact."[78] By the late 1920s psychologists rarely used the term "character." Instead, they defined "personality" as an entity that could be broken down into particular traits, measured, and compared across whole populations.[79] The new research about personality discounted unique instances and strove to formulate general principles. "The psychology of the concrete particular individual is not a science," Arthur Bills later explained in his 1938 presidential address to the Midwestern Psychological Association. "A better name for such a concrete approach would be biography, and biography is not a science."[80] Showing how personality was not a distinctive trait of individuals but subject to abstract laws was ideally suited to demonstrate the scientific nature of the field.

Psychologists Focus on Normality

In addition to overcoming the Kantian divide that placed mental phenomena on the cultural side, psychology confronted a second major obstacle to its development as an independent scientific discipline. In the first half of the twentieth century medically trained psychiatrists monopolized the treatment of mentally disordered individuals. Nearly all psychiatrists diagnosed mental illnesses and treated disturbed individuals in sites such as hospitals, clinics, and outpatient practices. In these settings psychologists were subject to supervision by physicians who opposed their efforts to gain clinical licensing privileges. This channeled psychologists into institutions—especially schools, corporations, and the military—that primarily dealt with normal, not ill, populations.[81] In these places, and only in these places, were they free from medical regulation.

The inability of psychologists to penetrate clinical settings had a profound impact on the knowledge base of the field. If psychiatrists monopolized the diagnosis and treatment of mental illness, psychologists would become the experts in detecting and sorting *normal* personalities. Working in institutions that served nondisordered populations, their mandate was to develop ways to identify and classify various types of normality, not of mental disorders. This led them to construct tests that they claimed could identify personality styles for schools to filter into optimal career paths, for the armed forces to recruit only normal soldiers, and for corporations to sort employees into appropriate jobs.[82]

If Wundt and Fechner pioneered psychology's incarnation as a natural science, English polymath Francis Galton (1822–1911) provided the means to legitimize the field's domain over normal personalities. In 1883, Galton observed, "The subject of character deserves more statistical investigation than it has yet received."[83] The following year he described some of his observations: "One of the most notable differences between man and man, lies in the emotional temperament. Some persons are quick and excitable; others are slow and deliberate. A sudden excitement, call, touch, gesture, or incident of any kind evokes, in different persons, a response that varies in intensity, celerity, and quality." Galton also observed extreme differences in temper across individuals: "Some men are easily provoked, others remain cheerful even when affairs go contrary to their liking." He concluded, "Character ought to be measured by carefully recorded acts, representative of the usual conduct. . . . It is the statistics of each man's conduct in small every-day affairs, that will probably be found to give the simplest and most precise measures of his character."[84]

Galton's work laid the foundation for the modern study of intelligence as well as other psychological phenomena. He was the major influence on French psychologist Alfred Binet, who invented the IQ test in 1904. Binet reasoned that intelligence nicely fit Galton's observations regarding bell curves. Any given individual's answers to a particular question could be compared to the answers that other people gave to the same question. The total number of correct answers from each individual could be summed and related to the summed scores of others who had taken the same test. These scores could then be placed on a statistical metric that yielded a clear value.

Intelligence tests became an almost instant success not just in France but especially in the United States for identifying superior, average, and deficient mental abilities. IQ tests seemed to be such an important step forward because they demonstrated that quantitative scientific techniques, which had made tremendous progress in exploring natural phenomena during the nineteenth century, also applied to an important human trait. The tests successfully predicted school performance (an unsurprising finding because of the similarity between the skills the tests measured and those used to attain grades). Moreover, they were very efficient. IQ tests could be administered simultaneously to large groups of people, rendering expensive and time-consuming interviews with individuals unnecessary. By the second decade of the twentieth century, educators were using IQ tests, by then known as Stanford-Binet tests, to evaluate the intellectual capabilities of millions of schoolchildren. They became the model for subsequent tests that measured personality.[85]

Individual Differences

The combination of psychology's turns toward the natural sciences and work in institutions that dealt with normal populations led to a third impact on the nascent discipline. Galton's development of statistical methods to measure individual differences became the dominant psychological approach in the twentieth century and remains so at present.[86] For Galton, individuals were not interesting for their uniqueness but only insofar as their attributes compared to others. This view led him to conceive of human traits as points along a continuous distribution. The individual difference model simultaneously made intensive explorations of individuals irrelevant and comparisons with others essential because the score of any individual could be linked to the mean scores of a group and their differences quantified.[87]

Psychologists came to be preoccupied with statistical comparisons of large numbers of subjects but disinterested in particular individuals. Their models relied on techniques where the meaning of any individual's score for some trait stemmed from its relationship to the scores that other people attained on the same measure. The personality trait of "introversion" is an example.[88] Subject A's introversion was assumed to be identical to subject B's introversion, differing only in the degree to which they possessed more or less of the same quality. Even such clearly interpersonal processes as "dependence" or "dominance" were detached from any interpersonal relations and attributed to individuals as a statistical quality. Personality traits were thus extracted from situational, historical, or social factors. These sophisticated quantitative methods allowed psychologists to reject intuition and accrue scientific legitimacy.

Individuals became of interest to personality psychologists only insofar as they were the medium through which abstract laws were expressed. "Individuals were now characterized not by anything actually observed to be going on in their minds or organisms but by their deviation from the statistical norm established for the population with which they had been aggregated," historian of psychology Kurt Danziger summarizes.[89] In addition, echoing Galton, psychologists viewed personality traits as falling along continuous dimensions that sharply contrasted with medicine's dichotomous conception of health and disease. The quantitative focus on individual differences in normal populations that emerged in early psychological research persists to the present. The development and spread of personality testing reinforced these trends.

Personality Tests Arise

Personality tests emerged in the shadow of intelligence tests. The overwhelming success of IQ tests in the early twentieth century provided the model for subsequent assessments of personality. During World War I, the US Army became concerned about the high number of soldiers who succumbed to what was then known as "shell shock" (what is now called post-traumatic stress disorder [PTSD]). The success of IQ tests led the military to approach psychologists who could develop measures that might identify which recruits were especially likely to succumb to psychic traumas.

At the time, most military physicians believed that preexisting personality weaknesses made particular soldiers susceptible to breakdown in combat. Identifying those recruits most vulnerable to shell shock before they entered the service would both save money and avoid the disruption to military discipline they created. Intelligence tests, which measured cognitive abilities, did not seem useful for this purpose. However, they provided a template for how standardized tests might detect the sorts of personalities liable to shell shock as well as others who might disrupt the cohesiveness and morale of combat units. Moreover, personality tests might predict the optimal fit between given individuals and particular roles in the military. They had the potential to identify qualities such as loyalty, respect, and leadership that could maximize the optimal functioning of the armed services.

The attempt to separate normal from abnormal recruits involved screening millions of men. The sheer magnitude of the task made individual diagnoses impractical and mandated the development of a short, easy-to-use, and readily scored instrument that could be administered to large groups of subjects. Individual responses had to be given numeric values and compared to the scores of large numbers of other men who took the same test so that appropriate selection decisions would result.

In the absence of observable measures, evaluators had to rely on self-reports of personality traits.[90] This created the problem that everyone is aware of which personal characteristics are praiseworthy and which are liable to criticism: patience is better than impulsiveness, conscientiousness than carelessness, or flexibility than rigidity. What people say they are like, then, partly reflects what they think they are supposed to be like. Even respondents who try to accurately describe what kind of people they are cannot separate their own evaluations from socially normative conceptions. Nevertheless, early personality testers had no alternative but to rely on self-reported attributes.

Psychologists who developed tests for the military were not so much interested in identifying personality disorders—the men the test detected as abnormal were not treated but sent home—as in making sure that only normal men entered the armed services and assigning them the most appropriate roles. Prominent military psychologist and future president of the American Psychological Association Robert Yerkes (1876–1956) thought that psychology's study of normal people would complement medicine's focus on the diseased. "We should not work primarily for the exclusion of . . . defectives," Yerkes explained, "but rather for the classification of men in order that they may be properly placed in the military service."[91]

At the request of the US military, Robert Woodworth (1869–1962), a Columbia University psychologist, developed the world's first personality inventory, the Personal Data Sheet (PDS). Woodworth examined psychiatric textbooks, compiled a list of 116 symptoms, and asked individuals whether they had experienced each: "Do you feel sad or low spirited most of the time?" "Are you ever bothered with feeling that people are reading your thoughts?" "Does the sight of blood make you sick or dizzy?" Responses were limited to yes or no.[92]

Woodworth assumed that those answers that indicated normal or abnormal personalities were obvious. In essence, normal meant "not mentally ill." He was not bothered by the fact that the most socially acceptable responses were clear since he believed that respondents would answer questions truthfully both because they were volunteers who were motivated to enter military service and because they would be subject to severe sanctions if false answers were detected. Nevertheless, a number of questions that were supposed to differentiate the normal from the disordered in fact did not. For example, normal controls were more likely than patient groups to affirm questions such as "Do you daydream a lot?" and "Do ideas run through your head when you sleep."[93] Despite its weaknesses, the PDS seemed to show that assessments of psychological life could be administered, measured, quantified, and compared across multitudes of individuals. Although it was never fully implemented before the war ended, the PDS served as the model for future efforts that measured personality traits.

Psychologists Enter Institutions

In the aftermath of World War I, personality became a core interest among American psychologists. The field boomed: between 1919 and 1939 the number of credentialed psychologists grew tenfold from just three hundred to three thousand professionals.[94] The study of personality was at the heart of the profession's growth. In 1932 psychologist A. A. Roback wondered, "Could anyone have predicted, even as late as a decade ago, the avalanche which bids fair to sweep away from the foreground nearly all interests in American psychology, to the exclusion of personality measurement?"[95]

Psychology's rise was especially associated with the growing visibility of psychological testing. From the beginning, the field's main mission was to facilitate the efficient operation of social institutions. The experiences of psychologists in World War I showed how they could perform valuable administrative and managerial tasks that aided organizational efforts to maintain conformity and promote adjustment. Corporations and schools, in particular, viewed tests as ways to identify various personality types and match them to optimal social positions. Personality tests indicated that psychologists could examine and classify large numbers of people without relying on expensive, time-consuming, and idiosyncratic explorations of individuals. Psychologists, not psychiatrists or teachers, became the recognized experts in identifying normal personalities.

After the war, inquiries flooded in from schools and businesses, and an era of mass psychological testing began.[96] The domain of psychology spread from the military and schools to businesses, where the loyalties of psychologists were to the organizations that employed them and not, as was often the case for psychiatrists and psychoanalysts, to the patients they treated. A subdiscipline of "industrial psychology" emerged where psychologists teamed with managers to identify which personalities would maximize worker output and which would lower it.

Corporations, in particular, desired tests that would allow them to efficiently select employees with personal traits that were best suited to particular positions. Most personality tests used the model of intelligence tests and assumed that personality traits, like IQ, could be isolated from particular individuals, assigned numerical scores, and then compared to the measurement of the same traits in other individuals. Someone with a normal personality answered test questions in ways that were comparable to the average group member among the statistical aggregate of people who took the same test.[97]

Although IQ tests might accurately predict school performance, they are far less successful in sorting people into different jobs. Indeed, more intelligent people might be better able to hide their undesirable personal qualities so that personality tests might actually work best among the less intelligent. Nevertheless, according to psychologist Albert Poffenberger, personality tests "would prevent the waste of high grades of intelligence in positions where it is not needed and would enable those of low intelligence to be located where their capacity would be adequate and where their character traits would make them successful."[98] Measures of personality styles such as dependency, leadership, tolerance for boredom, or autonomy could supplement tests of intelligence to enhance the match between individual traits and occupational positions.

Critiques of Personality Tests Arise

Personality tests flourished during the 1920s. Responding to demand from corporations, psychologists developed a number of tests to measure the kinds of personality traits that would be useful for particular jobs. Like Woodward's PDS, most of these tests relied on self-assessments of traits such as patience, regular habits, and good attention spans; contextual, cultural, or social variations were irrelevant. Ideally, these tests would slot creative people into autonomous work settings and filter those with high tolerance for boredom into routine and specialized work. For instance, a salesperson should be outgoing and gregarious while a forest ranger has to tolerate long periods of isolation.[99]

Yet testers found that it was far more difficult to measure personality than intelligence. One reason is that personality is considerably more complex. The definition of the most prominent US personality psychologist in the first half of the twentieth century, Gordon Allport, is illustrative: "Personality is the dynamic organization within the individual of those psychophysical systems that determine his unique adjustments to his environment."[100] Allport objected to the dominant psychological approach that fragmented integrated persons into discrete qualities, impoverished holistic selves by examining test scores, and abandoned the study of individuals in favor of considering what traits they shared with others. He insisted that, unlike intelligence, personality referred to a "dynamic organization," not to isolated traits. Moreover, the innumerable ways that personality organization can manifest itself resulted in "unique adjustments." Therefore, Allport argued for a personality psychology that both unified the various aspects of the self into a functioning whole and served as the major bridge between individuals and their environments.

In 1921, Allport wrote the first major critique of personality tests, which stressed how IQ tests were not a good model for measuring personality.[101] Allport and other critics recognized that personality tests confronted different problems. Because their answers stemmed from reliance on self-reported information, these tests could tap only people's *beliefs* about their personality traits. While individuals could reliably provide objective information such as their birthdate or number of siblings, they were much less dependable sources of information about their personal attributes. Most people have difficulty using language to describe feelings, don't know how their feelings relate to those of others, and naturally exaggerate their desirable traits and conceal their undesirable ones. The result was, as Sigmund Freud observed, that "the data of conscious self-perception, which alone were at its disposal, have proved in every respect inadequate to fathom the profusion and complexity of the processes of the mind, to reveal their interconnections and so to recognize the determinants of their disturbances."[102]

Allport and other critics also identified another fundamental distinction between IQ and personality tests. IQ tests have right and wrong answers. To determine IQ, testers need only sum the number of correct answers and then relate the resulting scores to the aggregate scores of others. In contrast, answers to questions such as "Are you generally happy?" or "Are you typically shy and introverted?" have no correct answers. Subjects might answer to the best of their ability, but neither they nor their testers can know whether their answers are "correct" or reflect idiosyncratic understandings of the meanings of the question, cultural ideals, and socially desirable traits.

One more fundamental difference between IQ and personality tests is that IQ scores run in a single direction, from low to high, with equal intervals between each unit. All individuals can be precisely ranked relative to all others, so a score at any point of the statistical distribution has a clear relationship to all other scores. An IQ score of 90, for example, is exactly 20 points worse than a score of 110. A serious problem, however, arises when values are placed on statistical distributions that define normal and abnormal personalities. There is no obvious way to establish where normality lies on the continuous distribution. Are both very low and very high scores abnormal so that middle-range scores are normal? Consider the continuum of compulsiveness on the high end and disorganization on the low end. "Normal" people score between both extremes. In other cases, such as paranoia or schizotypy, just one extreme but not the other might be abnormal. How to rank the value of many personality traits relative to other points on a distribution is anything but obvious.

Early psychologists confronted still another fundamental difference between IQ and personality tests. Very few people who take IQ tests intentionally strive to get a poor score; the overwhelming majority want to accurately answer as many questions as they can. In contrast, the test situation itself often generates motivation to answer questions about personality one way or another. Individuals can not only rationalize or misperceive their personalities but also deliberately try to falsify their reports to please their evaluators.[103] Subjects want to seem to be the kind of people that they think the testers want them to be and so tend to provide the answers that they think the test givers want. Someone taking a test to enter a management position will strive to exhibit qualities of leadership, getting along with others, and conformity to corporate norms. Military recruits who want to serve should seek to minimize undesirable personality traits. Other cases—draftees who don't want to serve or offenders who want to avoid prison and instead enter psychiatric treatment—might attempt to maximize pathology. Contextual factors, then, partly generate normality and abnormality.

A final, and perhaps most important, difference from IQ is that personality is intrinsically interactional. By its nature, expressions of personality vary widely across situations, roles, and relationships: an individual's coworkers might see him as cheerful, his children as despotic, his wife as neurotic, and his neighbors as stubborn.[104] Yet Allport observed how personality testing abstracts people from their actual social contexts so that they are not family members, friends, students, or parents but assemblages of traits isolated from social settings. Allport's brother, Floyd, similarly noted the inherently social nature of personality: "A man's self-assertion, submission, quickness of temper, suspicion, pride and inferiority are all dependent upon the existence of other human beings toward whom these attitudes may be displayed. . . . The hermit exhibits little personality, except in the sphere of pure intelligence."[105] Indeed, personality has little meaning aside from the particular contexts in which a person acts. For example, dominance and submission are often norms generated in particular social roles. Someone who is submissive when interacting with an employer or the police may be more dominant when encountering a student or employee. Or a ruthless person often acts humbly when it advances their own ends.

Existing personality tests might have sufficed for the military, which required adequate supplies of manpower, had little concern with fine-grained selection processes, and could assume that volunteers wanted to give honest answers, but these tests were more problematic when applied in other settings. Psychologists could not convincingly relate responses to personality tests to what people actually do in a variety of situations and in various social roles. Instead, they made the unrealistic assumption that personality was stable over diverse situations, independent of social roles, and uninfluenced by culture. Leading psychiatrist Karl Menninger critiqued the field in 1930: "Now, no human mind is ever shut up in a laboratory; at least no mind lives so. Human beings live in constant contact and interaction with other human beings, and the vast majority of mental processes concern these interactions." Psychological studies, however, were "far removed from the actual everyday behavior of human beings."[106]

Conclusion

The rise of a new, more individualistic social system in the last decades of the nineteenth century led to the demise of the notion of character and the rise of the then-new concept of personality. Asylum-based psychiatrists, however, focused on the psychotic, alcohol-related, and syphilitic conditions that dominated among institutionalized populations and rarely confronted people whose primary problems involved disturbed personalities. In its early decades, the revolutionary new field of psychoanalysis concentrated on the emergence of neurotic symptoms and seldom examined holistic personalities. Freud's later structural model of ego, id, and superego, however, provided a basis for what would become the centrality of personality (or character) in psychoanalytic theory.

The scant attention that psychiatry and psychoanalysis paid to personality disorders in the first decades of the twentieth century allowed psychologists to gain early jurisdiction over knowledge about personality.[107] They were firmly committed to establishing their field as a natural science that quantified and measured isolatable personality traits. To this end, they used the model of IQ tests to develop personality tests that showed how the scores of any given individual were similar to or different from the aggregate of other people's scores. Their clients were not individuals—indeed, it was generally not recommended that individuals receive their results on personality tests at all—but the corporate, educational, military, and legal institutions that employed them to identify who was normal and to screen out those who were unconventional. Psychologists developed tests that quantified and measured personality but at the cost of having nothing to say about the nature of any particular individual. The major developments in the study of personality in the next decade strove to remedy this state of affairs and create conceptions of personality that were grounded in situations, culture, and history.

CHAPTER THREE

Personality Becomes Social

Despite their otherwise radical differences, psychiatry, psychoanalysis, and psychology had one element in common before the 1930s: all neglected the study of sociocultural differences in personality. Psychiatrists' asylum-based theories were grounded in anatomy and physiology. What psychoanalysts called "character" was assumed to result from universal, not culturally determined, processes. Finally, psychologists' quests for scientific status led them to reduce personality to its most elemental components, which they took for granted to be timeless and placeless.

Psychoanalysts generated the initial turn toward examining the social components of personality in their responses to the new situation of the generation that came of age after World War I. Dramatic changes in social norms had transformed the nature of the problems that outpatients brought to therapy, from distressing symptoms arising from sexual repression to difficulties of adjusting to a more individualistic society. Intellectuals, bohemians, and artists, in particular, were attracted to Freud's view that civilization stifled individual dispositions. Young people were especially likely to reject traditional norms and turn toward the exploration of their inner selves. Hermann Hesse's *Demian*, the most popular novel among German youth in the postwar period, begins, "I wanted only to try to live in obedience to the promptings which came from my true self."[1]

These developments pushed psychoanalysts toward more intensive examinations of the total personality and its social determinants. This, in turn, led an important group of neo-Freudians to replace the earlier analytic emphasis on innate drives and inner conflicts with a thoroughgoing emphasis on social factors. They were aligned with anthropologists associated with the culture and personality school that rejected universal views of personality and focused on its local origins. The study of personality turned from past to present influences, from biology to culture, and from inner instincts to the social environment. By the end of the 1930s, culturally infused studies of personality and its disorders were prominent features of psychoanalysis and the social sciences.

Freud's Circle Turns to the Study of Personality

The impact of World War I led Freud to examine more closely the ways that people related to their present circumstances. It did not, though, lead him to alter his view that the new focus of analysis—the relationships among the ego, id, superego, and the external world—was universal rather than socially constituted. Postwar conditions, however, made a heightened focus on social processes virtually inevitable among Freud's circle. The 1920s featured a widespread rejection of previously taken-for-granted assumptions as new, much freer personality prototypes arose in Western societies.[2] Women, in particular, embraced the broadening of acceptable character styles. Their growing independence, however, was accompanied by unease over appropriate modes of adaptation to new circumstances. In addition, the two postwar centers of psychoanalysis, Vienna and Berlin, were rocked by intense political divisions as the rise of strong fascist, socialist, and communist movements heightened the turmoil in the social, cultural, and economic environments. Analytic clients increasingly featured problems associated with adjusting to radically transformed societies rather than dealing with specific neurotic symptoms that often arose in response to oppressive social norms.

A number of analysts moved away from studying unusual and sporadically appearing symptoms toward examining persistent character styles that were related to social processes. They drew on the earlier work of renegade analyst Alfred Adler (1870–1937), the first psychoanalyst to emphasize the social aspects of total personalities. Adler had been one of just four analysts who formed Freud's founding circle in 1902.[3] In 1910, Freud installed him as the first president of the Vienna Psychoanalytic Society.

Adler's publication of *The Neurotic Constitution* in 1912, which examined holistic personality structures, led to a sharp break with Freud and orthodox Freudians. This book highlighted the social roots of the ego and its attempts to adjust to the environment. Adler's approach sharply contrasted with Freud's focus on the unconscious, internal conflicts, and sexual instincts. Unlike the then-dominant psychoanalytic canon, Adler believed that patients' unified personality structures were the key to understanding any particular type of neurotic symptom they might have.[4] For him, the unconscious was less the source of powerful libidinous instincts than the repository of feelings of inferiority and powerlessness. These emotional states arise because of the prolonged period of helplessness and dependency that all infants experience. Many people subsequently respond to their inferiority complexes through compensatory attempts to denigrate other individuals and groups. Narcissism provides an example: while Freud emphasized how it stemmed from the infant's love of self, Adler stressed that it arose as a reaction against underlying feelings of inferiority.[5]

Adler, who himself was short and sickly as a child, considered inferiority complexes among adults especially likely to develop among those with physical deficiencies associated with particular bodily organs or childhood diseases. Sexual life, too, manifested the human need for power and domination. Adler's focus on how individual adaptations took on characteristic styles to compensate for inherent personal shortcomings sharply contrasted with the Freudian emphasis on the unconscious.[6]

Another of Adler's innovations was his argument that status seeking, competition, and social comparisons, which were products of particular social structures, led to characteristic types of people. Far more than other analysts, who emphasized parent-child dynamics, Adler stressed the formative role of siblings, peers, and other nonparental relationships in shaping personality. For him, none of these factors were universal but all were products of history, sociology, and culture. Finally, Adler's commitment to socialism and social change radically differed from Freud's single-minded attention to intraindividual forces and the therapeutic relationship. Accordingly, his generally lower- and working-class patients contrasted with the higher-status clientele of Freud and other analysts during the period before World War I.[7]

Adler's apostasy led Freud to expel him from the analytic movement. Freud's "History of the Psychoanalytic Movement" (1914) noted "how little gift Adler had in particular for appreciating the importance of unconscious material" and expressed "astonishment" at Adler for claiming priority over concepts Freud himself had developed.[8] Paradoxically, in light of Freud's own later turn toward ego psychology, he also attacked Adler for giving undue priority to ego-related processes at the expense of libidinal components. Freud concluded that Adler's "banal" and "superficial" work "has nothing to do with psycho-analysis."[9] He maintained his deep resentment and hostility toward his former acolyte for the rest of his life. Several decades later, however, Adler's writings became an influential source for the socially oriented neo-Freudians, including Erich Fromm and Karen Horney.[10]

"The great flowering of psychoanalysis occurred between 1918 and 1938," historian George Makari observes.[11] One aspect of this flourishing involved expanding the reach of analysis from its initial clientele of highly educated intelligentsia to a broader group encompassing the poor and working classes.[12] Many psychoanalysts became part of the postwar progressive movement that strove to reduce social inequalities and increase democratic participation. They established free or low-cost services for underserved groups in ten different European cities where "psychoanalysis was supposed to share in the transformation of civil society, and these new outpatient treatment centers were to help restore people to their inherently good and productive selves."[13] The rise of Nazism and resulting mass emigration of psychiatrists in the mid- to late 1930s abruptly ended the association of psychoanalysis with social and political activism.

The movement of analysts from studying neurotic symptoms toward issues related to personality was a second aspect of this blossoming. Karl Abraham (1877–1925), who founded the Berlin Psychoanalytic Institute in 1908, was one of Freud's closest allies. Abraham believed that psychoanalysts not only had to treat neurotic symptoms but also be able to overcome character abnormalities.[14] His writings, especially *Psychological Studies on Character Formation* (1925), focused on how character was related to both the particular developmental stages of childhood and the overall style of adaptations that people made to their environments.[15] He elaborated Freud's earlier sketches that related character to bodily regions and developed portrayals of oral, anal, and genital characters that strongly influenced future psychoanalytic formulations. Those with character disorders failed to move on from early developmental stages and established overly rigid modes of adaptation. For example, Abraham rooted what came to be called "dependent personality disorder" in the pleasure infants received from suckling at their mother's breast and the paranoid personality in the subsequent anal erotic stage.[16] Abraham's sudden death in 1925 precluded him from making further contributions to the study of personality disorders.

Another notable analyst associated with the Berlin school, Franz Alexander (1894–1964), used Freud's *The Ego and the Id* as the touchstone for his *Psychoanalysis of the Total Personality* (1929). Much like Abraham's writings, this book shifted the emphasis from isolated neurotic symptoms toward habitual modes of maladaptive behaviors. "More and more," Alexander wrote, "we are coming to regard neurotic illness as a manifestation of the whole human being."[17] He noted how psychoanalysis, which focused on the unconscious and libido in the early stages of its development, was coming to emphasize the ego as it matured. He colorfully compared the id to a terroristic weapon, the superego to a corrupt secret police, and the ego to long-suffering citizens.[18]

Alexander also attempted to define the difference between normal and disordered personalities. In the former, the three core aspects of ego, superego, and id "form a more or less coherent and integrated whole in which they cooperate harmoniously." In contrast, "in the neurotic psyche this cooperation is disturbed, the different agencies are mutually hostile, the integrity of the personality is lost, and the individual parts acquire an extensive mutual independence."[19] In other words, personality disorders did not refer to particular character styles so much as to the failure of individuals to integrate the different aspects of personality into a unified system. This approach blurred the boundaries between normal and disordered personalities: upstanding character traits among adults could stem from childhood fears of castration that arose from fears of parental authority.[20] Alexander was also the first analyst to focus on antisocial behaviors. In *The Roots of Crime* (1935), he distinguished neuroses where "the emotional conflict results in symbolic gratifications of unsatisfied urges" from criminal behaviors that involve "overt misdeeds."[21] A complex interplay of constitutional dispositions, intrapsychic conflicts, and social forces determined whether personality dynamics resulted in neurotic or behavioral outcomes.

Like many of his contemporaries, Alexander joined the migration of analysts to the United States in the 1930s, becoming a leader of the American psychoanalytic movement and president of the American Psychoanalytic Association. He urged the field to turn away from its focus on unobservable concepts such as the unconscious toward discernible and measurable processes. This approach could lead psychoanalysis to bridge medicine, on the one hand, and social science, on the other hand.[22]

Wilhelm Reich (1897–1957) was the major transitional figure between traditional psychoanalysts and the next generation of neo-Freudians. He strove to understand how neurotic symptoms expressed the whole personality, which in turn resulted from social forces. Reich, who was a Communist in the 1920s before his expulsion from the party, was the most politically oriented analyst at the time. He called for the destruction of repressive cultural forces in order to liberate innate sexual instincts. To this end, his work blended the tenets of psychoanalysis with those of Marxism.

Reich founded the field of character analysis, which placed character at the heart of the ego's self-protection from the demands of the id and superego and the dangers of external forces. He defined "character" as "the typical mode of reaction of the ego towards the id and the outer world."[23] Reich contrasted his approach with the traditional analytic emphasis on hysterical, obsessional, or phobic symptoms that were distressing and ego-alien. In contrast, Reich viewed neuroses as manifestations of underlying character problems such as psychopathy or masochism that are not isolated traits but essential aspects of who a person is. His approach broadened the scope of analysis because, while relatively few people displayed neurotic symptoms, everyone has a personality (or character).

Reich's emphasis on how problematic characters lay beneath the emergence of many types of neuroses was a particularly important development because it viewed specific symptoms as malfunctioning aspects of underlying character structures.[24] Neuroses were no longer foreign bodies but instead were bound to the history and functioning of the whole personality. Individuals developed what Reich called "character armor" to defend against threats from both inner and outer forces: "Character armor manifested itself in a person's way of talking, walking, their affectations, their giggles, smiles and sneers, their politesse and their rude guffaws."[25] It became independent of original intra-psychic conflicts as the ego was "transformed into chronic attitudes, into chronic automatic modes of reaction."[26] This process led Reich to emphasize rigidity as a defining quality of personality disorders, while its opposite— emotional flexibility—indicated mental health.[27] Reich's ideas also influenced analytic practice. Character armor led patients to resist analysts' attempts to change their neurotic traits. This meant that therapeutic efforts were especially difficult for the personality disorders because one of character armor's major functions was to serve as a defense mechanism against efforts to transform them.

Reich, who was a Marxist, came to link character styles to distinct social configurations. He was influenced by anthropologists such as Bronislaw Malinowski, who emphasized the cross-cultural relativity of different character structures. Cultural forces such as political ideologies, religious beliefs, and moral systems became embedded in personality structures. The family was the major channel through which these forces were transmitted to individuals. Reich noted how lower-middle-class families were factories "for authoritarian ideologies and conservative character structure" because of the ruthless sexual repression they imposed on children.[28] Unlike Freud, who emphasized that the needs of civilization inevitably led to the repression of libidinous instincts, Reich argued that inhibited character structures arose from particular social formations such as Nazism. In effect, Reich inverted the traditional reverence for the notion of "character," using the term to refer to unyielding deference to despotic authority.

In his book *The Mass Psychology of Fascism* (1933), Reich tied the rise of fascism to sexual repression within families: "Suppression of the natural sexuality in the child, particularly of its genital sexuality, makes the child apprehensive, shy, obedient, afraid of authority, good and adjusted in the authoritarian sense."[29] Reich's portrayal of bourgeois families as breeding grounds for later subordination was a major influence on work about the authoritarian personality in the later writings of Erich Fromm, Max Horkheimer, and Theodor Adorno.

Perhaps Reich's most important innovation was his insistence that sexual liberation was the best panacea for disturbed personalities. "I have become convinced," Reich wrote, "that sexuality is the center around which revolves the whole of social life as well as the inner life of the individual."[30] Far more than other analysts, Reich celebrated the id and denigrated the attempts of the ego to control it. Unlike Freud, who believed that the needs of civilization demanded that humans repress their instincts, Reich advocated for their full expression. Conversely, while Freud demonstrated much sympathy for the ego's delicate attempts to negotiate the demands of the id, superego, and external world, Reich was concerned with limiting the restraints that the ego placed on the full expression of instinctual drives: "It is the inhibition of sexuality ... which makes aggression a power beyond mastery, because inhibited sexual energy turns into destructive energy."[31] He pressed for reforms that dismantled oppressive social structures and norms that impeded the expression of sexual instincts. This was especially important for adolescents, whose character development could be permanently maimed when their natural sexuality was repressed.[32]

Reich's work reinforced the blurry boundaries between normality and pathology in psychoanalytic thinking. "What has to be explained is not the fact that the man who is hungry steals or the fact that the man who is exploited strikes, but why the majority of those who are hungry *don't* steal and why the majority of those who are exploited *don't* strike," Reich wrote in *The Mass Psychology of Fascism*.[33] He grounded neurotic and normal characters alike in the oral, anal, and phallic developmental stages. His work also attempted to transform analytic practice from uncovering past traumas to understanding how current character structures prevented the achievement of mental health. Reich's portrayals of masochistic and narcissistic character anticipate current analytic descriptions of these personality types.[34] His notion of character armor also initiated a long-standing belief among analysts that the personality disorders were far harder to treat than the symptom-based neuroses.

Reich's view of character placed him within the boundaries of accepted psychoanalytic thought during the 1920s and early 1930s. His later works, written after his emigration to the United States, put him far outside the analytic (or any other) mainstream. Eventually, Reich's commitment to viewing sexual freedom as the key to human liberation led him to develop orgone accumulators, which were wooden cupboards insulated with steel wool, that he asserted could not only enhance sexual energy but also cure cancer and schizophrenia, among many other diseases. His claims led the Food and Drug Administration to prosecute and convict him for making false statements about the health benefits of these machines. Reich died of a heart attack in 1957 while confined in a federal prison.

Austrian analyst Otto Fenichel (1897–1946), who became a leader of the American psychoanalytic movement after he immigrated to the United States, also moved the field in a more social direction. Although he was a devoted Marxist, unlike Reich, Fenichel never abandoned his commitment to psychoanalytic orthodoxy. In 1908, Freud had written, "The permanent character traits are either interchanging perpetuations of original impulses, sublimations of them, or reaction formations against them."[35] Fenichel used this sketch as the basis for classifying character traits. He proposed that libidinal energy could develop into character structures that did not suffer from inner conflicts and contrasted reactive character traits, which could be either avoidant or oppositional, with sublimation types that successfully channeled instinctual demands into valuable forms of social activity. While the latter types were not of much interest to students of neuroses, they were of "greatest importance" for the study of character.[36] This approach moved analytic emphasis away from pathology toward normality.[37]

For Fenichel, "character" referred to the usual ways that individuals integrated internal and external demands.[38] Far from intruding on the self, as the neuroses did, they were the typical responses of individuals to both inner and outer stimuli. Both character and character disorders were habitual forms of reactions that differed by the degree of plasticity they allowed. Disorders were characterized by rigid and enduring patterns that limited the flexibility of the ego to react to instinctual impulses, on the one hand, and environmental demands, on the other hand. Fenichel also insisted that instincts and character structures varied historically and so would appear in different guises in different societies.

By the mid-1930s the mainstream of psychoanalysis had moved from the study of neurotic symptoms to a focus on character disorders.[39] This immensely broadened its reach because the new character-based view was applicable to normal as well as disordered people. The new emphasis on character pushed analysis in a far more social direction because sociocultural forces determined what was "disordered" or "normal." Fenichel observed, "What is 'order' in one milieu is 'disorder' in another." While heredity and individual upbringing had some influence, "in most cases, however, the special attitude has been forced on the individual by the external world."[40]

During its initial decades, psychoanalysts generally ignored culturally specific factors and studied what they assumed were universal influences over human behavior. The rise of ego psychology, however, led to a heightened focus on how culturally specific values and social organizations led to various character types. Because a major purpose of the ego was to mediate between individuals and their environments, it followed that its functioning would vary across different groups. Different social settings produced more or less repression, different styles of defenses, the need for independence or dependence, and the like. Moreover, character types were not constant but altered according to situations: "The same persons may be extraverts under certain circumstances, introverts under others. . . . All this makes it evident that the influence of the social milieu is of even more importance in shaping the character than in giving form to a neurosis."[41] This recognition led to the emergence of a new style of thinking among a group that came to be called the "neo-Freudians."

The Neo-Freudians

The neo-Freudians had common roots with mainstream analysts in the Berlin school that Karl Abraham led. By the 1920s the major center of analytic training had moved from Freud's Vienna to Berlin. "Berlin is clamouring for psychoanalysis," Abraham wrote to Freud.[42] The Berlin school operated in a city racked by sharp political divisions, the rise of anti-Semitism, intense conflicts between fascists and Marxists, many political assassinations, and an extraordinary rate of inflation and consequent economic suffering. It was impossible for politically oriented Freudians to sustain a focus on inner life in an environment of such constant turmoil and threat. Their new social focus was also compatible with the values of a postwar generation that rejected traditional ideologies. During the 1930s the analysts associated with the Berlin school began to agitate for social and cultural reforms through integrating psychoanalysis with Marxism. Reich, who had moved from Vienna to Berlin, noted how the analysts there were "far more progressive in social matters than the Viennese."[43]

Karen Horney and Erich Fromm were the two most prominent neo-Freudians. Influenced by Abraham and Reich, they strove to show how social and cultural forces led to diverse character orientations. At the same time, they minimized the influence of libidinous drives and unconscious forces on character development. Personality resulted from historical, structural, and economic factors far more than from universal, biological underpinnings. As their writings evolved, the neo-Freudians came to almost completely shed the Freudian aspects of their work and to develop a thoroughly social view of personality.

Karen Horney

The German-born psychiatrist Karen Horney (1885–1952) trained with Abraham in Berlin. Although she was not Jewish, she immigrated to the United States in 1932 when the Nazis began to take power in Germany. Her early works, which focused on how socially induced conflicts led women to develop distorted personality structures, provided one of the first feminist critiques of psychoanalysis. Horney criticized Freud because "till quite recently the minds of boys and men only were taken as objects of investigation. The reason for this is obvious. Psychoanalysis is the creation of a male genius, and almost all those who have developed his ideas have been men."[44] As her thought evolved, she came to reject such core analytic concepts as the Oedipus complex, penis envy, and the dominant role of fathers in character development, instead building a theory of personality grounded in cultural ideologies and interpersonal relationships.

Uniquely among analysts at the time, Horney initially focused on the social norms that limited women's achievement and resulted in their precarious psychological situation in modern societies. Culture, not instinctual needs, distorted female character structures. Horney emphasized how social constraints that confined women in the home led to the ideal "of woman as one whose only longing is to love a man and to be loved by him."[45] The economic dependence of women on men coupled with their lack of sexual autonomy led to a situation where "it is hard to see how any woman can escape becoming masochistic in some degree, from the effects of the culture alone."[46] Masochistic character structures were thus neither biological nor sexual in origin but stemmed from conflicts between social norms and desires for self-fulfillment.[47] Women could find satisfaction only through overcoming the demands of a stifling civilization.

Horney turned previously male-focused analytic explanations on their heads. For example, social restrictions on female—but not male—achievement accounted for penis envy. Similarly, her mother-centered view of family processes contrasted with Freud's father-centered focus. Moreover, she believed that changing social conditions even without addressing intrapsychic issues could resolve women's problems. In further contrast with Freud, who assumed that the demands of civilization must inevitably suppress individual needs, Horney regarded this conflict as a result of particular modern settings that could be overcome through changing social circumstances. Even such phenomena as the Oedipus complex, which Freud had considered a result of universal family processes, were instead associated with social conditions that generated hostility among family members. Horney also inverted Freud's view of sexual problems: "Sexual problems, although they may sometimes prevail in the symptomatic picture, are no longer considered to be in the dynamic center of the neuroses. Sexual difficulties are the effect rather than the cause of the neurotic character structure."[48]

Horney was especially attuned to the changing influence of social norms on evaluations of character: "The conception of what is normal varies not only with the culture but also within the same culture, in the course of time. Today, for example, if a mature and independent woman were to consider herself a 'fallen woman,' 'unworthy of the love of a decent man,' because she had had sexual relationships, she would be suspected of a neurosis, at least in many circles of society. Some forty years ago this attitude of guilt would have been considered normal."[49] In the short period between Freud's development of his sexually grounded theory and the 1930s, cultural attitudes had shifted to such an extent that sexual repression no longer had major consequences for neuroses.

After Horney settled in the United States, her attention turned from the specific situation of modern women to the forces that produced neurotic character structures more generally. Her associations with anthropologists including Ruth Benedict and Margaret Mead led to her tenet that historical, social, and cultural factors led to various personality styles: "The standards vary with culture, period, class and sex [so that] there is no such thing as normal psychology, which holds for all mankind."[50] Competitive modern cultures, which emphasized the need to succeed, rendered women and men alike prone to anxiety and insecurity. Neurotic personalities "are essentially produced by the difficulties existing in our time and culture."[51]

In 1937 Horney published what became an extraordinarily popular book, *The Neurotic Personality of Our Time*. Its emphasis radically differed from those of traditional analytic approaches: "specific cultural conditions under which we live" more than "incidental individual experiences" produced neurotic characters.[52] Moreover, character problems stemmed from the way people use defenses against social demands as adults to a greater extent than through inner conflicts that originated in earlier periods of life. The past might generally shape character structures, but personality styles become autonomous systems that exert their influence through their present functioning. Culture, far more than biology, generated personality difficulties.

Another major contrast between Horney and classical Freudian views was her assertion that sexual forces underlay the neuroses only in "exceptional cases." Horney denied the importance of the core Freudian assumption that biologically based sexual drives are a primary influence on lifelong behavioral styles, instead asserting that sexuality itself was dependent on cultural attitudes: "A great deal of what appears as sexuality has in reality very little to do with it, but is an expression of the desire for reassurance. If this is not taken into consideration one is bound to overestimate the role of sexuality."[53]

Horney sharply distinguished character, which referred to the overall nature of personality structure, from symptoms such as phobias, depressions, or psychosomatic conditions.[54] Character was the most important influence over human behavior, including the formation of neurotic symptoms. The first page of *The Neurotic Personality of Our Time* makes clear that personality is the central dynamic in all neuroses: "I am not concerned here with any particular type or types of neuroses, but have concentrated on the character structure which recurs in nearly all neurotic persons of our time in one or another form."[55]

Horney asserted that social formations, not sexual or aggressive instincts, create character structures. US culture promoted intense competitiveness in both the economic and interpersonal spheres, which produced people who had at the core of their characters a basic anxiety, "a feeling of being small, insignificant, helpless, deserted, endangered, in a world that is out to abuse, cheat, attack, humiliate, betray, envy."[56] This anxiousness drove the characteristic individual in the mid-twentieth century to feel hostile, emotionally isolated, and inferior. Neurotics rarely confronted these feelings directly but instead projected them onto objects, situations, political events, or indistinct feelings of doom. Likewise, they employed a number of defenses against these mental states, such as the quest for affection from others, power, prestige, and material possessions.[57] These interpersonal and intrapersonal conflicts were not innate but stemmed from the cultural contradictions of modern life.

A fundamental inner insecurity that made people excessively dependent on gaining approval and affection from others marked contemporary neurotic characters. These emerged from contradictory social norms that led to perpetual states of psychic tension. Horney used the example of how, on the one hand, cultural expectations urged people to conform to the biblical injunction "thou shalt love thy neighbor as thyself."[58] Yet, on the contrary, they also received constant messages to succeed by outperforming others: "The neurotic person, however, pursues two ways that are incompatible: an aggressive striving for a 'no one but I' dominance; and at the same time an excessive desire to be loved by everyone."[59] The neurotic character, therefore, was marked by internal structural incompatibilities rather than any particular style. Conforming to the demands of a sick society produced and perpetuated neurosis. This thoroughly relativized the concepts of normal and neurotic, because in repressive societies neurotics who did not accept oppressive conditions could be healthier than conformists.

Horney also discussed what made some character types disordered. Character disorders had two distinctive qualities. First, they were overly rigid and so lacked the flexibility to react to changing situations: "The normal person, for instance, is suspicious where he senses or sees reasons for being so; a neurotic person may be suspicious, regardless of the situation, all the time, whether he is aware of his state or not."[60] Second, a character disorder prevented someone from self-actualization even in the absence of external constraints. Neuroses that responded to circumstances displayed "only a momentary lack of adaptation to a given difficult situation."[61] Character disorders, in contrast, might feature identical symptoms but were disorders because they resulted from deformations that were present before any particular situation and persisted after the situation is over. In other words, people with character disorders were their own worst enemies. In her later work Horney asserted that different cultures could be evaluated through the degree to which they promoted or hindered self-realization.[62]

Just before World War II, Horney published *New Ways in Psychoanalysis*, where her break with classical analytic principles became even clearer than in her past work. She replaced Freudian libido theory with a sociological orientation. Rejecting core notions such as the importance of early childhood experiences, inner drives, and the Oedipus complex, Horney insisted that personality and personality disorders alike arose through environmental influences. Inverting Freud, sexual problems resulted from character problems. After Otto Fenichel criticized the book for its neglect of sexuality, Horney responded that "I see [instinct theory] as something that must be overcome."[63]

Horney's lasting achievement was to reveal the sexism at the core of analytic views of female character. Her work was celebrated in the general culture as exemplifying the power of the "New Woman" that had emerged in the interwar decades. Traditional Freudians, however, including her former allies in the Berlin school, did not look kindly on her rejection of psychoanalytic orthodoxy. Franz Alexander, for example, wrote that Horney's *New Ways* presented a cartoonish, one-dimensional portrayal of both Freud's and her own views.[64] Her heresy eventually led to her expulsion from analytic institutes, although her influence in the general culture persisted for decades.

Erich Fromm

Another popular neo-Freudian émigré from Germany, Erich Fromm (1900–1980), also propelled the study of personality in a social direction. Like Horney, he trained at the Berlin Institute, in his case after receiving a doctorate in sociology. Fromm immigrated to the United States in 1934, where he lived with Horney for the rest of the decade. Both neo-Freudians joined with participants in the culture and personality movement to create an alternative to mainstream psychoanalysis.

Fromm was uninterested in exploring the personality dynamics of particular individuals. Instead, his goal was to uncover the social factors that differentiated typical personalities in various groups: "We are interested, however, not in the peculiarities by which these persons differ from each other, but in that part of their character structure that is common to most members of the group."[65] Understanding the social nature of character was particularly important during the 1930s because it revealed the human needs that lay behind the lure of authoritarian political ideas in vulnerable socioeconomic systems.

Fromm's major project was to merge Freud's insights with those of Karl Marx. Marx was committed to altering social conditions to bring about radical social change but ignored individual psychology. Freud, in contrast, resolutely focused on inner psychological dynamics, disregarded social differences, and was deeply pessimistic about the possibility of making fundamental social transformations. Fromm's accomplishment was to show how the prevailing social and economic system in a person's society was "a primary factor in determining his whole character structure."[66] Economic structures, social conditions, and shared ideologies were the dominant forces shaping character types. Their influence was so pervasive that even unconscious experiences and libidinal structures gained expression from socioeconomic conditions.[67]

Fromm's central concept was "social character," which his biographer Lawrence Friedman calls "the signature theoretical contribution of his career."[68] It provided the missing link between Freud's libidinous drives and Marx's socioeconomic base. Instincts and unconscious dynamics were powerful but, like conscious behaviors, were socially shaped. Character structures, too, had libidinal roots but were molded by the prevailing family structures and social conditions in each society. For example, in his early work Fromm posited that bourgeois character traits such as possessiveness and rationality were rooted in anal erotic dynamics. "The social character," Fromm wrote, "comprises only a selection of traits, the *essential nucleus of the character structure of most members of a group which has developed as the result of the basic experiences and mode of life common to that group*."[69] It followed that changes in the nature of society would in turn lead to changes in social character.

Fromm's popular work, *Escape from Freedom* (1941), treated anxiety as the central problem of modern society. In contrast to Freud, Fromm rooted modern anxieties in the particular conditions of each society rather than in biological or psychological constants. For instance, the Oedipus complex was not universal. Matriarchal societies in prehistoric times did not give rise to oedipal struggles but promoted free and unconditional love. Patriarchal societies, however, placed sons in competition with their fathers because they would inherit their property after their death.[70] When the social relations that gave rise to oedipal feelings changed, this complex would disappear. "Individual psychology," Fromm asserted, "is fundamentally social psychology."[71]

Character, too, was a social product. The combination of Protestantism and capitalism forged people who were marked by a compulsion to work, thriftiness, asceticism, and a readiness to submit to the demands of external authorities.[72] Fromm used the anal complex as an illustration: it arose from the rationality, possessiveness, and puritanism that characterized bourgeois society rather than from any universal developmental stage or libidinous instincts. Similarly, like Horney, Fromm viewed femininity and masculinity as derivations of socially determined norms, not as innate sexual differences.

For Fromm, unchecked capitalism, periodic structural unemployment, overpopulation, and a host of other social ills produced the fundamental conditions of life in the modern world. Lacking the security of encompassing belief systems found in earlier societies, many individuals turned to totalitarian movements that protected them from the anxiety, isolation, and loneliness that freedom engendered. Authoritarian ideologies allowed them to "escape" from these afflictions because they channeled insecurities into reverence for a strong leader. The sadomasochistic personalities that resulted involved deference to superiors and contempt for inferiors.

Fromm also discussed how twentieth-century capitalist societies produced individuals with a "marketing orientation" that molded their personalities to fit whatever expectations others had of them but that did not allow them to develop a genuine self of their own.[73] The change in economic focus from production to consumption led to fearful and passive people unable to construct meaningful identities. For members of modern societies, "everything is transformed into a commodity, not only things, but the person himself, his physical energy, his skills, his knowledge, his opinions, his feelings, even his smiles."[74] In the resulting marketing orientation, "success depends largely on how well a person sells himself on the market, how well he gets his personality across. . . . Since success depends largely on how one sells one's personality, one experiences oneself as a commodity. . . . The premise of the marketing orientation is emptiness, the lack of any specific quality which could not be subject to change."[75] The key problem people faced was not their instincts or unconscious repressions but understanding and overcoming an exploitative society. Integrated personalities could only arise after socioeconomic changes made the emergence of truly fulfilled selves possible.

Personality disorders, too, were more products of cultural than of inner dynamics, as Fromm's writings on sadomasochistic personality demonstrate. Analysts, following Freud, had considered sadomasochism as the result of arrested inner processes of psychosexual development.[76] In contrast, Fromm viewed this condition as a socially determined response to authority: "He admires authority and tends to submit to it, but at the same time he wants to be an authority himself and have others submit to him."[77] Social movements such as Nazism capitalized on the sadomasochistic character structures of their followers that allowed them to find love through cherishing strong leaders and superiority through despising alien groups. These negative qualities were not rooted in individual pathology but in the cultural, political, and social class dynamics of historically specific societies. Fromm's later writings remained hugely popular but became less scholarly, more spiritual, and relatively unconcerned with issues surrounding personality.

The neo-Freudians gained much attention and admiration in popular culture; their work was written in an accessible style aimed at a wide readership. Fromm and Horney's books were best sellers. *Escape from Freedom* sold more than five million copies in twenty-eight languages.[78] *Time* magazine placed Horney on its cover in 1946 as one of six "big-league practitioners" of psychoanalysis.[79]

Orthodox psychoanalysts denigrated the neo-Freudians. They condemned them for rejecting the crucial role of the unconscious, early childhood influences, and instinctual forces. They thought the neo-Freudians naively adopted a romantic view that individuals were naturally good before social institutions corrupted them. Other criticism of the neo-Freudians came from the political Left, which attacked them for ignoring the potentially revolutionary consequences of unleashing sexual forces, minimizing the degree of conflict between individuals and society, and failing to advocate radical political solutions. For example, Herbert Marcuse indicted the neo-Freudians because "the 'personality' and its creative potentialities are resurrected in the face of a reality which has all but eliminated the conditions for the personality and its fulfillment."[80] Personality development was impossible, Marcuse and other radicals claimed, as long as society itself was repressive.

Mainstream analysts did not appreciate the cultural renown the neo-Freudians achieved or their radical deviations from Freudian assumptions. They expelled Fromm as well as Horney from analytic institutes. The failure of the neo-Freudians to establish their own institutional base precluded them from influencing psychiatric theory and practice at the time. Although they lost the intra-professional war for legitimacy within psychoanalysis, the neo-Freudians garnered huge popular acclaim from the late 1930s through the 1960s. Along with the culture and personality movement, they did more than anyone to propel personality into public consciousness.

Culture and Personality

The disciplines of anthropology and psychology both emerged toward the end of the nineteenth century when the Kantian divide between the natural and the cultural approaches dominated. As the previous chapter described, psychologists pursued a quantitative path that rejected intuitive explorations of inner feelings and strove to uncover universal laws. Anthropologists took the opposite track, intensely studying lived experiences in specific societies. They used inductive rather than deductive methods, emphasized the unique rather than common qualities of the groups they encountered, and focused on the influence of social as opposed to universal forces in molding individual personalities. Most thoroughly rejected Freudian notions that all humans followed common stages of personality development and argued that the power of cultural influences overrode any biological factors.

A few anthropologists did apply Freudian principles to the study of cultural processes. The most influential was Hungarian-born Géza Róheim (1891–1953), who posited that individual psychology lay behind all significant cultural phenomena, including personality: "There can be many types of personality but only one Unconscious."[81] Like Freud, Róheim advocated for the psychic unity of humanity: group myths, folklore, and cultural artifacts resulted from unconscious processes such as the Oedipus complex. He claimed that his fieldwork among native peoples of Australia showed that infantile traumas, usually related to the separation anxiety between infants and their mothers, produced the characteristic symbols of societies.[82] Róheim's student and analysand George Devereux, who founded the field of ethnopsychiatry, was another figure who used both anthropological and analytic perspectives. Devereux maintained an orthodox analytic stance, while at the same time insisting that cross-cultural studies were essential for full understandings of personality.[83]

American Abram Kardiner (1891–1981) was another notable psychoanalyst who integrated Freudian insights with an anthropological perspective.[84] He postulated that the primary institutions of family organization, childcare practices, and sexual training shaped modal personality structures in all groups. Because these institutions differed across cultures, so did the resulting cross-cultural personality styles. Socially typical personalities in turn shaped the secondary cultural institutions of religion, myth, thought patterns, and other prominent symbolic systems. Kardiner used data from the Alor people of the Dutch East Indies to conclude that their apathetic, suspicious, and insecure personalities resulted from the maternal neglect they experienced in infancy.[85] While his work maintained many basic analytic principles, at the same time it recognized that other analytic assumptions were culture-bound products of Freud's time and place.

Róheim and Kardiner, however, were outliers. Most anthropological studies rejected psychoanalytic views of personality. Anthropologists affiliated with the culture and personality movement scorned the psychological reductionism of traditional psychoanalysis. On the one hand, they disputed Freudian appeals to universal, organically grounded aspects of human nature. For them, personalities did not follow any predetermined sequence of development but were aspects of unique cultural configurations that had to be understood on their own terms. Cultures were all-powerful shapers of personality. On the other hand, anthropologists claimed that Freudian portrayals of personality reflected a culture-bound notion that might typify certain groups in Western societies but that were far from universal. Cultural differences in personality, a topic that psychologists and analysts alike neglected, became anthropology's abiding source of concern.

By the early 1930s personality had become perhaps the central concept in the field, but anthropologists found themselves confronting psychoanalysis, which was immensely popular at the time. Traditional analytic assumptions challenged core anthropological beliefs. They regarded processes such as the Oedipus complex, stages of human development, or sexual and destructive instincts as universal to all societies. Moreover, they were relatively impervious to cultural shaping. Likewise, analysts viewed personality as a product of intraindividual conflicts that resisted cultural influences. The emergent anthropological worldview was diametrically opposite each of these assumptions.

In addition, anthropologists were propelled by their opposition to eugenics, a prominent intellectual current in the United States at the time. If Francis Galton's statistical approach to mental phenomena inspired psychologists, his enthusiasm for improving the human race through selective breeding guided eugenicists. The driving force behind Galton's work was to show how the natural side of the nature/nurture divide was by far the most powerful influence on human behavior. "Nature," Galton stated, "is all that a man brings with him into the world; nurture is every influence from without that affects him after birth."[86] He passionately believed that Darwin's principle of natural selection was not limited to biological processes but also powerfully molded character. Mental and physical properties alike were inherited results of natural selection. Moreover, this process not only determined individual differences but also the superiority and inferiority of different cultures and races.

One of Galton's US followers, eugenicist Paul Popenoe, proclaimed in 1915, "Heredity is not only much stronger than any single factor of the environment, in producing important human differences, but is stronger than any possible number of them put together."[87] Another leading eugenicist, Charles

Davenport, linked personality traits such as seclusiveness, stinginess, insincerity, and deceit to genetic factors.[88] American eugenicists were highly regarded, well resourced, and influential shapers of thought in law, education, and popular culture.[89]

American anthropologists were appalled at eugenicists' racist views as well as their elevation of nature and degradation of nurture. They set out to develop a totally divergent approach that emphasized the cultural determinants of human behavior where "in the great mass of a healthy population, the social stimulus is infinitely more potent than the biological mechanism."[90] In addition, they rejected the notion that some cultures were superior or inferior to others but regarded all as morally equivalent. By the mid-1920s the most potent academic debate in the United States was the relative importance of biological and cultural factors in shaping human behavior.

Based on the writings of Franz Boas (1858–1942), a German immigrant to the United States, and his students Ruth Benedict (1887–1948) and Margaret Mead (1901–1978), anthropologists insisted that human behavior was not innate but varied enormously across cultures. Boas was committed to the idea of "the complete moulding of every human expression—inner thought and external behavior—by social conditioning."[91] People learned how to feel, think, and behave: to the extent that inherited natural propensities existed, they were so malleable that they were "capable of infinitely multiform solution."[92]

The culture and personality school that came to dominate anthropological thinking in the 1930s was allied with the neo-Freudians. Members of both groups read each other's works and socialized together. For both, cultural relativism replaced the universal, instinctual complexes that had marked Freud's work. Most fundamentally, they posited that cultural influences overrode any common hereditary endowments. History, circumstance, and environment were the primary forces that shaped lifestyles, human relations, and moral codes, as well as personality, in each culture. These forces were powerful enough to prevail over whatever inherited traits humans shared with members of other groups.

Polish-born Bronislaw Malinowski used his fieldwork among the Trobriand Islanders during the 1920s to provide one of the first anthropological critiques of Freudian personality dynamics.[93] His study of this matrilineal group found that their social organization was grounded on the strictly nonsexual relationship between women and their brothers, who exercised discipline over her children. In contrast, fathers had no socially established authority over their offspring. Trobriand boys came to fear their mother's brother, not their own father, with whom they had affectionate relationships. Malinowski also claimed that their incestuous longings were displaced from their mothers to their sisters.

On these grounds, Malinowski rejected the universality of the Oedipus complex, which he claimed grew out of the particular constellation of family relationships in the Western groups that Freud studied. He quoted US philosopher John Dewey's complaint that psychoanalysts "treat phenomena, which are peculiarly symptoms of the civilization of the West at the present time, as if they were the necessary efforts of fixed native impulses of human nature."[94] Nevertheless, he recognized that his findings also suggested that oedipal feelings were grounded in biological predispositions that were attached to whatever family figures were available in particular cultures.[95] They were, however, subject to change when social structural conditions changed. Malinowski observed that fathers in Western societies were losing their positions of authority, so that "psycho-analysis cannot hope, I think, to preserve its 'Oedipus complex' for future generations, who will only know a weak and henpecked father. For him the children will feel indulgent pity rather than hatred and fear!"[96] Therefore, Freud went astray in ignoring the wide variation in family structures across various societies and over historical time that determined oedipal dynamics. Malinowski's study provided an early illustration of the culturally specific factors that shaped personality development.[97]

Other anthropologists went beyond Malinowski's efforts and strove to develop a new discipline entirely freed of biological influences. Benedict's immensely popular *Patterns of Culture* (1934) posited that learned, culturally specific values defined all forms of human behavior: "Not one item of his tribal social organization, of his language, of his local religion is carried in his germ cell."[98] Benedict used examples of ancient Greek definitions of homosexuality, the catatonic trances of native healers, and paranoid character traits among the Dobuan Islanders of New Guinea to assert that virtually all behaviors our society views as abnormal other cultures consider normal. For Benedict, individuals were conditioned from birth by the character of the culture into which they were born. Culture, not psychology, was the dominant influence over personality.

Benedict, like other members of the culture and personality school, described entire cultures as organized around a single, unique personality trait. The Dobuans provided a prominent example. A constant fear of poisoning ran through Dobuan life but was seen as normal rather than paranoiac behavior. Conversely, they considered behaviors that were normalized and even rewarded in our culture as abnormal. The Dobuans, Benedict suggested, would regard a person who is always cheerful, happy, and outgoing as deviant. Normal and abnormal personality traits thus resided in culturally approved conventions, not in universal psychological standards of appropriate functioning. "All our local conventions of moral behavior are without absolute validity," Benedict concluded.[99]

Well-adjusted personalities conformed to culturally patterned behaviors. Cultural influences were so powerful that they would shape the personalities of most people born into a particular culture into the dominant prototypes. In *Patterns of Culture*, Benedict distinguished "Apollonian" cultures that emphasized conformity, regulations, and rules from "Dionysian" cultures that highlighted individualism, expressiveness, and freedom. Benedict concluded that accepting the dictum that all cultures had equal validity allowed people to arrive "at a more realistic social faith, accepting as grounds of hope and as new bases for tolerance the coexisting and equally valid patterns of life which mankind has created for itself from the raw materials of existence."[100]

Benedict's younger colleague Margaret Mead was another major spokesperson for the culture and personality view. Like Benedict, she was a thoroughgoing cultural determinist who insisted that biology was irrelevant for explaining human behavior: "We are forced to conclude that human nature is almost unbelievably malleable, responding accurately and contrastingly to contrasting cultural conditions."[101] Her study of personality among the Samoans, *Coming of Age in Samoa* (1928), became the best-selling anthropology book ever written up to that time.[102] Mead's work on three tribes in New Guinea, *Sex and Temperament in Three Primitive Societies* (1935), was also a cultural sensation. These writings could hardly be more different from the psychological and psychoanalytic views of personality.

As a twenty-three-year-old graduate student in 1925, Mead conducted her dissertation research in American Samoa. She focused on the differences between the sexual freedoms among the adolescent girls she studied there with the harsh restrictions placed on this group in the contemporary West. "The girls' minds were perplexed by no conflicts, troubled by no philosophical queries, beset by no remote ambitions," she wrote of the Samoans. They had "the sunniest and easiest attitudes toward sex."[103] Indeed, they were "one of the most amiable, least contentious, and most peaceful peoples in the world."[104] The book's cover design, which featured a topless young woman running with a young man through palm trees under a tropical moon, helped propel interest in *Coming of Age*.[105]

Mead's work in New Guinea emphasized the profound cultural distinctions among the three groups she studied: "In one, both men and women act as we expect women to act—in a mild parental responsive way; in the second, both act as we expect men to act—in a fierce initiating fashion; and in the third, the men act according to our stereotype for women—are catty, wear curls and go shopping, while the women are energetic, managerial, unadorned partners."[106] These differences seemed to indicate the arbitrary nature of gender-linked personality styles.

For Mead, temperament was wholly a product of cultural, not biological, forces. Babies were born without instincts or individual predispositions but learned how to feel and act from siblings, peers, parents, and other adults. Anthropologists should not focus on the personalities of particular individuals but instead examine how different societies produced standardized traits in their members. Most people in a given society came to share personality qualities because of social learning and pressure rather than psychological dynamics. The culture and personality movement gave the impression that cultural norms were all-powerful shapers of personalities that gave little room for individual deviations.[107]

If almost all people conformed to preferred cultural styles of personality, what constituted a personality *disorder*? In fact, people whom psychiatrists might call "disordered" were those who deviated from culturally specific patterns of behavior. For example, a mental illness conceived as a violation of the laws of nature, such as transgressing gender norms, is really just a violation of culturally specific rules. Mead provided examples of the people of Papua New Guinea who assigned roles of "fisherman" to women and "painter" to men. Those who deviated—artistic women or men who liked fishing—were social nonconformists; they did not have mental disorders.[108] What psychiatrists might consider to be a "personality disorder" was more a product of Western stereotypes of undesirable character traits than of any natural reality.

Anthropologists produced an outpouring of works that related personality styles to particular social structures. Leslie White, for example, viewed individualistic, extraverted personalities as unlikely to emerge in groups with crowded living conditions, such as the Pueblo Indians: "And the distance between individuals in a pueblo is very small. A pueblo is no place for an individualist; an aggressive 'go-getter' is especially obnoxious. He makes life unbearable for his neighbors. Close contact within a pueblo tends to wear off the sharp corners and edges of a personality and make it smooth and inconspicuous, like a water-worn pebble."[109]

Most work in the culture and personality tradition focused on far-distant and, to Westerners, "exotic" groups. Social psychologist John Dollard's *Caste and Class in a Southern Town* (1937) brought the culture and personality tradition to bear on a US region. Dollard set out to study the personalities of African Americans but soon discovered that their lives were so deeply rooted in their caste-based communities that their personalities were inextricable from social context. Expressions of personality responded to the demands of concrete social positions. A person "will tend to develop the feelings appropriate to his life reality situation and, as a corollary, all men in the same situation will tend to develop essentially the same feelings."[110]

Dollard found that the descendants of formerly enslaved people showed common emotional traits. They displayed the personality types that they believed their subordinate positions compelled them to adapt. Most accepted their actual social situations as defined in the Deep South and renounced expressions of protest and aggression. They affected a performance style where they appeared to be ignorant, shiftless, and happy-go-lucky, although they did not believe these traits characterized their true selves. Dollard quoted another sociologist who found, "without any permanent place in the economic life of the community, the Negroes are thoroughly cowed, meek, humble and generally silent."[111] In contrast, when among their own people they showed their "real" personalities. Dollard's work indicated how people used personality as a strategic resource in given situations.

Although Benedict, Mead, and other leaders of the culture and personality school typically studied small, faraway, and isolated groups, their work became enormously influential in the United States. Like the neo-Freudians, they assumed that central analytic concepts such as the Oedipus complex and penis envy resulted from power dynamics in patriarchal societies rather than universal psychological processes. Anthropologists did not influence therapeutic practice, but their broader conceptions of how personality related to the dominant cultural patterns in groups, not to biological factors, remained prominent for decades. At the same time, they left little room for the uniqueness of individual personality or for the systematic comparative study of personality across different societies.

Conclusion

The radical changes that World War I and its aftermath brought about reoriented the study of personality in a far more social direction. Psychoanalysts, neo-Freudians, and anthropologists all came to focus on the social determinants of character structures. During the 1930s, the mass immigration of European refugees led the center of personality studies in each field to move to the United States.

By the eve of World War II, three well-developed—but thoroughly divergent—models of personality had emerged. Psychological portrayals of personality abstracted character traits from social circumstances, quantified them, and compared individual scores to the means of aggregates. The psychoanalytic emphasis was the opposite of the psychological worldview in each way. Analysts examined character traits as aspects of the total self, which they tried to interpret through deep explorations of particular individuals and how they adapted to their environments. They rarely worked in institutions but served individual clients who sought their help in overcoming personal problems. Finally, the neo-Freudian and culture and personality schools eschewed the study of individuals and their differences, instead examining the social shaping of personality. They scorned the universalistic methods of psychologists and analysts alike, instead closely scrutinizing modal personalities in various groups and societies. They rarely worked in either nonacademic organizations or private practices, instead targeting a broad readership in the society at large. The onset of World War II would propel personality to a central place in mainstream psychiatry as well as in psychology, psychoanalysis, and the social sciences.

CHAPTER FOUR

Personality Flourishes

The attention paid to personality in US culture spiked in the period between the country's entry into World War II in 1941 and the publication of the *DSM-III* in 1980. The appeal of personality spread through three major routes. The first was psychoanalysis, which had fully embraced its study by the time Freud died in 1939. Especially in the United States, analysis was a resounding public success. "In America today," sociologist Philip Rieff observed in 1959, "Freud's intellectual influence is greater than that of any other modern thinker. He presides over the mass media, the college classroom, the chatter at parties, the playgrounds of the middle classes where child-rearing is a prominent and somewhat anxious topic of conversation."[1] In this period, analytic interest focused on personality styles, especially narcissistic and borderline types.

Social scientists forged the second pathway for the enormous popularity of personality. In the wake of the influential neo-Freudian and culture and personality schools in the 1930s, postwar books such as *The Authoritarian Personality* (1950), *The Lonely Crowd* (1950), and *Organization Man* (1956) gained much public, as well as academic, acclaim. Cultural relativism became a dominant theme in the study of personality as the rise and fall of Nazism discredited biological approaches to all forms of human behavior. Finally, the mass application of personality tests to soldiers during World War II spread throughout the educational and corporate realms in the postwar period, propelling psychologists to prominence within these spheres. The eminence of personality persisted up to the revolutionary transformations of psychiatric diagnosis that the *DSM-III* brought about in 1980.

World War II

World War II propelled personality disorders to far greater importance than ever before. The US military tried to identify disordered recruits before they entered service, to deal with problematic personalities who did join the armed forces, and to help discharged soldiers who struggled with readjusting to civilian life. Military psychiatrists developed sophisticated techniques for addressing personality disorders at each stage. Their efforts were highly publicized: psychiatry in general and psychoanalysis in particular were thrust into cultural prominence during and after the war as newspapers, magazines, movies, radio, and, later, television featured their efforts to confront the mental health problems of soldiers and civilians.

Harry Stack Sullivan (1892–1949) was head of the William Alanson White Institute, probably the leading psychoanalytic institute in the world at the time. In collaboration with neo-Freudians, sociologists, and anthropologists, he developed influential theories of the social genesis of personality disorders.[2] Sullivan believed that a proper understanding of personality could arise only through direct observation of interpersonal relationships. His theory accordingly defined personality as "the relatively enduring pattern of recurrent interpersonal situations which characterize a human life."[3] This view of personality residing within interactions rather than interior selves evokes Allport's earlier invocation of Crusoe and Friday.

When the United States entered World War II, Sullivan became the leading psychiatric advisor to the Selective Service Commission. Sullivan and his colleagues emphasized the need to identify those recruits who were not necessarily mentally ill when they appeared before draft boards but whose personalities could make them prone to become mentally ill in the future. They urged physicians to disqualify those who displayed such personality "deviations" as "instability, seclusiveness, sulkiness, sluggishness, discontent, lonesomeness, depression, shyness, suspicion . . . [and] recognized queerness and homosexual proclivities."[4] It was especially important for physicians to identify such men before they entered the military because their mental disturbances could not only make them unfit to fight but also disrupt their combat units.

Sullivan developed a fifteen-minute interview that screened all potential recruits to determine their fitness for combat. It was not so much concerned with particular symptoms of mental illness as with whether personalities were suited for military service and whether a recruit had sufficient ego strength

and emotional stability to adjust to his combat unit. Conversely, it could identify those with overly aggressive or passive personalities or homosexual tendencies that would disqualify them as soldiers. For example, traits such as
difficulty in making friends, being recognized as a follower in school or later
life, and lack of purpose and spontaneity differentiated soldiers who might
become psychiatric casualties from those who might not.[5] Skilled interviewers
not only used verbal responses but also observed factors such as "the way that
the person seats himself, what he does with his body, with his posture, his
restlessness" to assess personality.[6]

Screening efforts led a full quarter of potential recruits, 1.75 million men,
to be rejected for neuropsychiatric reasons.[7] Sullivan's procedure became a
victim of its own success: the military discontinued it in 1942 because it dramatically lowered available manpower. Nevertheless, it focused attention on
the importance of personality characteristics as possible predictors of adjustment to the military. Later in the war, the armed services came to use personality tests as one method of determining the fitness of recruits to enter combat
and to select officer candidates. The belief grew that these tests could inform
decisions to match individuals with the kind of military positions that best
suited their personal characteristics.[8]

Ultimately, the screening effort failed, and not only because of the enormous number of rejections. Despite the effort to detect defective personalities
before they entered the service, more than a million US soldiers received mental health treatment during the war. Psychiatric reasons accounted for about
half of all medical discharges from the military.[9] Yet the causes of mental
breakdowns had little to do with the sorts of personality problems that screening interviews were designed to identify. Instead, by far the most important
predictor of psychological collapse was the intensity of combat itself.[10] Most
breakdowns occurred among those without predispositions that screening
might have identified before they entered military service. The military's chief
psychiatrist, William Menninger (1899–1966), concluded that the "history or
the personality make-up" was less important for successful adjustment to the
military than "the force of factors in the environment which supported or
disrupted the individual."[11]

Although psychiatrists came to believe that the intensity and duration of
combat experiences were the most important predictors of which soldiers
would be psychic casualties, they also realized that personality could have
some impact. Psychiatrists urged a focus on the total personality within the
context of a wartime environment that demanded extreme adjustments. Men-

ninger reported that more than half a million men were discharged because of "personality disturbances."[12] During the war, passive-aggressive conditions were the most frequently diagnosed type of personality disorder, accounting for 6 percent of all admissions to army hospitals.[13]

Perhaps the most interesting finding was that personality disorders could be advantageous in certain kinds of combat situations. Psychopaths provided one case.[14] On the one hand, they often got into fights, went AWOL, and were subject to various punishments. Yet, on the other hand, the same belligerence and impulsivity that led psychopaths to get into trouble outside of combat could lead them to act heroically in battle. Military psychiatrists Roy Swank and Walter Marchand noted how the less than 2 percent of soldiers who had "aggressive psychopathic personalities" could endure combat for inordinate lengths of time before breaking down.[15] Obsessive-compulsive personality types were another case. Their rigid behaviors made them steady and reliable bomber pilots who were better able to withstand the terrors of air combat.[16]

Personality difficulties were not just of interest at the screening and inservice stages. They also often created serious problems once veterans returned home. The same personality traits served very different functions inside and outside the military. Aggressive personalities who performed well in the war had particular trouble adjusting to peacetime conditions. And men with dependent personalities who especially relied on support and affection from closely knit military groups found it harder to adjust to the greater individualism that post-service life entailed.[17]

World War II also featured the military's adoption of anthropological efforts to define national character structures. It embraced the notion that personality traits usually associated with individuals—independence and dependence, dominance and submission, extraversion and introversion—could also characterize entire cultures and so be helpful for understanding adversaries. The US Office of War Information enlisted Ruth Benedict to write an analysis of Japanese national character that became *The Chrysanthemum and the Sword* (1946). This book, which sold more than two million copies in Japan, characterized the Japanese as "both aggressive and unaggressive, both militaristic and aesthetic, both insolent and polite, rigid and adaptable, submissive and resentful of being pushed around, loyal and treacherous, brave and timid, conservative and hospitable to new ways."[18]

Benedict's colleague, Margaret Mead, published a similar study of American character, *And Keep Your Powder Dry* (1942), which emphasized the strengths of Americans' antiauthoritarian, competitive, and loyal personality traits. Around the same time a close friend of Mead's, British anthropologist Geoffrey Gorer, explained what he considered to be the manic-depressive aspects of Russian national character through the lasting effects of their toilet training.[19] Similarly, Gorer attributed the contrast between the outward gentleness and inward brutality of the Japanese to the severity of their early hygiene practices.[20] These anthropological studies heralded an obsession with the social determinants of personality that arose in the postwar era.

Diagnostic Manuals

World War II led to a total transformation of psychiatric diagnostic manuals. As the previous chapter discussed, personality disorders were an afterthought in the reigning prewar *Statistical Manual*. They could be recorded only if they rose to psychotic severity and, even then, were not diagnosed in the presence of other kinds of psychoses. The war dramatically elevated the status of personality disorders in psychiatry.

Medical 203

William Menninger was a psychoanalytically oriented psychiatrist who rose to brigadier general, the highest rank a psychiatrist had ever attained in the army. He was a member of the royal family of US psychiatry: with his father, Charles Frederick, and his younger brother Karl, he founded one of the preeminent psychiatric inpatient facilities in the United States, the Menninger Clinic in Topeka, Kansas. During the war he was in charge of developing a new psychiatric diagnostic manual for the army, which he thought could also be used in civilian settings. The manual, *Medical 203*, was published in 1946.

While the wartime experiences of military psychiatrists were the immediate generator of *Medical 203*, the earlier writings of William's brother, Karl, largely influenced its content. Karl Menninger (1893–1990) was one of the earliest US proponents of psychoanalysis. In 1931 and 1932 he had undergone a training analysis with Franz Alexander at the Chicago Psychoanalytic Institute and visited Freud in Vienna two years later.[21] "Freud did not treat me very nicely," Menninger admitted, "but none the less, I think his ideas, his grasp, his formulations are so infinitely ahead of anything else that has been proposed, that I have nailed my banner on his mast, and I'll defend it against assault for the rest of my life."[22] Menninger's expansive theory combined Freudian psychodynamics with Adolf Meyer's account of mental disorders arising when individuals' reactions were inadequate to their environments.

Karl Menninger's book *The Human Mind* was the best-selling volume about mental health in US history at the time.[23] First published in 1930, it was in its third edition (1945) when *Medical 203* came out. The book's very first sentence asserted, "I have tried to put down in a systematic fashion the conception I have of the human personality."[24] For Menninger, "personality" was an extremely broad concept that involved examining "the individual as a whole. . . . It means all that anyone is and all that he is trying to become."[25] Like Meyer, Menninger emphasized how personalities had to adjust to aspects of the external environment. Apparently referring to Kraepelin, Menninger concluded the personality section with the observation that "the evolution of psychiatric thought . . . signalizes the transfer of emphasis from the final stages of mental disaster to the study of the constituents of personality. . . .What we call the 'disease' is the logical outgrowth of the particular personality in its efforts to solve a particular problem. The disease is a part of him, not an intruder or an invasion from without."[26]

In Theophrastian style, Menninger laid out a number of character types—the man who is always sick, the nagging wife, the impulsive thief. He then presented seven types of broken personalities that were "prone to have unusual difficulties on being put to adaptational strain."[27] These were the somatic, hypophrenic (mentally deficient), isolation, schizoid, cycloid, neurotic, and antisocial types. Four of these—isolation, schizoid, cycloid, and antisocial—directly entered *Medical 203*, and variations of the other three were clearly visible in the manual. Echoing Karl Menninger's view, *Medical 203* gave pride of place to personality and its deformations. They accounted for two of just five general classes of mental disorders and also played some role in two other classes, psychoneuroses and psychoses. The only set of conditions that had no connection with personality was the final class, disorders of intelligence.[28]

Reflecting the nature of psychic casualties during the war, "transient personality reactions to acute or special stress" was the first category in *Medical 203*. These diagnoses referred to how established patterns of reaction that people typically applied when overwhelming fear or flight situations led them to break down under conditions of extreme stress such as combat. They were distinguished from other types of mental disorder because they arose because of some external precipitant and were usually reversible. Each of its assumptions—that the afflicted did not have preexisting mental disorders, that their reactions stemmed from the external environment, and that their conditions were not chronic—starkly contrasted with the diagnoses found in the extant *Statistical Manual*.

The second class of personality disorders replaced the old grab-bag label of "psychopathic personality" with a category of "character and behavior disorders." These were pathological personality types that, unlike neuroses and psychoses, did not entail distress. Such disturbances rarely came to the attention of hospital-based psychiatrists in civilian settings but were potentially important sources of disruption within closely knit combat units. Their diagnostic criteria used an individual's conduct as the basis of classification. *Military 203* developed an elaborate conception of such conditions: its three subtypes encompassed seven kinds of pathological personality types (schizoid, paranoid, cyclothymic, inadequate, antisocial, asocial, and sexually deviant), addictions, and five kinds of immaturity reactions. All referred to nonpsychotic characterological problems that were absent from the prewar diagnostic manual. Despite the new descriptors, disorders such as "antisocial personality," "asocial personality," and "sexual deviant" retained the moralism of the discarded psychopathic personality condition.

The importance of personality extended beyond these two central classes. The psychoses were "characterized by a varying degree of personality disintegration." The psychoneurotic diagnosis of dissociative reaction arose when personality disorganization was sufficiently strong that overwhelming anxiety led to "aimless running or 'freezing.' "[29] The manual also directed clinicians to record personality predispositions for every diagnosis. *Medical 203* left no doubt that disordered personalities were a—and often *the*—fundamental aspect of mental disorders.

DSM-I *and* -II

Medical 203 was the basis for the first edition of the *Diagnostic and Statistical Manual of Mental Disorders* (*DSM*) that the American Psychiatric Association published in 1952. The *DSM* personality disorders involved typical patterns of adjustment to internal and external stressors. This distinguished them from other classes that featured particular symptoms rather than holistic character structures. Second, unlike the other categories, personality disorders caused minimal or no distress and anxiety. Third, they were not episodic but lifelong behavior patterns. The *DSM* characterized twelve types of personality disorders that it divided into three major groups.[30] Personality pattern disturbances—inadequate, schizoid, cyclothymic, and paranoid—were so deeply rooted that they "can rarely if ever be altered in their inherent structures by any form of therapy."[31] The second group were the emotionally unstable, passive-aggressive, compulsive, and a more general category of "other" that disintegrated when faced with stressful conditions.[32] Reflecting the significance that the passive-aggressive personality had for military psychiatrists, the manual contained three subtypes of pure passive-aggressive, passive-dependent, and aggressive. The final group of sociopathic personality disturbance contained those who were antisocial, dyssocial, sexual deviants, or addicted to alcohol or drugs.[33]

Each *DSM* description was riddled with social values. The four sociopathic personality disturbances were overtly evaluative. People who had them were "ill primarily in terms of society and of conformity with the cultural milieu, and not only in terms of personal discomfort and relations with other individuals." Those with inadequate personalities were characterized by "inadaptability, ineptness, poor judgment, lack of physical and emotional stamina, and social incompatibility." Passive-aggressive types featured "pouting, stubbornness, procrastination, inefficiency, and passive obstructionism." Such people were clearly unlikeable, difficult to deal with, or engaged in objectionable behaviors. It is not clear, however, why they were "disordered" in any medical sense.[34]

The next edition, the *DSM-II* (1968), considered the personality disorders (renamed "personality disorders and certain other non-psychotic mental disorders") as one of ten classes of mental disorders. This manual abandoned the tripartite division of personality patterns, personality traits, and sociopathic disturbances but continued to list eleven particular types, each of which was "characterized by deeply ingrained maladaptive patterns of behavior that are perceptibly different in quality from psychotic and neurotic symptoms."[35] It also unified the three subtypes of pure passive-aggressive, passive-dependent, and aggressive personalities into a single passive-aggressive type. The *DSM-II* added explosive, hysterical, and asthenic (low-energy) types and separated sexual deviance, alcoholism, and drug dependence, which constituted "certain other non-psychotic mental disorders," from the personality disorders. Otherwise, the descriptions of each type were similar to those found in the first *DSM*. Notably, neither narcissistic nor borderline conditions appeared in the *DSM-II* despite their growing centrality in psychoanalytic writings during the 1960s.

Unlike the manuals that followed, neither the *DSM-I* nor -*II* contained any general definition that stated what made any of their conditions "mental disorders." The *DSM-I* was silent about what made its personality types disorders except for the general and undefined characteristics of "developmental defects or pathological trends in the personality structure."[36] The *DSM-II* was equally nonspecific, noting that "this group of disorders is characterized by deeply ingrained maladaptive patterns of behavior that are perceptibly different in quality from psychotic and neurotic symptoms."[37] The result was that there was no way to differentiate personality disorders from culturally undesirable personality traits, nonconformity, or eccentricity.

Psychoanalysis

Before World War II the field of psychoanalysis was almost completely independent of traditional asylum-based psychiatry. Analysts trained in autonomous institutes and practiced in community settings. In prewar Europe, most analytic institutes welcomed laypeople as well as medically trained physicians. In his "The Question of Lay Analysis" (1926), Freud explicitly rejected the idea that analysts needed medical training and urged the development of a sovereign discipline of psychoanalysis. This involved establishing training institutes outside of universities and medical schools. European analysts comprised a mix of medical doctors, social scientists, psychologists, philosophers, and literary types. They gained their professional credentials through undergoing an analysis themselves, a process unique to the field. Only those who were analyzed were qualified to practice psychoanalysis. "We have been obliged to recognize and express as our conviction that no one has a right to join in a discussion of psychoanalysis who has not had particular experiences which can only be obtained by being analyzed oneself," Freud mandated.[38] This was because "the teachings of psycho-analysis are based on an incalculable number of observations and experiences, and only someone who has repeated those observations on himself and on others is in a position to arrive at a judgement of his own upon it."[39]

The European analysts who immigrated en masse to the United States in the 1930s encountered analytic institutes that were strictly limited to physicians. For example, the New York Psychoanalytic Society mandated, "The practice of psycho-analysis for therapeutic purposes shall be restricted to physicians (doctors of medicine) who are graduates of recognized medical schools, have had special training in psychiatry and psycho-analysis and who conform to the requirements of the medical practice acts to which they are subject."[40] Because of this, analysis was almost completely absorbed into American psychiatry in the postwar period. Indeed, psychoanalysis came to dominate the theory and practice of psychiatry in the postwar era. "By the mid-1960s, psychiatry had come in the mind of the American public to mean psychoanalysis," historian Edward Shorter observes.[41]

World War II was a second factor leading psychoanalysis to enter the mainstream of the psychiatric profession. William Menninger ordered that every military doctor should receive training in basic analytic principles.[42] After the war the size of the profession—newly infused with analytic principles—exploded, more than doubling between 1940 and 1948 from 2,300 to 4,700. By 1976 twenty-seven thousand psychiatrists practiced in the United States.[43] The locus of the field also moved from the asylum to the community. Before the war, two-thirds of psychiatrists worked in institutions; soon after the war ended, most had outpatient practices.

Perhaps most crucially, in contrast to the prewar era when psychoanalysis was independent of traditional psychiatry, after the war this boundary evaporated. Although only about four hundred analysts practiced in the late 1940s, the dominance of analysis in the general culture led them to have an outsized influence over the profession. Psychoanalysts became leaders in academic departments of psychiatry, psychiatric education and training, and the American Psychiatric Association.[44] Analysis became part of the medical establishment: it was "no longer an out-group discipline, but one which has been integrated extensively within the field of psychiatry."[45]

Psychoanalytic influence exploded in the general culture as well as within the psychiatric profession in the postwar period. "Nowhere was psychoanalysis more popular and professionally successful than in the USA in the first two decades following World War II," historian Dagmar Herzog notes.[46] Psychoanalysis became the prevailing psychological language of the educated middle and upper middle classes from the postwar period through the mid-1960s. "In New York City in 1946, there was an inevitability about psychoanalysis," literary critic Anatole Broyard observed. "Psychoanalysis was in the air, like humidity or smoke. You could almost smell it."[47]

Personality disorders came to take the central place in American psychiatric theory from the 1940s through the 1970s. After World War II what historian George Makari calls the "Hartmann era" began in American psychiatry. Heinz Hartmann (1894–1970) "set the theoretical agenda for American ego psychology for the following three decades" after World War II, Makari summarizes.[48] A German émigré psychiatrist who had studied with both Freud and eminent sociologist Max Weber, with other ego psychologists, he developed an ambitious agenda to apply psychoanalytic principles to normal as well as pathological phenomena.

Hartmann's ego psychology, which "represents a turning point in the development of modern psychoanalytic theory," placed the study of the total personality at its heart.[49] While Freud had highlighted how the ego must control both the dangerous biological impulses of the id and the unreasonable demands of the superego, Hartmann focused on how the ego adapted to and attempted to master the external world. This led him to emphasize the ego's relationship with social norms and social experiences, providing a bridge between the terrains of psychoanalysis and sociology.[50] Various character structures arose through adaptations to particular social circumstances that had the power to shape not only processes related to the ego but to underlying drives as well. Personality disorders, in turn, resulted from faulty ego development. Both normal and pathological personalities suffered from conflicts that "are part of the human condition," but the latter were more intense and less flexible than the former.[51]

Hartmann and other ego psychologists led orthodox psychoanalysis to confront the social, cultural, and historical settings in which people acted; the traditions that shaped their identities; and the actual interpersonal relationships through which they lived their lives.[52] For them, personalities could arise independently of instinctual drives and inner conflicts. Correspondingly, the focus of treatment shifted from uncovering unconscious memories toward strengthening the patient's capacity to cope with social demands. By 1946 a coalition of ego psychologists and orthodox Freudians controlled the American Psychoanalytic Association.[53]

Personality Disorders in Psychiatric Treatment

Before World War II most treatment of mental illness in the United States occurred in inpatient institutions. Outpatient therapy was rare and mostly limited to a few large cities. The postwar period involved a vast expansion of community-based practices. In 1947 *Life* magazine reported a sudden "mass demand for psychiatric help that has swamped facilities and practitioners alike."[54] Personality disorders accounted for much of this demand.

The prominent place of personality disorders in postwar diagnostic manuals both influenced and reflected psychiatric practice in the decades following World War II. Analytic patients at the time displayed very different types of problems than patients in earlier decades who presented hysterical symptoms, compulsions, frigidity, impotence, and the like that were often linked to repressive sexual norms and harsh superegos. The difficulties of the new generation were more likely to reflect personality styles connected to frustrated ambitions, narcissism, and the impulsivity of borderline patients.[55] People with diagnoses of personality disorders came to constitute a substantial proportion of psychiatric outpatients. One survey of psychoanalytic practice in 1976 summarized that there were "fewer good classical neurotics" and more "psychotics, borderlines, narcissistic characters, and patients with problems in development."[56]

Sociologist Charles Kadushin's study of 1,500 patients in ten psychiatric clinics in New York City in 1959–1960 provides a prominent example. Although different clinics had widely varying diagnostic practices, personality disorders were the single most common type of diagnosis.[57] The overall percentage of patients receiving these labels ranged from 16 to 65 percent, averaging about 45 percent. Psychoanalysts diagnosed 36 percent of their patients with some personality disorder, somewhat below the 42 percent they considered as neurotic. Kadushin found that clinics considerably differed in the type of personality conditions they favored. For example, schizoid diagnoses ranged from nonexistent in some facilities to 62 percent in others. Passive-aggressive was the favorite diagnosis in two clinics but was rarely used in others.[58]

Another survey of 440 psychiatrists in private practice the American Psychiatric Association conducted in 1970 indicated that 24 percent of clients received diagnoses of some personality disorder. Aside from the neuroses, which constituted 64 percent of diagnoses, the amount of personality disorder was far higher than any other category. A quarter of analytic patients and 17 percent of nonanalytic patients received a diagnosis of some personality disorder. This survey also indicated that people with personality disorders rarely entered inpatient treatment: only about 5 percent of inpatients had a personality condition.[59]

One aspect of the personality disorders that distinguished them from the psychoneuroses was the varying ways that the two classes came to enter treatment. Neurotics generally sought professional help to relieve distress from their unwanted symptoms. In contrast, personality disorders rarely involved distress. Therefore, other people including family members, educational authorities, the police, or other agents of social control typically pushed them to get therapeutic assistance.[60] Unfortunately, no studies exist about the particular pathways through which people with personality disorders entered treatment in this era.

The heady position psychoanalysis assumed in the 1940s and 1950s began to decline in the mid-1960s. It faced attacks from many fronts: medically minded psychiatrists derided it as un- or even anti-scientific. The antipsychiatry movement that arose at the time mocked it as part of a repressive establishment. Gay people loathed its homophobia while feminists mocked patriarchal concepts such as "penis envy." The conventional analytic emphasis on the individual came to seem more and more outmoded as identity increasingly focused on social categories such as gender, race, and sexuality. "By 1968," historian Eli Zaretsky observes, "the psychoanalytic church stood rigid, orthodox, ossified, and nakedly hypocritical. Ideas it had once bravely pioneered had become doxa."[61]

Narcissism

In the face of such widespread criticism, analysts focused on the concept of narcissism in their attempts to reconstruct the field.[62] From the late 1960s through the 1970s the view emerged of the narcissist as a distinct character type that was not just a collection of transient symptoms but an enduring and stable way of relating to the world. The novelist and critic Tom Wolfe famously labeled this period the "Me Decade," "the greatest age of individualism in American history," when "all rules are broken!"[63] One face of the new formulation attempted to reconcile analysis with the major aspects of the 1960s counterculture that featured self-expression, loosening of sexual mores, and antiauthoritarian values. Centered on the Chicago-based analyst Heinz Kohut (1913–1981), this group moved the focus of analytic attention "from Oedipus to Narcissus."[64]

Kohut strove to replace what he saw as the ossified state of Freudian analysis with a new system centered on the positive aspects of narcissism and its resonance with youth culture themes of self-expression and freedom from oppressive social norms. In thoroughgoing contrast to traditional Freudian conceptions, which emphasized the repression of instincts, Kohut's works—much like Reich's earlier efforts—celebrated the indulgence of desires. They emphasized the creative and fulfilling aspects of the individualism that the counterculture promoted. Kohut's vision contrasted both with the vision of Freud, who saw the conflict between individuals and civilization as universal and timeless, and with that of critics of the counterculture, who saw it as embodying social decline. Kohut celebrated the dominion of the self that the critics lamented and instead associated it with joy and liberation.

Kohut did not reject the postwar economic abundance and plenitude that seemingly lay behind the emergence of widespread narcissism. He developed a "self-psychology" that he contrasted with conventional instinct-based theories. Its tenets became integrated into a new analytic mainstream.[65] The pseudonymous psychiatrist, Aaron Green, the central figure in Janet Malcolm's *Psychoanalysis: The Impossible Profession*, noted how Kohut's disciples "think that his is the true psychoanalysis—that he has introduced something radical and revolutionary, and that psychoanalysis is going to have to assimilate it."[66]

In fact, psychoanalysis did absorb Kohut's self-psychology. "Despite the audacity and ferocity of his attacks on Freud and Freudian analysis, Kohut is very much part of, by some accounts at the center of, the analytic mainstream today," historian Elizabeth Lunbeck observes.[67] Kohut transformed the value connotations of narcissism. Western societies traditionally placed higher value on altruistic concern for others than on the self. In contrast, Kohut promoted self-love as the basis for achieving emotional maturity. He paved a path for the self-esteem movement that led people to elevate their own well-being above values of duty, honor, and community responsibility. Kohut thus inverted traditional evaluations of character, although he used the language of science, not morality.[68] Narcissism did not fit a traditional medical paradigm of disease but instead was "a way station on the road of man's search for a new psychological equilibrium."[69]

Kohut did not ignore the pathological side of narcissism. He emphasized how narcissistic disorders, like other personality disorders, resulted from parental indifference or rejection during early developmental stages.[70] Narcissistic disorders were defects in selves that arose in infancy because of mothers' lack of empathy and often psychotic-like behavior: "In the great majority of cases, it is the specific pathogenic personality of the parent(s) and the specific pathogenic atmosphere in which the child grows up that account for the maldevelopments, fixations, and unsolvable inner conflicts characterizing the adult personality."[71] Responses to such environments involved developing a compensatory false self to protect a deeply wounded inner core. In the relatively short time since tight family structures led parents to be overinvolved with their children, by mid-century parents seemed underinvolved in their children's development.[72]

The second thrust of psychiatric research on personality disorders was led by another European émigré, Otto Kernberg (b. 1928). Kernberg, who was the most prominent American analyst during the 1970s and 1980s, emphasized how the failure to integrate good and bad representations of the self and others prevented ego integration, which in turn made individuals vulnerable to developing personality disorders. He viewed disordered conditions as pathologies of personality organization that stemmed from problematic object relations in the pre-Oedipal period. Character pathologies were thus deeply rooted aspects of internal personality organization that led to profound problems in both identity and interpersonal relationships. Kernberg emphasized borderline as well as narcissistic conditions, which both involved the inability to integrate good and bad images of the self and others.[73]

Unlike Kohut's rejection of classical analytic ideas, Kernberg's portrayal embraced the drive-based foundation of orthodox analysis. In contrast to Kohut, Kernberg viewed narcissists as outwardly charming and seductive while inwardly seething with anger and aggression. They embodied a contradictory combination of appealing and repellant personal qualities. Although narcissists might appear to be self-confident, independent, and successful, internally they were empty and full of rage. They were incapable of forming fulfilling interpersonal relationships, instead exploiting other people and then turning against them. Narcissists were pathological because their relations with others were not integrated with their self-images. In addition, their character pathology ruined not only their lives but also those of their closest relations. Kernberg also rejected the neo-Freudian notion that narcissistic characters were social products. Following Freud, he insisted that narcissistic tendencies arose early in life but were not outgrown; they persisted independently of social norms.[74]

In addition to narcissism, Kernberg focused on borderline personality.[75] This term originally referred to patients who fit neither the psychotic nor the neurotic categories but fell somewhere between them. Kernberg accepted this formulation of borderline as a level of severity and also postulated that, because of their early experiences with rejecting, aloof, and aggressive parents, usually mothers, adults who developed borderline conditions split external objects into all good or all bad, shifting abruptly between the two. They thus developed patterns of highly intense, yet highly unstable, relationships. This deep sense of rage made them particularly difficult patients for therapists to deal with. As the next chapter discusses, borderline conditions became the focus of research about the personality disorders following the publication of the *DSM-III* in 1980.[76]

Together, Kohut and Kernberg illustrate the normal and pathological sides of narcissism that Freud's 1914 essay had already laid out: narcissism was a normal and healthy stage of development that could become a disorder when it was not overcome as people matured. "Narcissism," Lunbeck summarizes, "has always been simultaneously pathological and normal."[77]

In 1979, historian Christopher Lasch's *The Culture of Narcissism* transformed the analytic concept of narcissism into a searing indictment of popular culture.[78] The analytic concern with the concurrently grandiose yet emotionally needy patient was emblematic of the selfish character structure that an affluent and materialist twentieth-century capitalist society produced. Lasch's outwardly confident and seductive narcissists fumed with inner emptiness and repressed fury. Lasch associated the emergence of narcissistic characters with the rise of consumerism, lax family structures, and lenient social norms. He thus yoked the analytic concept of narcissism with the neo-Freudian approach that connected character structures to social conditions.

The ego psychologists' studies of subjective experiences and personal narratives linked them far more strongly to interpretative disciplines such as literature and history than to more quantified fields such as psychology and medicine. Psychoanalysis, Kohut maintained, was the "empathic-introspective immersion of the observer into the inner life of man."[79] The postwar period saw the rise of not just ego psychology but also a vigorous new sociological approach to personality.

Social-Scientific Studies of Personality

During the postwar period psychoanalysis became integrated with not only traditional psychiatry but also the social sciences. The leaders of the Frankfurt Institute for Social Research, which came to be called the Frankfurt School, were part of the wave of emigration to the United States during the 1930s. They faced a different task than did the psychoanalysts, whose worldviews could easily merge with their American counterparts. In contrast, European social science was far more theoretically driven and nonquantitative than comparable fields in the United States. The Frankfurt School prioritized theory over fact gathering, deduction over induction, and political involvement over detachment. "The most difficult intellectual adjustment," historian Martin Jay observes, "involved coordinating the philosophically grounded social research practiced by the Institute with the rigorous antispeculative bias of America social science."[80]

Philosopher and sociologist Max Horkheimer (1895–1973) directed the Frankfurt Institute. Like his colleagues, Horkheimer was primarily concerned with wedding the writings of Sigmund Freud to those of Karl Marx. For example, he suggested that the Oedipus complex might have existed in bygone economic eras when sons aspired to replace their fathers in positions of authority. Under present circumstances, however, sons were detached from their fathers and more oriented toward peer groups. This led to a situation where "it is no longer the son's fear of the father that is the typical psychological fact but the father's secret fear of the son."[81] The Frankfurt School was deeply immersed in contemporary political developments, especially the relationship between personality styles and the rise of totalitarian movements in Europe. Horkheimer wrote that authoritarian characters featured "a mechanical surrender to conventional values; blind submission to authority together with blind hatred of all opponents and outsiders; anti-introspectiveness; rigid stereotyped thinking; a penchant for superstition; vilification, half-moralistic and half-cynical of human nature; projectivity."[82]

Philosopher and social critic Theodor Adorno (1903–1969) also focused on the relationship between social forces and personality types. Adorno argued against the unity of the personality and insisted, as Freud had, that modern personalities were disjointed and riven by conflict.[83] He wrote about the emergence of a new character type that responded to the material gratifications promised by mass culture. Western societies were no longer marked by sexual repression but by the fetishism of commodities.[84] German workers did not fulfill Marx's prophecy of instigating a socialist revolution that would abolish capitalism, instead identifying with their possessions and allegiances to authoritarian social movements. The emergence of fascism as a mass ideology in many European societies in the 1930s seemed to reinforce the Frankfurt School's belief that pathological social movements were rooted in particular character styles. In particular, totalitarian political regimes capitalized on unconscious intraindividual dynamics that made people susceptible to manipulation by demagogic leaders. "There is a Hitler, a Stalin in every breast," Arthur Schlesinger Jr. observed in 1949.[85]

After immigrating to the United States, Adorno collaborated with a number of US social scientists to produce *The Authoritarian Personality* (1950), which quickly became a classic social-scientific study. It was, one early reviewer claimed, "an epoch-making event in social science."[86] This massive project surveyed more than two thousand respondents and also involved clinical interviews and projective testing of large groups. It grounded the anti-Semitic appeal of fascism in the paranoid character structures that capitalist societies produced. Authoritarian characters simultaneously displayed sadistic and masochistic drives that led them to become willing participants in fascist political movements. Adorno and colleagues argued that their findings showed that authoritarian personalities were products of families that practiced harsh and arbitrary discipline. Such families themselves resulted from particular social formations racked by status anxiety and insecurity.

At the heart of the appeal of fascism was the principle that "personality may be regarded as a *determinant* of ideological preferences."[87] The book concludes:

> A basically hierarchical, authoritarian, exploitative parent-child relationship is apt to carry over into a power-oriented, exploitively dependent attitude towards one's sex partner and one's God and may well culminate in a political philosophy and social outlook which has no room for anything but a desperate clinging to what appears to be strong and a disdainful rejection of whatever is relegated to the bottom . . . [and] the formation of stereotypes and of ingroup-outgroup cleavages. Conventionality, rigidity, repressive denial, and the ensuing breakthrough of one's weakness, fear and dependence are but other aspects of the same fundamental personality pattern, and they can be observed in personal life as well as in attitudes toward religion and social issues.[88]

For Adorno and his collaborators, authoritarian characteristics were not so much innate aspects of individuals as results of specific social configurations. Changing such personalities required altering the social organization of capitalist societies, not the psychological characteristics of particular people. Authoritarian tendencies, they concluded, "are products of the total organization of society and are to be changed only as that society is changed."[89]

Critics questioned why the book associated authoritarian characters only with fascism rather than a broader spectrum of totalitarian societies that included communism. They also claimed that the authoritarian concept combined a disparate group of personality traits found in a variety of social settings. In addition, they criticized the study's sampling, questionnaires, and interviews.[90] Nevertheless, the book was an enormous success. It was particularly notable for linking the European penchant for general theoretical concerns that addressed pressing social and political issues to an Americanized style of quantitative investigation.

The project of relating individual psychological development, family dynamics, and social structures to personality types would preoccupy the social sciences for the next decade. The huge popularity of *The Authoritarian Personality* stimulated a flock of works centered on the relationship of contemporary society and personality styles. By the 1950s postwar affluence had spread consumer culture to a much broader swath of American society. At the same time, the manufacturing economy was starting to decline, replaced by a postindustrial society centered on service industries. The best-known work in this vein was sociologist David Riesman's *The Lonely Crowd: A Study of the American Character*, which "quickly became the nation's most influen-tial and widely read mid-century work of social and cultural criticism."[91] It was the most popular sociology book in history, selling more than 1.4 million copies.[92] In 1954, Riesman became the first social scientist to appear on the cover of *Time* magazine.

Riesman claimed that psychoanalysts and psychologists overestimated the lasting influence of childhood experiences on adult personality.[93] Instead, he focused on how major institutions, which changed over time, shaped the dominant personality/character styles in different social groups. "Character" referred to the "more or less permanent socially and historically conditioned organization of an individual's drives and satisfactions—the kind of 'set' with which he approaches the world and people."[94] Societies had evolved since Freud's time to the extent that television, advertising, and consumer culture affected personality styles as much as, or even more than, familial influences.

The Lonely Crowd documented a shift among Americans from a life gov-erned by an unquestioned body of beliefs to one dominated by sensitivity to peer groups and the mass media. It argued that a progression of three char-acter types marked American history. Originally, "tradition-directed" per-sons lived in stable, preindustrial communities that produced personalities anchored in group membership inherited across the generations. Next, the "inner-directed" personalities that marked the nineteenth century internal-ized strong norms that promoted self-reliance but were relatively indifferent to the approval of others. In both tradition- and inner-directed societies, "fixed social characters could be maintained by fixed beliefs."[95]

Unlike these ideal types, the prototypical "outer-directed" personalities that emerged in the twentieth century were more concerned with relationships to other people and so would rather be loved than esteemed. In contrast to the familial focus of psychoanalysis, young people in the post–World War II era were most attuned to their peers and so became "more like each other than any one of them is like his father or mother."[96] Typical American personalities had become more oriented to marketing and consumption than to moral values and production. A preoccupation with consumption as a way of life had replaced the self-restraint that marked the earlier culture of character. Echoing Horney and Fromm, Riesman argued that postwar economic abun-dance drove Americans to crave acceptance by their peers. As adjustment and conformity became dominant ideals, anxiety about achievement replaced both shame and guilt in promoting adherence to social norms. Riesman's work implied that the problems of psychiatric patients shifted from neuroses arising from harsh superegos to failures of adequate adaptations to the demands of others. He also speculated that modern life presented so many possible character types that "increasingly, the differences among men will operate across and within national boundaries" so the notion of "national character" would become anachronistic.[97]

At the same time, analytically oriented psychologist Erik Erikson popularized the concept of "identity" in *Childhood and Society* (1950). In contrast to Freud, Erikson posited that the ego was not fixed at early ages but developed throughout the life course. In addition, he emphasized how Freud's oral, anal, and phallic stages involved not just varying instinctual drives but also different interpersonal tasks. His model, which became immensely popular in the 1960s, placed identity at the core of individual existence. Identity provided selves with continuity over time, the capacity for intimacy, and a sense of their relatedness to others. He took a historical view of the concept, noting how "the patient of today suffers most under the problem of what he should believe in and who he should—or, indeed, might—become; while the patient of early psychoanalysis suffered most under inhibitions which prevented him from being what and who he thought he knew he was."[98]

Erikson's conception also bridged analytic and social conceptions of personality. People could realize their core identities only through anchoring them in the roles their societies provided them. Identity emerged within concrete historical events, interpersonal relationships, families, communities, cultures, economies, and political systems as well as from intraindividual dynamics. Erikson coined the popular term "identity crisis" to refer to the natural process among youth who strove to discover their true selves. This grounded the study of personality in normal, not disturbed, processes. Moreover, Erikson also applied his model cross-culturally to show how early bodily and interpersonal experiences led to varying adult personalities in groups such as the Native American Sioux and Yurok.[99] His work was an integrative model of how personalities embodied interactions between instinctual forces, the unfolding of new capacities across the life course, and socially available forms of identity.

In the mid-1960s, the other-directed conformists that Riesman and other social commentators depicted gave way to the expressive and rebellious countercultural youth. Mostly raised in an affluent society, these rebels scorned the material values celebrated in the decades following World War II. Group-oriented selves that emphasized social and political dimensions of identity replaced the individual focus of postwar culture. Their dominance marked what Lunbeck calls "a culture in characterological freefall."[100]

Psychology

World War II and its aftermath had a dramatic impact on the discipline of psychology as well as psychiatry and the social sciences. Before the war, psychologists had little presence in clinical settings but were mainly limited to teaching in academic departments or to administering tests in institutional contexts.[101] Yet psychiatrists were unable to fill the surging demand for mental health services that followed in the wake of the war. In response, the federal government funded large efforts during the immediate postwar period to train psychologists to practice in clinical settings, particularly veterans' hospitals. The field grew tenfold, from less than three thousand in 1939 to more than thirty thousand professionals in 1970.[102] Nevertheless, the prestige of the new clinical wing remained lower than that of the dominant experimentalists and statisticians. Lee Cronbach's 1957 presidential address to the American Psychological Association—"The Two Disciplines of Scientific Psychology"—was exemplary. It considered experimental and statistical psychology to be scientific but did not mention clinical psychology.[103]

While psychologists entered the clinical realm in the postwar era, compared to the analysts, neo-Freudians, and culture and personality anthropologists, they had little presence in the general culture. They did, however, penetrate many social institutions through their refinement of personality testing. Although statistical methods had been an important component of the psychological discipline since its inception, their influence intensified in the postwar period. "In their search for scientific certainty," historian James Capshew notes, "psychologists had moved from attempting to define their work in terms of content (whether in terms of consciousness or behavior) to an almost obsessive concern with research design and quantitative methods."[104] B. F. Skinner, too, observed that the use of statistical methods "has become a shibboleth to be used in distinguishing between good and bad work."[105] The Minnesota Multiphasic Personality Inventory (MMPI) exemplified the kind of personality test that developed in this period.

The MMPI Era

Personality had been a central object of psychological concern over the course of the twentieth century. "By the time of World War II," sociologist William

Whyte observed, "the use of aptitude and intelligence tests had become so widespread that it was almost impossible for any white-collar American to come of age without having taken a battery at one time or another."[106] During the war, the military relied on psychologists as well as psychiatrists to develop suitable tests that screened recruits and sorted them into appropriate positions as well as rejected undesirable ones, especially gay persons. By the end of the conflict, twenty million soldiers had taken sixty million standardized tests.[107] In the postwar period the professional prestige of psychologists soared as many organizations eagerly sought their services. The number of corporations using psychologists increased from 14 percent in 1939 to 50 percent in 1947 and 75 percent in 1952.[108] By 1970, more than five hundred personality tests had been developed.[109]

Psychologists primarily assessed personality through tests that used self-reported responses to closed-ended questions.[110] Schools used them to steer students into appropriate careers, prisons to filter inmates into suitable rehabilitation programs, and corporations to match people to apt jobs. Employers were especially attracted to these tests because they not only promised to identify dependable, honest, and rule-following employees but also to exclude those who would cheat the company, abuse absence policies, and have behavioral problems.[111]

The Minnesota Multiphasic Personality Inventory became the most widely used personality test in the world. In the United States alone, about fifteen million people still take an MMPI each year.[112] University of Minnesota psychologist Starke Hathaway and physician J. C. McKinley created the MMPI in 1939 to measure psychopathology. Their goal was to develop a diagnostic test that would not be subject to the personal biases of particular clinicians or the specific practices at different clinics. They also wanted a test that would be immune to criticisms that personality inventories were untrustworthy because respondents would manipulate their answers to achieve their desired ends. Although the MMPI was originally designed to diagnose various types of mental illnesses in clinical settings, it was soon widely adopted in schools, corporations, government, and courts.

Hathaway and McKinley began by accumulating more than 1,000 items from psychiatric texts, earlier personality tests, and their own clinical experience and then used their judgment to cut them down to 550. They then gave the selected items to two groups. The first were patients in treatment at psychiatric clinics in Minnesota. The second was composed of a total of about 1,500 relatives of these patients, high school graduates in the community, and government workers. Because they screened out people who were under a doctor's care, the latter group "could be reasonably assumed to be normal in mind and body."[113] Hathaway and McKinley expected that the answers the control group gave would provide valid indicators of normality while those stemming from the responses of the patient group would show abnormality. They took for granted that high scores on pathological indices indicated mental illness but never resolved the issue of what low scores meant. Decisions based on the test were insulated from arbitrary clinical judgments because machine scoring produced results that were presumably unbiased.

Both the treated and control groups were extremely homogeneous. Hathaway summarized: "Each subject taking the MMPI, therefore, is being compared to the way a typical man or woman endorsed those items. In 1940, normal adults in Minnesota were about 35 years old, married, lived in a small town or rural area, had had eight years of general schooling, and worked at a skilled or semiskilled trade (or was married to a man with such an occupation level)."[114]

Remarkably, the MMPI items established in the late 1930s persisted until 1990, so the millions of scores obtained across the country and worldwide were compared to "normal" Depression-era Scandinavian farmers of Minnesota and their "disordered" diagnosed counterparts. Hathaway explained the reason for not revising the scale: "We cannot change or leave out any items or we lose an invaluable heritage of research in mental health. To change even a comma in an item may change its meaning."[115] Even after the MMPI items were revised around 1990, using a nationwide sample of about 1,100 men and 1,500 women, the test's content remained very similar to the original version—84 percent of items were identical between the two tests.

Hathaway and McKinley focused on those items that distinguished the treated from the community groups. They assumed the mentally ill and normal groups were homogeneous and that there would be a sharp distinction between them. "Normality" meant responses that were closer to those Minnesotans who didn't have psychiatric diagnoses compared to those who did. The responses of the depression-era Minnesotans became the basis for deciding who was normal or disordered in the military and thousands of businesses, courtrooms, schools, hospitals, and clinics for many subsequent decades.[116]

The MMPI's major innovation was that questions with no face validity, that is, truth value, of their own could be used to distinguish between the presumably normal and abnormal groups. In other words, the tests were dependent on respondents' interpretations of questions because there was no solid way of knowing what the words the test relied on really meant.[117] Hathaway and McKinley didn't view this as a problem: the items had no meaning in themselves but only became significant when related to the patterns of answers that separated the treated and untreated groups. For example, a group of diagnosed sociopaths might be more likely to answer "false" to "I have been quite independent and free from family rule," even though the face validity of the question might suggest otherwise. Nevertheless, the question was useful because, regardless of whether sociopaths are actually less independent of family rule, they are more likely than members of the control group to say that they are. The item was valuable not because it is accurate but because it helps discriminate between sociopaths and others. The statement "I go to church every week" provides another example. In response to an irritated inquirer who wondered whether using this question to screen police officers violated the separation of church and state, Hathaway stated that the item had no meaning, even to him. What it did do was separate the mentally ill from others and so was useful in screening police officers for mental illness. Regardless of their truth value, such questions allowed the test to distinguish normal from disordered people.[118]

Indeed, for Hathaway, the "best" items were exactly those that had no obvious answer so that subjects couldn't try to outwit the testers. The final test included those items that showed the most difference between the two groups. They were often very strange: "I have never had any black, tarry-looking bowel movements." "I believe there is a Devil and a Hell in the afterlife." "I think I would like to belong to a motorcycle club." "I think that Lincoln was greater than Washington." Science journalist Annie Murphy Paul observes, "The test Hathaway and McKinley ultimately produced was without a doubt one of the weirdest creations in the history of man's attempts to understand himself."[119]

Nonetheless, defenders of the MMPI justified the test because of its predictive power. "I want to make it very clear," Hathaway asserted, "that the item counts, not because some clinician or somebody thought that the item was significant for measuring something about human personality, but it counts because in the final analysis well-diagnosed groups of maladjusted, sometimes mentally ill persons answered the item with an average frequency differing from the average frequency of the normative group."[120] The meanings of the items were irrelevant: all that mattered was that people diagnosed with mental illnesses answered them differently than those that were not. "I am often asked," Hathaway explained, "what specified items mean. I do not know because the scoring of the scales has become so abstracted that I have no contact with items."[121]

Notable University of Minnesota psychologist Paul Meehl favorably contrasted the MMPI's "cookbook method" with diagnoses that relied on clinical judgments: "Using the cookbook method, we don't need a clinician; instead, a $230-per-month clerk-typist in the outer office simply reads the numbers on the profile, enters the cookbook, locates the page on which is found some kind of 'modal description' for patients with such a profile, and this description is then taken as the best approximation of the patient."[122] Meehl claimed that cookbook methods, which rely solely on explicit rules similar to recipes in a cookbook, have far greater predictive power than clinical decisions guided by individual discretion. Aggregate judgments of many scores invariably were more accurate than even the most insightful clinician's diagnosis. "The clinical interpreter," Meehl concluded, "is a costly middleman who might better be eliminated."[123]

The fact that the test items had no meaning in themselves transferred knowledge about the meaning of personality from subjects to testers because subjects would not know the implications of their responses to each item. The truth value of the test stemmed from statistical comparisons of a subject's answers to those of other subjects, not whether it actually corresponded to some personal trait. Because the items had no obvious answers, it was difficult for respondents to either exaggerate or downplay their attributes. Psychologists alone held the knowledge about how the item discriminates between different groups required to interpret the responses.

The MMPI had another major consequence for transferring authority over the interpretation of personality from subjects to testers. Because personality tests served the interests of organizations, most subjects want to provide answers that they think will please their evaluators. In some situations— when employers use the test to select employees, police departments to screen recruits, or courts to award custody of a child to the most suitable parent— subjects are motivated to deny pathology. In other settings, such as seeking disability payments or using an insanity defense to deny responsibility for a crime, subjects might want to overreport disorder. For example, MMPI scores of litigants trying to keep their children in custody cases are about two standard deviations lower than those among personal injury plaintiffs who want to seem disabled.[124]

Because test takers often strive to provide answers that are most in line with the impressions they want to create, the MMPI devised an impressive range of weapons to detect subjects who did not provide straightforward answers. Among them was a lie scale that consisted of items that everyone ought to endorse such as: "I do not always tell the truth" or "I gossip a little at times." The MMPI also contained scales of test defensiveness, randomness of responses, and inconsistency as well as a scale indicating exaggerated claims of pathology. The result was an imposing array of controls over subjects who provided the "wrong" patterns of answers.

The weeding out of subjects who did not answer questions truthfully left open the question of what "truthful" answers really meant. Because no particular MMPI item has any meaning, the scale is only interpretable when a given subject's answers are compared to the answers that other people who have taken the same test have given. The only possible meaning of an MMPI profile is statistical: the answers a subject gives are either more or less common than the answers that others have given to the same items.

Sociologist William Whyte insightfully analyzed the MMPI and similar tests in an appendix to his classic book *Organization Man,* called "How to Cheat on Personality Tests." "When an individual is commanded by an organization to reveal his innermost feelings," Whyte asserted, "he has a duty to himself to give answers that serve his self-interest rather than that of The Organization. In a word, he should cheat."[125] According to Whyte, after World War II, corporations came to emphasize conformity, cooperation, and adjustment. They relied on personality tests to screen out potential employees who might be disruptive, different, or eccentric and, conversely, to identify and select conformists.

Whyte advised test takers to strive for scores in the middle of the bell curve, between the fortieth and sixtieth percentile. That is, they should not answer questions in a way that they think actually characterizes themselves but instead how they think most people would answer. Optimal scores stem from the most conventional, run-of-the-mill answers possible. Whyte reminded subjects to always keep in mind what they think the test makers want to hear, not what they believe themselves to be. "The important thing," Whyte emphasized, "is to recognize that you don't win a good score: you avoid a bad one. What a bad score would be depends upon the particular profile the company in question intends to measure you against."[126] When the conventional answer is not obvious, test takers shouldn't reflect too much or think too hard but give the first answer that comes to mind. They should strive to assure testers that they will conform to corporate norms. In other words, they must show they are "normal," as the 1950s culture of conformity defined this term.

Paradoxically, personality, as measured by the MMPI and similar tests, is not an individual characteristic but stems from a statistical distribution. Personality psychologists assumed that personality is like intelligence so that scores can be placed on a linear scale that precisely compares any individual score to the scores of all other test takers. Statistical metrics provide the only possible criteria for defining normality: normal personalities are ones who give answers that are most like those that others provide. Conversely, those with personality disorders respond differently than most others. For example, women who score higher than normal on the masculine/feminine scale are "typically more aggressive and dominating than most women are; they may be coarse, rough and tough in their manner." Conversely, men who score low on this scale "may be effeminate and have greater involvement with aesthetic and artistic interests than most men do."[127] One result of the reliance on statistical norms is that the same personality characteristic can be normal or abnormal depending on the aggregate personality characteristics of people in the comparison group. For example, an outgoing person might be normal in the United States but deviant in Japan. Ultimately, normality as the MMPI and similar personality tests defined it rested on statistical norms, not universal psychological or biological processes.

The context of the test-taking situation posed another problem. For example, a job applicant taking a personality test for some organization might be asked, among many other questions, "Do you daydream frequently?" Although the test might say there is no right or wrong answer, a savvy test taker will answer "no" in this context. "In many companies a man either so honest or so stupid as to answer 'yes' would be well advised to look elsewhere for employment," Whyte advised.[128]

By their nature, the MMPI and similar personality tests ignore the natural conduct of people in socially significant situations. None ground the personality in individuals who have particular life histories, who interact with other people, and who function in specific cultures. They do, however, serve the pragmatic organizational function of identifying those who are most and least likely to conform to institutional norms.

A Note on Projective Tests

Although quantitative tests such as the MMPI dominated psychological testing, an undercurrent of qualitative research was also present. The Rorschach test, developed by Swiss psychiatrist Hermann Rorschach (1884–1922) in 1921, was the first projective method. This test asks subjects to interpret ten inkblots that have no inherent meaning. Trained clinicians then use responses to help uncover the personality dynamics that presumably underlie the answers. Although developed by a European psychiatrist, the Rorschach test became especially influential among US clinical psychologists.[129]

Projective tests that strove to uncover the total personality of subjects through qualitative methods flourished in the 1940s and 1950s. Along with the Rorschach, the Thematic Apperception Test (TAT) developed by Harvard psychologist Henry Murray in 1935, was the most popular interpretative test.[130] The TAT shows subjects stick figures in a variety of nonspecific situations and asks them to make up stories about them. Tests of this nature were as popular as quantitative inventories between the early 1940s and mid-1950s but fell into disrepute because of their subjective assessments, low reliability, time-consuming scoring, and uncertain relationship to actual behavior.[131] Ortho-dox psychologists never accepted their validity, but they proved to be highly popular among the general public and many clinicians.

Conclusion

In the postwar period no discipline, whether psychology, psychoanalysis, or any social science, attempted to link personality to any organic factor. This was not a handicap at the time, but they were vulnerable to a looming scientific upheaval about the biological determinants of human behavior. During the 1950s and 1960s genetic and brain-based views were just beginning to regain prestige within science. From the 1970s onward, however, organic models of personality dominated. Psychoanalysis, in particular, was ill suited to confront the revolution in psychiatric practice that the biological revolution would bring about. The *DSM-III*'s (1980) turn toward defining disorders through their symptomatic manifestations and excising any reference to their causes would signal the death knell of psychoanalysis within psychiatry. Thereafter, the study of personality disorders would increasingly become mechanized, quantified, and removed from individual experience. In addition, the social emphasis that dominated views of personality from the 1930s through the 1960s would almost entirely disappear in the new paradigm that arose in 1980.

CHAPTER FIVE

Personality Disorders in the *DSM-III*

The flourishing of general cultural interest in personality that began in the 1930s lasted for about a quarter of a century after World War II ended. During this period personality and its disorders took center stage not only in psychoanalysis but also in psychology and the social sciences. Only psychiatric researchers, whose professional power was steadily growing, resisted their lure. The influence of this group, along with developments in the social matrix surrounding the mental health professions, would come to overshadow and eventually recast views of personality disorders (PDs).

In the postwar period there was little need for psychiatric diagnoses, including those of personality disorders, to go beyond the vague, brief descriptions found in the first two *DSM*s. Most of the definitions in these manuals were imprecise, and many were infused with untestable psychoanalytic assumptions. "American psychiatry was a mess and needed clarity in diagnosis," according to prominent psychiatrist George Vaillant.[1]

Beginning in the 1950s and sharply accelerating over the next two decades, psychiatric researchers launched a crusade to overhaul the field's diagnostic system. By the early 1970s researchers realized the *DSM-II* was not well suited for a variety of forces: the evolving culture of medicine, the rise of a powerful new group of biologically oriented investigators, opposition from the antipsychiatry movement, rapidly changing funding mechanisms for clinical treatment, pressures from federal agencies, and the market demands of the pharmaceutical industry. Psychiatric diagnosis required a revolutionary new approach, which eventually led an entirely new classification to emerge in 1980.

Pressures for a New Diagnostic System

Many interests converged to propel this transformation, in particular, by bringing the principle of *specificity* to the forefront of diagnostic criteria. The *DSM*'s cursory diagnoses were outliers among medical specialties, which used specific indicators to distinguish one disease from others. Psychiatric researchers, who barely existed before the 1960s, wanted the field to view mental illnesses as precise entities comparable to the diseases other areas of medicine defined and treated. As this group steadily gained professional power during the 1970s, it pressed psychiatry to adopt a similar taxonomy. As long as they lacked a medical-like classification, psychiatrists would face the charge that their field was not scientific. Personality disorders were especially vulnerable to this accusation because they involved general relationships between individual adaptive capacities and social environments that were difficult to quantify and shot through with value judgments.

At the same time, biologically oriented psychiatrists were developing a new somatic paradigm. Joseph Schildkraut's (1934–2006) catecholamine hypothesis of affective disorders, which proposed that depression might be associated with an absolute or relative deficiency of particular neurotransmitters, was the best-known theoretical work. This article, which was published in the *American Journal of Psychiatry* in 1965, "captured the imagination of the field and helped us to understand the biology of psychiatric disorders."[2] It became the most frequently cited article in the history of this journal and served as a model for the exploration of the neurobiological grounding of mental disorders. "There are now substantial indications that serious mental illnesses derive from chemical, rather than psychological, imbalances," prominent biological psychiatrist Seymour Kety proclaimed eleven years later.[3]

Psychiatry also faced highly damaging attacks from an influential antipsychiatry movement that developed in the 1960s and persisted into the 1970s. Led by renegade psychiatrists Thomas Szasz and R. D. Laing and propelled by influential empirical research, especially psychologist David Rosenhan's renowned study of pseudopatients, anti-psychiatrists claimed that the profession was unable to define and measure its most central concepts such as "mental illness" and "schizophrenia."[4] Only a radically new type of diagnostic system that defined mental disorders in comparable ways to organic diseases could restore the profession's credibility.

In addition to changing professional and lay cultures, highly practical concerns pushed psychiatry to adopt a diagnostic system grounded in specificity. Beginning in the 1960s and sharply accelerating over the following decade, private and public insurers paid for an increasing portion of clinical treatment. These third parties would only reimburse clinicians who treated patients with specific diagnoses. They were suspicious of the generality of many *DSM-II* conditions, which did not seem to be genuine diseases that warranted payment. They cast an especially wary eye on the personality disorders, which often involved lengthy, yet frequently unsuccessful, treatments.

The new imperative for drug companies to market their products was another powerful stimulus for replacing the existing diagnostic model. In 1973 the Food and Drug Administration mandated that all psychiatric drugs coming on the market must treat some particular mental disorder.[5] This pushed psychiatrists involved in drug-related research to develop explicit diagnostic criteria for the conditions they studied. Because no drug specifically targeted the personality disorders, this issue was not central for these conditions but was a potent force driving changes in the overall diagnostic system.

Finally, the National Institute of Mental Health (NIMH) had been the major funder of mental health research and education since its inception in 1949. For its first two decades, the NIMH had little involvement with diagnostic concerns, instead focusing on expanding community-based treatments. By the end of the 1960s, however, the agency had come under blistering political attacks for its support of socially oriented programs. A new diagnostic system modeled on specific, disease-like conditions would help restore the agency's scientific credibility. It, too, would benefit from the perception that the mental health professions dealt with genuine mental disorders and not broad psychosocial problems of living.

A New Diagnostic Model

Several principles guided the development of the diagnostic model that the *DSM-III* would implement in 1980. The first struck at the heart of the psychodynamically inflected *DSM-II*: the new manual would not take sides in theoretical disputes. It would be theory neutral. Its diagnostic criteria would employ descriptive, observable, and measurable symptoms without inferences about their causes. Therefore, its approach shed psychodynamic concepts that relied on interpretations of what symptoms mean. The first two *DSM*s did not explicitly formulate the personality disorders through psychoanalytic principles, but this class was closely identified with analytic theory. Although proponents of the *DSM-III* anticipated that the manual's new diagnoses would open a path for biological psychiatrists to discover the particular neurotransmitters (e.g., dopamine, noradrenaline, serotonin) associated with various disorders, the manual's definitions would not be grounded in biological, or any other, causal assumptions.

A second core tenet of the new manual was that all diagnoses were based on readily measurable indicators. The leaders of the *DSM-III* revision believed that a major defect of the *DSM-II* was its reliance on unobservable processes such as the unconscious and on overgeneralized terms such as "neurosis." In its place, they strove to install diagnostic criteria that could easily be operationalized. Using the new system, clinicians in, say, New York, Los Angeles, or Topeka would agree on what particular disorder any given patient had. This would allow the *DSM-III* to overcome the low reliability of the *DSM-II*, whose cursory descriptions did not allow different users to reach the same conclusion about the most appropriate diagnosis. Standardized measures would provide the foundation for psychiatry to stand alongside other medical specialties, which had well-established notions of what constituted different diseases.

A third goal of the medically minded classification was that, unlike the extant model, each specific *DSM-III* diagnosis would be independent of other diagnoses. The assumption that mental, like organic, disorders were autonomous disease processes implied that there would be limited overlap, or "comorbidity," between diagnoses. Therefore, the new classification should minimize connections among presumably distinct entities. This perspective thoroughly contrasted with the capacious role that general processes such as "anxiety" or "neurosis" played in the *DSM-II*.

Finally, the *DSM-III* used the empirical literature on each condition to develop its diagnostic criteria. Each diagnosis would stem from research-based evidence, not from untestable theoretical assumptions. Only those conditions that gained justification from empirical findings would enter the new manual. The theory-neutral, observation-based, autonomous, and research-grounded *DSM-III* diagnoses would radically depart from the *DSM-II*'s analytic, untestable, overlapping, and weakly supported conditions.

Developing the DSM-III

In 1974 the American Psychiatric Association (APA) appointed a task force to begin work on developing the *DSM-III*. It selected Robert Spitzer, a research-oriented psychiatrist, to chair the task force and select the members of fourteen advisory committees on particular classes of disorders and other diagnostic issues. Spitzer clearly stated his intention: "DSM-III will not only be a radical departure from DSM-II—it will be revolutionary!"[6]

The *DSM-II* was clearly an unsuitable foundation for a new classification based on specificity. Instead, the *DSM-III* built upon a diametrically opposed diagnostic paradigm, the Feighner criteria, which originated in the Washington University Department of Psychiatry.[7] In the 1960s this department was a rare outpost of medically oriented psychiatric research. It was the major institutional base of the newly emerging research psychiatrists who defined themselves in opposition to the then-dominant analytic wing of the profession.

The Washington University group used operational definitions to develop homogeneous categories of distinct mental illnesses. They advocated for a strict medical model that viewed each mental illness as consisting of clusters of observable symptoms that were separable from each other, from non-disordered conditions, and, especially, from idiosyncratic clinical interpretations. For them, anything worth studying had to be measurable; unless they could be quantified, subjective processes had no place in the diagnostic process. Diagnoses were not just important; they were *the* central aspect of the discipline because all other psychiatric concerns—determining the etiology, prognoses, and treatment of mental illness—depended on the accuracy of its diagnostic system. In 1972 the Washington University psychiatrists published what came to be known as the "Feighner criteria" after the psychiatric resident who recorded the definitions of the fourteen conditions for use among researchers.[8] Despite the fact that the extant research base for these criteria was minimal, this article became the most widely cited piece in the history of psychiatric journals.[9]

Using the Feighner criteria as a model for the *DSM-III* posed several formidable obstacles. They were developed for use by researchers, but the *DSM* had to serve clinical, as well as research, purposes. The extent to which clinicians would be willing to use the specific, empiricist Feighner diagnoses was an open question. An even greater problem was that the Feighner criteria contained just fourteen diagnoses, far fewer than the *DSM-II*. Just one of these, antisocial personality disorder (ASPD) was a personality disorder. Therefore, they did not incorporate the conditions of many patients in clinical treatment. Unlike researchers, who could focus on a limited number of disorders, clinicians required a far more expansive diagnostic system.

Finally, the major goal of the Feighner criteria—to eliminate subjectivity as the grounds for diagnosis—struck at the heart of clinical expertise, which relied on understanding each patient's particular problems. The stark opposition between the perspectives of researchers and clinicians would become the central dynamic in the antagonistic process that ultimately resulted in the publication of the *DSM-III* in 1980.

Challenges in Measuring the Personality Disorders

Issues surrounding the personality disorders took a prominent role over the six-year period when the *DSM-III* was developing. The major political conflict in the construction of the new manual—the struggle between empirically driven researchers and analytically oriented clinicians—was especially visible for these conditions. Foremost among Spitzer's concerns was the need to reconcile the highly divergent views of researchers and clinicians toward the personality disorders. "Spitzer was preoccupied with the diagnostic category of Personality Disorder," historian Hannah Decker observes.[10]

As the previous chapter noted, the *DSM-II* contained eleven personality disorders. From the outset, it was clear that they would be very difficult to mold into the kind of entities that Spitzer and the task force wanted to formulate. Indeed, in every respect the personality disorders were virtually the opposite of the specific, measurable, and standardized mental disorders that featured particular symptoms. High comorbidity also marked this group. Most people who met criteria for one type of personality disorder also qualified for a diagnosis of at least one other type as well as of a number of symptom-based conditions. In addition, they involved aspects of individual identity that were difficult to quantify and that resisted extraction into impersonal disease entities.

Spitzer and the task force recognized the formidable challenges that the personality disorders presented. A planning workshop in 1976 summarized some of the fundamental issues: "How do we deal with the fact that personality disorders are 'fuzzy at the edges?' Pathology shades into normal problems of everyday life. Related is the question of how one distinguishes personality 'disorders,' which are pathological, from everyday personality 'traits.'"[11] Another concern was whether personality disorders were categorical or dimensional. A basic principle of the new *DSM-III* classification was that each of its diagnoses required a certain number of symptoms to qualify as a disorder. Patients who did not display enough symptoms did not have the condition. In contrast, many researchers believed that the personality disorders better fit a dimensional model that ranged continuously from normal personality traits, through mild pathology, and then to severe states. In the 1976 memorandum Spitzer wrote, "Is it possible in diagnosing personality disorders to have a diagnostic axis focusing on distinctions along a continuum (spectrum) of severity of impairment extending into normality (such as with high blood pressure, for example)? Of course, the spectrum concept does not easily lend itself to diagnoses based on discrete subdivisions, which were being espoused for DSM-III."[12] As Spitzer recognized, the possible dimensionality of the personality disorders was ill suited for the categorical *DSM-III* paradigm.

The personality disorders presented other potent diagnostic challenges. One was that they were marked by deeply embedded character traits that were indistinguishable from who a person *is* rather than by particular symptoms. Because they referred to holistic character structures, personality disorders were intrinsically difficult to fit into preestablished molds. They invariably contained terms such as "manipulative," "impulsive," "dependent," "shallow," or "unstable," which required clinical judgments that resisted standardized definitions.

Another core problem was how to separate personality disorders from deviant behaviors and conflicts between individuals and society that were not mental illnesses. The sole personality disorder in the Feighner criteria, antisocial personality disorder, illustrates this difficulty. The ASPD diagnosis sustained the long tradition of moralistic definitions of what originally was called "psychopathic personality." Overall, antisocial personalities "demonstrate a consistent pattern of recurrent and repeated antisocial, delinquent, and criminal behavior beginning in childhood and lasting well into adulthood."[13] The Feighner criteria defined antisocial personality through problems in school, running away from home, trouble with the police, poor work history, marital difficulties, rage, fighting outside of school, sexual promiscuity, vagrancy or wanderlust, and persistent lying.[14] The line between psychiatric disorder, social deviance, delinquency, and criminality was very thin.

Probably the dominant issue in discussions of the personality disorders in the *DSM-III* deliberations involved how to reconcile the views of researchers and clinicians toward these conditions. Personality disorders were not a central concern for the researchers who dominated the *DSM-III* process. Indeed, many of them scorned these conditions, viewing them as nonspecific, unmeasurable, value laden, and not true mental disorders. Prominent psychiatrist Aaron Beck, for example, believed that the very concept of personality disorder was a "construct so artificial and removed from observables, that it is probably of little utility and, even worse, it is probably a misleading fiction."[15] In addition, they were often nonresponsive to drug treatments and so were of little interest to biologically oriented psychiatrists and pharmaceutical companies.

Many researchers believed that personality disorders were not independent entities but were aspects of mood, anxiety, or psychotic conditions. Others considered certain personality types to be predisposing factors to mental
disorders, but not disorders in themselves.[16] Some worried that, although the
DSM's general definition of mental disorder required the presence of a "dysfunction," it was not clear what a dysfunction of personality was a dysfunction *of*. Instead, many of these conditions, such as ASPD, seemed more related to "conflicts between an individual and society," which the *DSM-III*
definition of mental disorder explicitly excluded.

Researchers also believed that the manual should contain only diagnoses
with a firm grounding in empirical evidence. In their view, the *DSM-III*
should not include any type of mental disorder that lacked such a body of
proof. Yet, because they disdained the personality disorders, psychiatric researchers had not compiled the needed body of findings about many of them,
and their analytic proponents rarely conducted research at all. A potent challenge would be how to ground diagnostic criteria for the personality disorders in empirical evidence.

Unlike psychiatric researchers, psychologists had conducted numerous
studies of personality, yet these posed problems as a model for the new *DSM*.
On the one hand, the thoroughgoing empiricism of psychological studies was
well suited to the goal of constructing an evidence-based classification. Yet,
on the other hand, most psychologists studied nonclinical populations and
were generally unconcerned with issues about mental disorders. Moreover,
the measures that psychologists used such as Cattell's 16 Personality Factor
model or Eysenck's three-dimensional PEN (psychoticism, extraversion, and
neuroticism) model did not correspond to the extant personality disorders
in the *DSM-II*.[17] Their sophisticated quantitative studies of untreated groups
were generally alien to clinicians, who worked with particular patients and
lacked both the skills and the interest in using statistical models. Few clinicians did any kind of replicable research at all. Therefore, little evidence existed that could help build new diagnostic criteria for most of the personality
conditions.

Although psychiatric researchers neglected or derided the personality disorders, they were central to clinical theory and practice. By the 1970s, ego
psychology, which featured the personality disorders, had become the core
framework of analytic theory. Clinical concerns were practical as well as theoretical. Unlike researchers, clinicians needed the new manual to incorporate
the conditions suffered by all the clients they saw in their day-to-day practices,

especially those with personality disorders, who stayed in therapy for long periods of time. Aside from the psychoneuroses, they were the most commonly diagnosed conditions among outpatients in the *DSM-I* and *-II* era. By 1970 this class accounted for a full quarter of psychiatric diagnoses in outpatient settings.[18] Clinicians, therefore, needed assurance that they would be reimbursed for treating patients with personality disorders. They insisted that the manual must retain all categories that were clinically useful regardless of their grounding in empirical research.[19] For example, Otto Kernberg wrote that the *DSM-III* would be "weakened" if its diagnostic criteria "deviate too far from . . . present clinical understanding and practice."[20]

Establishing Criteria for the DSM-III

The development of criteria for the personality disorders followed the same procedure as for the other diagnostic classes. Spitzer appointed all members of the various advisory committees who would design new measures based on the extant research literature. The Advisory Committee on Personality Disorders (ACPD) consisted of eight psychiatrists, including Spitzer himself; one psychologist, Theodore Millon; and one epidemiologist, Lee Robins from Washington University. The divergent concerns of researchers and clinicians posed the most serious problem for the ACPD. The limited interest psychiatric researchers had in the personality disorders meant that the committee lacked a robust body of empirical findings to construct new diagnostic criteria. The extensive body of evidence from personality psychology that did exist was too divergent from clinical significance to be relevant. Psychiatrist John Gunderson, who went on to become the chair of the *DSM-IV* personality disorders work group, noted how the *DSM-III* committee made its decisions in the almost complete absence of empirical data: "For most of the personality disorder categories there was either no empirical base (e.g., avoidant, dependent, passive-aggressive, narcissistic) or no clinical tradition (e.g., avoidant, dependent, schizotypal); thus their disposition was much more subject to the convictions of individual Advisory Committee members."[21]

The conflicting interests of researchers and clinicians, differing nature of personality conditions from other mental disorders, and absence of an extensive body of empirical evidence led the development of diagnostic criteria for the personality disorders to take place in a highly politicized context. As psychologist Lee Anna Clark later observed, "It is no secret that the official classification of personality disorders . . . embodied in the DSMs represents a compromise among the often competing interests of clinicians, researchers, educators, and statisticians with various training backgrounds and orientations."[22]

A New Multiaxial System

The contending perspectives and interests of researchers and clinicians about the personality disorders posed the major challenge for Spitzer and the ACPD. Many researchers would have been happy to eliminate the class completely. However, this would have been disastrous for clinicians, whose practices were filled with patients they believed had personality disorders. Spitzer developed an ingenious solution to this conflict by implementing what the *DSM-III* called a "multiaxial" system.

As far back as 1969, Spitzer had expressed interest in developing a diagnostic system "under which individuals are described in terms of more than one clinical dimension."[23] The multiaxial classification of the *DSM-III* realized this goal. All patients would be evaluated on three different axes. The first, Axis I, encompassed all clinical syndromes other than personality disorder (or developmental disorder). Axis II was reserved for the personality disorders, and all patients would be assessed for these conditions. If no personality disorder was present, clinicians had the option to record any personality traits that might be related to an Axis I diagnosis. Patients could have a diagnosis on Axis I, Axis II, or both axes. In addition, the evaluation would note any relevant physical conditions on Axis III. Two optional axes, IV and V, were also available to record the severity of psychosocial stressors and the highest level of adaptive functioning in the past year.

Some participants in the manual's development expressed concerns about placing the personality disorders on a separate axis from other mental disorders. One of the original goals for the new manual was to synchronize the *DSM* system with the World Health Organization's diagnostic manual, the *International Classification of Diseases*, ninth revision (*ICD-9*). Kurt Nussbaum of the Social Security Administration worried that the multiaxial system conflicted with that goal. In addition, the placement of personality disorders on a separate axis might make them seem nonmedical and jeopardize the ability of clinicians to obtain reimbursement for treating them. This in turn "would most likely eliminate the psychiatrist from dealing with the personality disorders, as is already happening."[24] Nussbaum suggested that Axis II be reserved for the underlying personality structure, while Axis I would contain the primary diagnosis, including one of some personality disorder. The ACPD, however, judged that the multiaxial system had substantially more advantages than flaws and rejected Nussbaum's suggestion.

In retrospect, Spitzer claimed that the implementation of the multiaxial system was the *DSM-III*'s most important innovation.[25] ACPD member Theodore Millon went even further, asserting, "The formal adoption of the multiaxial schema in the DSM-III signifies a reformulation of the task of psychodiagnoses that approaches the magnitude described by Kuhn . . . as a paradigm shift."[26] Although Spitzer and the ACPD touted the multiaxial system as an innovative and newly comprehensive way to understand mental disorders, in fact, it resurrected a very similar system that appeared in William Menninger's *Medical 203*. This nomenclature stated that a complete diagnostic evaluation must record the severity of symptoms; presence of accompanying physical disorders; type, degree, and duration of accompanying stressors; degree of personality predisposition; and degree of disability.[27] The multiaxial system in the *DSM-III* was more a return to the classification that preceded the *DSM-I* than a novel paradigm shift.

The implementation of the multiaxial system turned out to be a shrewd political compromise on Spitzer's part, helping to resolve the intense disputes between researchers and clinicians. The manual both maintained a class essential for clinical use and allowed psychiatric researchers to keep their distance from these conditions. In certain respects, the multiaxial system even elevated the position of the personality disorders. Unlike the case in previous *DSM*s, all patients would be assessed for personality disorders and accompanying personality traits. This meant that, at least among clinicians who heeded the manual's instructions, the *DSM-III* would facilitate gathering a more complete set of information that always included assessments of personality.

The major problem with Axis II was that it undermined the *DSM*'s goal to classify self-contained entities that were independent of other diagnoses. An unforeseen result of the multiaxial system was the emergence of a huge amount of comorbidity, where patients received more than one diagnosis. Indeed, the multiaxial schema that required recording both Axis I and Axis II conditions virtually mandated a vast extension of multiple diagnoses. For example, those with compulsive personality disorder would almost inevitably have an obsessive-compulsive anxiety disorder. The criteria for borderline personality disorders overlapped with almost every other personality disorder.[28] The manual noted of narcissistic personality disorder, "Frequently, many of the features of Histrionic, Borderline, and Antisocial Personality Disorders are present."[29]

The need for insurance reimbursement also facilitated the growth of co-morbid diagnoses. As Nussbaum predicted, insurance companies were often suspicious about the medical reality of the personality disorders and were especially loath to pay for the extended treatments that they often required. Therefore, many clinicians provided their patients with a diagnosis of some Axis I disorder along with an Axis II personality disorder. This resulted in extremely high comorbidity rates, which defeated the purpose of a classification that was meant to isolate specific disorders.

Despite the mixed results of the multiaxial system, it remained a core feature of the *DSM-III-R* (1987), *DSM-IV* (1994), and *DSM-IV-TR* (2000). In 2013 the *DSM-5* incorporated the personality disorders into the main diagnostic categories and eliminated the remaining three axes. This restored the personality disorders to the equivalency with other classes of mental disorders they had in the *DSM-I* and *-II*.

Types of Personality Disorders in the *DSM-III*

As with all its diagnoses, the *DSM-III* criteria for the personality disorders were more specific and elaborated than earlier definitions. The manual included eleven particular types that were grouped into three clusters.[30] The first were disorders that featured odd or eccentric behaviors: paranoid and schizoid personality, retained from the *DSM-II*, and the new condition of schizotypal. The second cluster involved behaviors that were dramatic, emotional, or erratic. Two of these, histrionic and antisocial, were held over from the *DSM-II*, and two, narcissistic and borderline, were found for the first time in the *DSM-III*. The final cluster concerned anxious and fearful conditions including the *DSM-II*'s compulsive and passive-aggressive types and the new diagnoses of avoidant and dependent personality disorders. Finally, a residual category of atypical, mixed, and other personality disorder could be used when individuals did not qualify for one of the explicit conditions. The *DSM-III* did not retain the *DSM-II*'s cyclothymic, explosive, asthenic, and inadequate types. The manual's personality disorders were especially concerned with people who deviated from social norms that demanded outgoing behaviors.

Introversion and Extraversion

Since the publication of Carl Jung's *Psychological Types* in 1921, introversion and extraversion were considered to be key dimensions of personality. Jung posited that introverts dwelled on the inner world of their thoughts and feelings while extraverts were drawn to the external world of interpersonal relationships and activities. He presented both extraversion and introversion as variants of normal, not disordered, personalities. Jung did not consider one type superior to the other but found them equally valuable ways of being. Nor did he see them as totally dichotomous: "There is no such thing as a pure extrovert or introvert. Such a man would be in a lunatic asylum."[31]

Although Jung's types gained little traction among psychiatrists, many personality psychologists came to see someone's position on the introvert–extravert spectrum as a central part of their personality. It was one of the Big Five personality traits and one of Eysenck's three dimensions and had a devoted, albeit small, following among clinical psychologists who identified themselves as Jungians. It also served as a basis for the hugely popular Myers-Briggs Trait Index, which parsed people into sixteen personality types, all of which were normal.[32]

Jung's types emerged at a time when personality was replacing character as the dominant mode of describing individuals. Simultaneously, it gained traction as extraversion was becoming the preferred personality style in the general culture over the course of the twentieth century. The words most associated with personality in general typified extraverted people: "fascinating," "attractive," "magnetic," "creative," "dominant," "forceful." The United States, in particular, contained what historian Warren Susman called a "culture of personality" that celebrated dominant and forceful extraverts and denigrated quiet and shy introverts.[33] "Society is itself an education in the extrovert values, and rarely has there been a society that has preached them so hard," William Whyte summarized in 1956.[34] More recently, Susan Cain contrasts introversion, "now a second-class personality trait, somewhere between disappointment and pathology" with extraversion, "an enormously appealing personality style."[35]

The class of personality disorders in the initial *DSM*s mirrored the cultural values placed on extraversion and introversion. Four of the eleven personality disorders in the *DSM-I*—inadequate, schizoid, passive-dependent, and compulsive—were related to the introverted style. None concerned extraversion, although cyclothymic personalities alternated between periods of depression and elation.[36] The *DSM-II* maintained this unbalanced ratio, although it added a type of hysterical or histrionic personality disorder that featured the sort of high-intensity and attention-seeking behaviors associated with extraverts.[37]

A central topic of discussion in the ACPD was how to characterize conditions related to introversion.[38] The committee spent considerable time discussing a proposal to establish a diagnosis of "introverted personality disorder" that had not appeared in previous manuals. This plan generated a torrent of criticism. Psychoanalyst Ralph Crowley wrote to Spitzer, "I do not disagree with being labeled Introverted Personality, but Disorder, No! And in bringing in the personal, I mean to speak for all others of my kind." Jungian psychologist Naomi Quenk protested, "It is a gross disservice to the valuable and well-functioning introverts in our society to have a pathological label attached to their normal and healthy attitude. It is discouraging that the psychiatric community has seen fit to encourage the extraverted bias characteristic of our society." Another psychologist, Mary McCaulley, citing her own research indicating about half of college students had introverted personalities, reasoned the proposal would pathologize a huge proportion of the population.[39]

Alarmed by the intense criticism the proposal attracted, Spitzer wrote to the ACPD that "there are more Jungians in this country than I had realized."[40] He circulated a memo to the group asking them to devise a better label for the condition. After considerable internal dissension the advisory committee finally decided to drop the label of "introverted" and instead expand the *DSM-II* category of schizoid personality disorder (SPD). People who fit this category possessed traits such as "close friendships with no more than one or two persons," "emotional coldness and aloofness," and "indifference to praise or criticism."[41] They prefer to be by themselves and display no need to form close relationships with others. Unlike those with avoidant PD, who actively withdrew from others, those with SPD withdrew passively. ACPD member Donald Klein objected that the category of "schizoid personality confused two quite separate groups of people: the shy, socially backward, inept, obedient person who is fearful and therefore isolated but appreciates sociability and would like to be part of the crowd; and . . . the asocial, eccentric . . . person who seeks to be alone and has difficulty in relationships with his peers, frequently resulting in social ostracism and scapegoating."[42]

The *DSM-III* wound up dividing the *DSM-II* schizoid diagnosis into three separate personality syndromes: a more limited schizoid category that referred to those who were incapable of forming social relationships, schizotypal personalities marked by eccentric communications and behavior, and avoidant personality disorder (AVD). The new AVD diagnosis had not appeared in prior manuals. It applied to people who were preoccupied with feelings of inadequacy but desired affection and acceptance, were hypersensitive to rejection, distanced themselves from close personal attachments, and required "uncritical acceptance" before they would enter relationships.[43] In addition to

these three types of introverted disorders, the *DSM-III* also contained a category of dependent personality disorder for the individual who "passively allows others to assume responsibility for major areas of life," "subordinates own
needs to those of persons on whom he depends," and "lacks self-confidence."[44]
Psychiatrist A. James Morgan unsuccessfully urged the work group to view
avoidant personality as a continuum that ranged from normal shyness to active avoidance to avoidance accompanied by distress or disability to psychotic
breaks.[45]

Considerable controversy also accompanied the diagnosis of another condition that fell on the introverted spectrum, schizotypal personality disorder.
This, too, was a new diagnosis that was meant to capture a personality structure that resembled schizophrenia in some respects but lacked a history of
psychotic episodes. Those who received this label did not meet criteria for
schizophrenia although they showed characteristics such as magical thinking, recurrent illusions, and odd speech. Such individuals featured "social
isolation, e.g., no close friends or confidants."[46] Because profound social isolation characterized both schizotypal and schizoid personality disorders, it
was very easy to confuse the two diagnoses. One member of the ACPD noted,
"Using both schizoid and schizotypal is asking for trouble. I have a nagging
feeling that if we cut out schizoid and leave schizotypal then what will happen
is that people will equate schizotypal with schizoid and not understand the
other term."[47] Compulsive personality disorder was the final diagnosis related
to introversion. Its "essential feature" was "restricted ability to express warm
and tender emotions."[48]

The *DSM-III* thus found multiple ways to turn various facets of introversion into a personality disorder, including the dependent, avoidant, schizoid,
schizotypal, and compulsive types. In contrast, it contained just two conditions that involved qualities related to extraversion. Histrionic personality disorder applied to people who were "lively and dramatic and are always drawing
attention to themselves."[49] Narcissistic personality disorder referred to those
who require "constant attention and admiration."[50] The skewed ratio of personality disorders related to introversion and extraversion implicitly reflected
the cultural devaluing of the former and admiration of the latter.

Antisocial Personality Disorder

Antisocial personality disorder is the oldest recognized personality disorder.
Theophrastus, for example, portrayed the shameless man who "is the sort who,
after shortchanging someone goes back to ask him for a loan. . . . When shop-

ping he reminds the butcher of any favors he has done him. And then, standing next to the scale, he throws on some meat. . . . If he gets away with it, fine
and dandy. If not, he grabs some ox guts from the table and goes away laugh-
ing. When his foreign guests have bought theater tickets, he joins them without paying for his seat, and does the same the next day, on which occasion
he includes his sons and their tutor in the party."[51] Indeed, for many decades
when it was called "psychopathic personality," ASPD was the sole personality
disorder that psychiatry acknowledged. From the outset, it was difficult to
separate the criminal and deviant behaviors associated with this condition
from presumably deeply ingrained and pervasive personality characteristics.
Most early formulations of ASPD involved lists of behaviors that were unified
only through their deviation from social norms. Prichard's original definition
of moral insanity noted cases where "the moral or active principles of the
mind are strangely perverted or depraved."[52] Kraepelin described seven classes
of psychopaths including the excitable, the unstable, the impulsive, the eccentric, liars and swindlers, the antisocial, and the quarrelsome.[53] From the
earliest nineteenth-century efforts to the present, most persons who received
a psychopathic diagnosis were involuntary patients, often incorrigible criminals, who were placed in forensic mental health services and so bridged the
mental health and criminal justice systems.[54] Others entered treatment through
mandates of probation or parole offices. Unsurprisingly, clinicians regarded
persons with ASPD as the most distasteful and intimidating patients they
encountered.[55]

Such formulations of psychopathic personalities faced a serious problem.
They failed to separate a variety of negative social consequences, which could
stem from many diverse personality styles, from the results of a specific personality configuration. US psychiatrist Hervey Cleckley (1903–1984) developed the most influential conception that tried to resolve this difficulty. His
book, *The Mask of Sanity: An Attempt to Clarify Some Issues about the So-
Called Psychopathic Personality*, first published in 1941 and then undergoing
four subsequent revisions, posited that the unique aspect of psychopathy was
its concealment. Psychopaths' outwardly appealing, seductive, and intelligent
qualities masked their manipulative, dissembling, and self-absorbed inner
pathology. The sixteen criteria Cleckley used to define the psychopath focused on traits such as superficial charm, insincerity, lack of shame, and poor
judgment rather than on criminal and deviant behaviors.[56]

Cleckley's focus on internal personality dynamics contrasted with definitions that relied on patterns of antisocial behaviors, which risked overpathol-

ogizing disadvantaged people, who had frequent run-ins with the police and underpathologizing those whose social standing insulated their behavior from criminalization.[57] The same need to exert power, ruthlessness, callousness, and lack of remorse that characterizes ASPD can be found among many highly successful businesspeople, politicians, athletes, law enforcement and military personnel, and many other respectable occupations. The major difference between these reputable groups and criminals with similar personality dispositions is that the former are better able to conceal their psychopathic traits and maintain an outward appearance of normality.[58] "The diagnosis of characterological sociopathy has nothing to do with overt criminality," psychotherapist Nancy McWilliams explains, "and everything to do with internal motivation."[59]

Unlike previous diagnostic efforts, the *DSM-I* incorporated Cleckley's ideas that focused on core personality dynamics. It explicitly separated conflicts arising from failures to conform to social norms from "severe, underlying personality disorder."[60] Only those with such disturbances should be diagnosed with what this manual called a "sociopathic personality disturbance." Antisocial reactions were found among those who "are frequently callous and hedonistic, showing marked emotional immaturity, with lack of sense of responsibility, lack of judgment, and an ability to rationalize their behavior so that it appears warranted, reasonable, and justified."[61] The *DSM-II* similarly applied what it called "personality disorder, antisocial personality" to those who are "grossly selfish, callous, irresponsible, impulsive, and unable to feel guilt or to learn from experience and punishment." It also explicitly noted, "A mere history of repeated legal or social offenses is not sufficient to justify this diagnosis."[62] Although both manuals used the term "antisocial" rather than "psychopath," their diagnostic criteria were compatible with Cleckley's influential formulations.

The *DSM-III* returned diagnostic criteria to their original reliance on devalued social norms found among Kraepelin and his predecessors.[63] It converted the *DSM-II*'s personality disorder into a behavioral disorder, overtly refuting the preceding manual's caveat that a history of repeated legal or social offenses cannot justify the diagnosis.[64] ASPD in the *DSM-III* required the presence of behaviors such as truancy, delinquency, casual sexual intercourse, and vandalism before age fifteen along with later inability to sustain consistent work behavior, irresponsible parenting, criminal involvement, and failure to maintain enduring attachments to sexual partners.[65] It was the only personality disorder diagnosis that required persistent symptoms that initially arose in childhood.

ACPD member Theodore Millon called these criteria "a major regressive step that the DSM has returned to an accusatory judgment rather than a dispassionate clinical formulation; what we have before us is but a minor variation of earlier, ill-considered, and deplorable notions such as 'moral insanity' and 'constitutional psychopathic inferiority.'"[66] Millon observed how, on the one hand, only a small subset of people who come into conflict with legal and social norms have antisocial personalities and, on the other hand, many of those who do have antisocial personalities often succeed and thrive in valued social positions in politics, business, or the military.[67] For Millon and others the *DSM-III* criteria for ASPD hopelessly confounded negative value judgments with underlying personality disorders. They could have added that the criteria were also highly entangled with behaviors associated with poverty.

The ACPD ignored the relatively large body of literature—much of which relied on Cleckley's formulations—that had accumulated about ASPD by the late 1970s. Instead, their decision arose from the influence of one of the committee members, Lee Robins, an affiliate of the Washington University group. Robins's work, published as *Deviant Children Grown Up* in 1966, was the basis for the ASPD diagnoses in the Feighner criteria. She studied a group of more than five hundred delinquents referred to a child guidance clinic in one midwestern city and followed them into adulthood. Robins found that antisocial behavior in childhood was an important predictor of problems among adults, including alcoholism, divorce, and incarceration.[68] Her work was a puzzling basis for, first, the Feighner criteria and, next, the *DSM-III* because, although it made an important contribution to the literature on crime and delinquency, it did not deal with any personality characteristic or mental disorder.

The ACPD grappled with how to reconcile Cleckley's emphasis on underlying personality dynamics with Robins's focus on overt behaviors. ACPD member John Lion attempted to retain the *DSM-I* notion of "psychopathic personality," noting that he "rather like[d] Cleckley's idea of singling out this individual with his callousness, indifference to social norms and imperviousness to change or treatment . . . [so that it was time to] haul out the psychopath again, and put him in as a personality disorder."[69] Cleckley's traits, insincerity, lack of shame, and incapacity for love, however, required a considerable amount of clinical judgment. The variety of appraisals different clinicians could make about the presence of these qualities would imperil the *DSM-III*'s major goal to achieve diagnostic reliability. In contrast, Robins's and the related Feighner behavioral criteria were far easier to operationalize in a standardized way. For example, they specified truancy more than once a year, two or more non-traffic-related arrests, and two or more divorces. In the end, Spitzer and the ACPD did not alter Robins's proposal, which they believed would be the best way to achieve high reliability.[70]

The resulting *DSM-III* criteria for ASPD were fundamentally flawed. They hopelessly blurred violations of social norms with mental disorders. The ASPD diagnosis also did not fit the manual's definition of "mental disorder," which excluded conflicts between individuals and society. Their "antisocial" behavioral descriptors could easily stem from societal forces that led marginalized people to violate social and legal norms. Worse, they didn't refer to any underlying personality structure that might account for such behaviors. Most people who fulfilled conditions for ASPD were not psychopaths, because the behaviors they enumerated could stem from a wide variety of non-disordered and disordered personality types.[71] The ASPD criteria could also underdiagnose as well as overdiagnose. "Antisocial" character could become manifest in many ways, legal as well as illegal: "the harshly punitive father; the puritanical, fear-inducing minister; the vengeful dean; and the irritable, guilt-producing mother."[72] Psychopaths were often found in business, politics, law, and the military. Prominent psychologist Robert Hare argued that psychopathy was a far more virulent version of ASPD: "It's like having pneumonia versus having a cold."[73]

Those who met ASPD criteria might deserve punishment, but it was not clear why they needed psychiatric treatment. The result was that the ASPD diagnosis in *DSM-III* was no more advanced than its original nineteenth-century moralistic formulations.

Borderline Personality

The ACPD was preoccupied with how to characterize the diagnosis of borderline personality disorder (BPD). Kraepelin had described a predisposition to manic depression he called "irritable temperament" where "patients display from youth up extraordinarily great fluctuations in emotional equilibrium." This condition typically arose among women and featured frequent mood changes, distractibility, and suicidal thoughts. It could not be classified as one of his core entities but was "best conceived as *a mixture of the fundamental states*."[74] The explicit label of "borderline" first arose in 1938 when analyst Adolf Stern identified a grab bag of ten symptoms—narcissism, hypersensitivity to minor slights, psychic rigidity, low self-esteem among them—that were not psychotic but also were not readily assimilated into any neurotic condition. His term "borderline" represented a level of pathology in between psychotic disconnection from reality and symptom-based neuroses.[75] Stern also noted that these patients were especially resistant to traditional therapies and so were "extremely difficult to handle effectively by any psychotherapeutic method."[76] Subsequently, some clinicians continued to view "borderline" patients as "too sane to be considered crazy and too crazy to be considered sane."[77] Others, however, came to regard BPD as a type, not a level of severity, of personality disorder that was marked by impulsivity, identity confusion, and self-harm.

Neither of the first two *DSM*s mentioned borderline personality disorder; nevertheless, it was frequently diagnosed. BPD gained prominence in the late 1960s when leading analyst Otto Kernberg elevated it to a central position in analytic theory and practice. Kernberg stressed how "borderline" referred to a type of internal personality disorganization that featured impulsivity, inappropriate mood shifts, unstable interpersonal relationships, and occasional brief psychotic episodes. He also used the term to refer to a level of severity that went beyond the distress of the neuroses but did not reach the detachment from reality of the psychoses.[78]

BPD was becoming a rampant diagnosis even before the *DSM* officially recognized it; studies showed that about 10–15 percent of outpatients had this condition.[79] In addition, many inpatient hospitals developed units devoted to treating BPD. The vast majority of people with this diagnosis were women with long histories of self-harm, unstable relationships, anger, and identity confusion. In contrast to ASPD, most of them turned their destructive emotions inward.[80] Susanna Kaysen, who wrote a best-selling memoir (later made into a popular movie), *Girl, Interrupted*, about her confinement at McLean Hospital in Boston in the late 1960s, became the best-known case of BPD.[81] Kaysen reported having all of the central borderline symptoms including cutting, suicidal thoughts and attempts, compulsive sexual promiscuity, impulsivity, and depersonalization. Despite the severity of her condition, she did not experience psychotic symptoms such as hallucinations or delusions.

Its theoretical prominence and wide diagnosis insured that BPD must have a home in the *DSM-III*. Clinician Paul Chodoff expressed his concern to the ACPD that third parties might not reimburse a condition unless it referred to a distinct clinical syndrome.[82] He feared that the *DSM* process, which was dominated by researchers, would become disembodied from the actual patients clinicians saw in their offices. Yet extant definitions were problematic because borderlines did not show the egosyntonic features that marked the personality disorders. Nor did the term refer to any particular personality style that characterized other conditions in this class. It also lacked any essential feature, and its heterogeneity was difficult to fit into the sharply defined diagnostic categories that the *DSM-III* strove to operationalize. These qualities of BPD led many researchers to scorn what they regarded as an imprecise and unmeasurable label.

Psychiatrist Donald Goodwin, who wrote the primary psychiatric text in the Washington University tradition, summarized, "The borderline syndrome is a mess. . . . [It] stands for everything that is wrong with psychiatry and the category should be eliminated and that simply renaming it will not help matters."[83] Even the proponents of this diagnosis realized that "borderline" was a poor label because it was unclear what lay on each side of this "border." Yet, by the late 1970s BPD had become such a significant diagnosis that even changing its name would result in an undesirable upheaval in practice settings. One psychiatrist noted how BPD was not on the border of anything but that removing it from the manual "would be a grade 4 to 5 psychosocial stressor for many of our brethren who are still in a state of mourning over the loss of the 'neuroses.'"[84]

All members of the ACPD agreed that "borderline" was not a good term. Theodore Millon called it a "bad and misleading label."[85] Indeed, Millon wrote to the committee that *the label, borderline, is perhaps the most poorly chosen of all the terms selected for the DSM-III.*[86] Unlike other personality conditions, "borderline" did not refer to a distinct character style. Moreover, many saw borderline syndrome an indicator of severity, not of a particular personality feature.[87] Others, following Kraepelin's early formulation, believed that the impulsive and erratic moods of borderline conditions indicated they were a subset of manic-depressive moods.[88] The committee could not concur on what the condition should be called. Donald Klein proposed the label of "emotionally unstable character disorder," which he viewed as embodying Kraepelin's notion of "irritable temperament." In an unusually hostile response, Spitzer took Klein to task for not providing diagnostic criteria for the condition and for confusing it with the affective condition of cyclothymic disorder.[89]

Spitzer sent the ACPD and others a memo from psychiatrist Lawrence Rockland that noted the "conceptual and descriptive confusion" surrounding BPD and suggested that the label identity diffusion disorder (IDD) better conveyed the nature of the condition.[90] Although his proposal generated little support, it led to an extensive discussion involving issues of whether BPD was a distinct syndrome or encompassed several different disorders. Most agreed that BPD involved profound identity disturbance, conflicts in interpersonal relationships, anger, depression, impulsivity, sexual promiscuity, and misuse of alcohol and drugs. Yet others noted how many of these characteristics could also be elements of narcissistic and histrionic personality disorders. Klein observed how "every conceivable variety of character disorder has been described as borderline at one time or another."[91]

Kernberg wrote to Spitzer noting that IDD would be a more confusing label than BPD and urged keeping that term.[92] Psychiatrist Nathaniel Lehrman, however, urged the committee to drop the borderline label: "What is good for the psychotherapy business may not be what is good for America. We should drop 'Borderline Personality Disorder' from consideration for DSM-3." Lehrman suggested that "continuingly unstable personality" would be a more accurate depiction of the condition.[93]

In response to the utter confusion within the ACPD, Spitzer composed a memo to the group expressing his dismay at the lack of consensus over defining BPD. He compiled a list of about fifty traits with responses of yes or no and asked about four thousand APA members to respond whether each characterized a borderline condition.[94] Eight hundred and eight responded to his invitation to use these items to evaluate one patient they considered as borderline and one control patient. His analysis of the returned data led him to conclude that the borderline concept was not unitary but contained at least two types, corresponding to borderline cases of schizophrenia and the proposed diagnosis of continuously unstable or identity diffusion disorder.[95] The clinicians involved in this study had no objections to using the term "schizotypal" to refer to cases of borderline schizophrenia. However, they strongly resisted the label of "unstable" personality. First, they insisted that such people were *stably* unstable. Second, they contended that clinicians would never abandon the well-entrenched borderline personality disorder category.

Despite their serious misgivings, the advisory committee retained the borderline label. Spitzer bowed to clinical reality and kept a word—"borderline"—that the ACPD had unanimously concluded was terrible. The resulting BPD diagnosis in *DSM-III* reflects the uncertainty and lack of consensus in the extensive ACPD discussions. The criteria read, "The essential feature is a Personality Disorder in which there is instability in a variety of areas, including interpersonal behavior, mood, and self-image. No single feature is invariably present. Interpersonal relations are often intense and unstable, with marked shifts of attitude over time. Frequently there is impulsive and unpredictable behavior that is potentially physically self-damaging."[96] The hallmark of BPD was thus a chronic pattern of instability in emotion, interpersonal relationships, self-concept, and behavior. Individuals must meet five of eight accompanying characteristics (impulsivity, unstable relationships, inappropriate anger, identity disturbance, affective instability, intolerance of being alone, physically self-damaging acts, and chronic feelings of emptiness). The text also notes that "some conceptualize this condition as a level of personality organization rather than as a specific Personality Disorder. Borderline Personality Disorder is frequently associated with other Personality Disorders."[97]

The interests of clinicians in a diagnosis that was central to their practices trumped the goal of researchers to establish clear, homogeneous, and easily operational diagnostic criteria. Despite the confusion that accompanied the development of BPD, it went on to become the best-known personality disorder after 1980. Twenty years later, its criteria remained a mess. Because the diagnosis did not require the presence of any particular symptom, it could be met in 256 different ways![98] BPD was both extremely heterogeneous and comorbid with many other disorders. Indeed, nearly 70 percent of BPD patients had three or more other diagnoses.[99] Despite these difficulties, BPD thrived in the research literature: it was the only personality disorder to grow at a faster rate than the medical literature in general in the period 1966–1995.[100]

There is no doubt that the indicators of harmful emotional dysregulation, volatility, unpredictability, and self-injury render BPD a legitimate mental disorder. It is unclear, however, why the *DSM* classified it as a *personality* disorder. Its trademark indicator—emotional dysregulation—is virtually the opposite of the rigidity that characterizes a PD.[101] Moreover, unlike other PDs, but like mood conditions, the symptoms of BPD are not egosyntonic, cause great distress, and lead to efforts to get rid of them. Kraepelin's classification of borderline states as a kind of mood disorder marked by impulsivity, frequent mood changes, and irritability seems to better fit this condition than the inflexibility that marks the personality disorders. Indeed, recent research indicates that nearly half of people with bipolar diagnoses also meet criteria for BPD.[102] Subsequent *DSMs* maintain the seemingly mistaken placement of BPD as a personality, rather than mood, disorder.

Narcissistic Personality Disorder

Narcissistic personality disorder (NPD), like BPD, first appeared in the *DSM-III*. Freud's initial formulation of narcissism had featured many positive aspects: "People of this type impress others as being 'personalities'; it is on them that their fellow men are specially likely to lean; they readily assume the role of leader, give a fresh stimulus to cultural development or break down existing conditions."[103] As the previous chapter described, narcissism was central to the major analytic theorists of the 1960s and 1970s, Otto Kernberg and Hans Kohut. Especially in the materialistic, individualistic, consumer-oriented US society that marked the post–World War II period, narcissistic qualities of egotism, self-confidence, and self-assurance could evoke admiration and be conducive to success. Yet the outward grandiosity of narcissists could disguise an inner sense of inferiority and weakness.[104] Some narcissistic individuals with superior senses of pomposity alienated others, developed interpersonal problems, and faced conflicts in the workplace or other social settings that led them to enter psychotherapy. Narcissism had become such a central concept for clinical theory and practice, as well as a major product of postwar culture, that there was no way it could remain unacknowledged in the new diagnostic manual.

Given that narcissism was a widely known personality condition among clinicians as well as in society at large, it was expectable that it would generate considerable debate and dissensus within the ACPD. On the contrary, the committee's discussions contain virtually no record of NPD. The *DSM-III* criteria were virtually identical to those Millon initially proposed.[105] They required that the following characterize someone's current and long-term functioning, leading to either social or occupational impairment or subjective distress:

1. Grandiose sense of self-importance or uniqueness
2. Preoccupation with fantasies of unlimited success
3. Exhibitionism that involves constant attention and admiration
4. Either indifference or rage in response to criticism
5. At least two of the following mark interpersonal relationships: entitlement, exploitiveness, alternations between overidealization and devaluation, and lack of empathy[106]

Aside from small modifications, these criteria have persisted through the current *DSM-5*.

Mental Disorders or Devalued Conditions?

The *DSM-III* introduced the personality disorders section with the caution that "it is only when *personality traits* are inflexible and maladaptive and cause either significant impairment in social or occupational functioning or subjective distress that they constitute *Personality Disorders*."[107] It did not, however, specify why any of the personality disorders met the manual's definition that all mental disorders were "behavioral, psychological, or biological dysfunctions" as opposed to "social deviance" or conflicts "between an individual and society."[108]

The criteria sets for each personality disorder were riddled with negative value judgments. Paranoids were guarded and secretive, avoided accepting blame, questioned the loyalty of others, and lacked a sense of humor. Schizoids were emotionally cold, aloof, and indifferent to the feelings of others. Histrionics were overly dramatic, craved excitement, and constantly drew attention to themselves. Those with antisocial personalities virtually embodied conflicts between individuals and society: they had long histories of "lying, stealing, fighting, truancy, and resisting authority" that began in childhood. Compulsive personality disorder was also defined by interpersonal conflict: its sufferers "stubbornly insist that people conform to their way of doing things." Likewise, passive-aggressives displayed "resistance to demands for adequate performance in both occupational and social functioning." The *DSM-III* criteria left no doubt that those with personality disorders were unpleasant, difficult, or dangerous people; it was unclear, however, why they had "mental disorders" as the manual defined the term.[109]

Both clinicians and researchers accepted Spitzer's solution to place the personality disorders on a separate axis from other mental disorders, but their evaluative nature aroused the ire of a third group: feminists, who were deeply suspicious of what they regarded as psychiatry's pathologization of women. Although manifestos such as Betty Friedan's *The Feminine Mystique* (1963), Kate Millett's *Sexual Politics* (1969), and Germaine Greer's *The Female Eunuch* (1970) attacked psychiatry's oppressive control over women during the *DSM-I* and *-II* period, these manuals were so invisible that feminist critiques did not target them. The *DSM-III* process, however, infuriated many feminists. They were especially appalled at the value-laden aspects of the personality disorders.

As early as John Stuart Mill's *The Subjection of Women* (1869), female character styles were determined by the values of male-dominated groups. "All women are brought up from the very earliest years in the belief that their ideal of character is the very opposite to that of men; not self-will, and government by self-control, but submission, and yielding to the control of others," Mill wrote. He went on to say, "It may be asserted without scruple, that no other class of dependents have had their character so entirely distorted from its natural proportions by their relation with their masters."[110] In other words, personality disorders were entangled in sociocultural stereotypes that disguised oppressive power relationships. Friedan revived this critique in her penetrating analysis of the social norms that forced women to embrace subordinate personality styles so that their husbands could thrive.[111]

Several of the personality disorders were shot through with negative value judgments of stereotypical feminine qualities. One was histrionic personality disorder, which was "diagnosed far more frequently in females than in males." Among its criteria were terms such as "self-dramatization," "vain and demanding," and "dependent, helpless, constantly seeking reassurance."[112] Dependent personality disorder was another: "The essential feature is a Personality Disorder in which the individual passively allows others to assume responsibility for major areas of his or her life because of a lack of self-confidence and an inability to function independently; the individual subordinates his or her own needs to those others on whom he or she is dependent in order to avoid any possibility of having to be self-reliant."[113] Such diagnoses seemed to embody adverse value appraisals of stereotypical gender roles more than symptoms of a mental disorder. Feminists also pointed out how calling these conditions "personality disorders" ignored the social and economic constraints that kept women dependent. Mill would have recognized their claims that feminine behavior often represented strategic responses to oppressive situations more than natural personality traits. Feminist opposition to these conditions would escalate in the *DSM-III* revision process.

The Impact of *DSM-III*

The development of the *DSM-III* involved sharp conflicts between psychiatric researchers, many of whom scorned the personality disorders, and clinicians, who feared that new diagnostic criteria would preclude them from obtaining reimbursement for treating them. Surprisingly, the new multiaxial system led these conditions to flourish among both clinicians and researchers. One study that compared the proportion of patients receiving a diagnosis of some personality disorder in a large medical center found they increased from 19 percent during the last five years of the *DSM-II* to 49 percent in the first five years of the *DSM-III*.[114] Because most patients who presented with some PD also had one or more Axis I diagnoses, few clinicians had problems being reimbursed for their efforts.

In addition, because clinicians could ascertain and record the personalities

of all their patients on Axis II, researchers had a new source of data for studying the personality disorders. The unintended result of the *DSM-III* revolution
was to propel the personality disorders into the mainstream of psychiatric
research.[115] Compared to the meager 1.2 percent of articles published about the
personality disorders in the *American Journal of Psychiatry* in 1979–1980, 9.4
percent of *AJP* articles dealt with these conditions a decade later.[116] Across all
journals, the number of articles about some personality disorder grew from
69 in 1975 to 262 ten years later.[117]

This growth, however, was highly uneven across different personality disorders. In 1975, ASPD was the most studied condition, accounting for 37 percent of all articles, followed by BPD (18 percent) and histrionic PD (16 percent). By 1985, BPD accounted for 40 percent of the literature while ASPD
slipped to second place with 25 percent, followed by schizotypal (17 percent)
and narcissistic (15 percent). By 1995 only BPD, ASPD, and schizotypal had
thriving research literatures. Other conditions languished. Just 44 publications
concerned histrionic PD over a thirty-five-year period.[118] The research literature on dependent, narcissistic, compulsive, paranoid, and passive-aggressive
conditions was also very scant.[119]

Conclusion

A number of problems with the *DSM-III* criteria soon surfaced. Far from
being separable entities, there was huge overlap among the various personality disorders. For example, pure borderline conditions were a rarity: almost
all patients who met criteria for BPD also qualified for some other personality
disorder or disorders. The personality disorders were not just highly interconnected with each other but also internally heterogeneous. This meant
that patients with the same diagnosis often had little in common. Such heterogeneity precluded researchers from making much progress in finding the
etiology, prognosis, or treatment for any of the conditions. Worst of all, the
nonspecific atypical, mixed, and other diagnosis turned out to be the most
prevalent condition of all, indicating the amorphous nature of the personality
disorders.

The *DSM-III* thus did little to answer the questions that Spitzer had asked
in his 1976 memo. Not only did the "fuzzy edges" between normal and disordered personality traits remain, but it was unclear what made *any* condition
a personality "disorder." The eleven PDs clearly characterized people who
were dislikable, maladaptive, and, often, deviant. But it was not clear why any

of them had internal *dysfunctions*, which the *DSM* considered to be the essential quality of any mental disorder. The issue that feminists raised—the diagnostic criteria for the personality disorders reflected social values far more than mental disorders—also remained unaddressed. Another problem was that in some cases the manual's quest for high reliability might have impaired validity. As noted above, ASPD provided one example. Paranoid PD was another case. The *DSM-I* and *-II* considered it to result from projections of unacceptable inner motives, drives, and tensions onto external figures. Because determinations of projection involved subjective inferences, the *DSM-III* simply removed this core process from the diagnostic criteria.[120]

Finally, the *DSM-III* ignored the other major issue that Spitzer's memo posed: Was it possible to reconcile the dimensional qualities of the personality disorders with the manual's "discrete subdivisions" of these diagnoses? As research proceeded over the decades that followed the *DSM-III*, the question of whether the personality disorders better resembled the manual's categorical portrayals or continuous spectra took on growing importance. By the time psychiatry turned to another fundamental revision in its diagnostic manual around the turn of the century, the dimensional or categorical nature of the personality disorders would become the core issue in the entire *DSM* process.

Another result of the *DSM-III* was the demise of psychoanalysis within psychiatry. As late as 1980, prominent journalist Janet Malcolm could say that "psychoanalysis . . . has detonated throughout the intellectual, social, artistic, and ordinary life of our century as no cultural force has . . . since Christianity."[121] The *DSM-III*'s atheoretical approach abruptly brought an end to this sweeping influence and led to the severing of psychoanalysis from psychiatry. The theory-neutral stance of the manual disguised the deep hostility of its developers toward analytic conceptions. The overt opposition to analysis that surfaced in the *DSM-III* deliberations undermined the basis of the field's legitimacy within psychiatry. In addition, the profession's turn away from psychotherapy toward drug treatments left little room for analytic approaches. Psychoanalysis fell from its lofty pedestal and virtually disappeared from psychiatric curricula in the years following the adoption of the *DSM-III*. After 1980 most analytic trainees would come from nonmedical fields, especially clinical psychology and social work.[122]

The decline of psychoanalysis left a vacuum in the study of personality. Psychologists would fill this void with a quantitative, empiricist, and measurable perspective that was diametrically opposite to the analytic view but in certain ways was highly congruent with the *DSM-III*'s approach. Personality psychologists were poised to take control over the next revolution in constructing the personality disorders.

CHAPTER SIX

Personality Contentions in the *DSM-5*

An extraordinary spirit of optimism pervaded psychiatry in the years follow-ing the publication of the *DSM-III* in 1980. The manual itself was at the center of the field's resurgence. In contrast to the invisibility of its modest predeces-sors, the *DSM-III* and its successors, *DSM-III-R* (1987), *DSM-IV* (1994), and *DSM-IV-TR* (2000), became the touchstone for mental health practice and research. Each edition sold nearly a million copies and generated enormous profits for the American Psychiatric Association.[1] Most important, the man-ual's diagnostic system created a sense that psychiatry had solved its crisis of legitimacy and moved into a new era. Although the focus of the *DSM-III* revolution was to create a more reliable classification system where observers would agree on what condition a patient had, many believed that this im-proved reliability would soon lead to improved validity, where a diagnosis corresponded to the actual disorder that was present. In particular, the surge of neuroscientific research during the 1980s and 1990s was expected to un-cover the biological foundation of mental disorders that had eluded psychia-try for the past 150 years. "It seems that we are about to move into a period when genetics will define disease entities in psychiatry," a prominent review confidently predicted in 1989.[2]

The *DSM-III* revolution entrenched the manual in all facets of mental health—not just research and clinical treatment but also education, drug tri-als, epidemiology, hospital administration, the criminal justice system, and other institutions. As well, it bolstered psychiatry's position as the legitimate authority over the definition of mental disorder for all the mental health pro-fessions. Government agencies, professional organizations, pharmaceutical companies, advocacy groups, and political figures all sponsored campaigns widely promoting the idea that the *DSM* entities were genuine diseases in need of treatment from psychiatrists and other professionals.

Surging numbers of patients seeking mental health services accompanied these educational efforts. At the time the *DSM-III* was published, community surveys estimated that about 10 percent of individuals diagnosed with some mental disorder had contact with mental health professionals; ten years later this figure had soared to 25 percent; by the early 2000s about 40 percent received some kind of professional treatment.[3] As the number of patients soared, the fierce clinical opposition that the development of the *DSM-III* had engendered quickly withered. Moreover, the manual's theory neutrality allowed professionals of all persuasions to apply its many diagnoses to the full range of patients who sought their services. The new diagnostic system legitimized their claims to be treating real diseases and, crucially, provided them the means to obtain reimbursement from insurers.

The *DSM-III* revolution also thoroughly altered the status of the personality disorders within the mental health field. As the previous chapter recounted, before 1980 they were central to psychoanalysis and highly consequential for clinicians. Many researchers, however, derided the idea of a "disordered personality." Moreover, because they were holistic, they were difficult to square with the *DSM-III*'s precise, symptom-based system. Spitzer's multiaxial system in the new manual was an astute compromise that maintained the range of personality disorders on Axis II but separated them from the symptom-based conditions on Axis I. At the time, no one knew how the multiaxial system would influence psychiatric practice and research.

Personality Disorders in the *DSM-III-R* and *-IV*

The three manuals that followed the *DSM-III* tinkered with, but made no radical changes to, the personality disorders. Most of their revisions altered the wording of particular diagnostic criteria. Perhaps the major modification involved adding underlying personality dynamics to the behavioral ASPD criteria. The *DSM-III-R* reintroduced the notion of lack of remorse for antisocial behavior.[4] The *DSM-IV* went further, adding "contempt for the feelings of others," "superficial charm," and "lack of empathy" to the "associated features" of ASPD.[5] These revisions made the ASPD diagnosis more compatible with its formulations in the diagnostic manuals that preceded the *DSM-III*. The *DSM-IV* also downgraded the status of passive-aggressive PD, which had been the most common diagnosis during World War II, to an appendix.[6]

The major controversies involving the personality disorders in the two decades that followed the *DSM-III* stemmed from feminist advocacy efforts. Spurred by the proposal from the *DSM-III-R* personality disorders work group for a new diagnosis of "masochistic personality disorder," feminists launched highly publicized efforts to expose what they regarded as sexism in psychiatric diagnoses.[7] This disorder involved "a pervasive pattern of self-defeating behavior" as manifested in such actions as choosing relationships that lead to disappointment, rejecting offers of help, becoming depressed after positive events, and feeling hurt after provoking angry responses from others.[8] It excluded from diagnosis those who displayed such characteristics in response to or in anticipation of physical, sexual, or psychological abuse. The masochistic personality disorder diagnosis was quite similar to Wilhelm Reich's "masochistic character," which involved patterns of suffering, self-damage, complaining, and self-depreciation.[9]

In 1985, the chair of the American Psychological Association Committee on Women wrote to Spitzer charging that "the diagnosis has ominous implications for perpetuating damaging stereotypes of women and for fostering an unnecessarily pathological view of women's experience."[10] Psychologist Paula Caplan was the most visible opponent of this diagnosis. Caplan believed that masochistic personality disorder did not constitute a mental disorder so much as reflect social expectations that women should put other people's needs ahead of their own. She feared that the diagnostic criteria, such as choosing to remain in relationships involving maltreatment, rejecting attempts at help, and refusing opportunities for pleasure typified the behaviors that female victims of violence displayed. In effect, women in these situations would be doubly victimized, first by their domestic partners and then by psychiatrists.[11] Caplan engaged in widespread media campaigns, writing articles for the mainstream press and appearing on popular television programs where she belittled the proposal for a diagnosis related to women's masochism.

In response to criticism from Caplan and others, the *DSM-III-R* Advisory Committee on Personality Disorders (ACPD) met with members of feminist groups from a variety of mental health professions including, in addition to the two APAs, the National Association of Social Workers, National Association of Women and the Law, and the American Orthopsychiatric Association. A representative of the Feminist Therapy Institute told the committee that her group "had voted to invest all its financial and other resources in filing a lawsuit" if it approved this diagnosis.[12] This meeting generated considerable adverse publicity in the popular press regarding the *DSM-III-R* process. In response, the ACPD changed the label of masochistic personality to self-defeating personality disorder (SDPD), which the feminists still considered to be victim blaming. They also noted how the *DSM* contained no parallel diagnosis for traditionally male behavior. These groups organized highly visible and widely publicized demonstrations at the 1986 APA meeting.

The central question regarding SDPD was whether including it in the *DSM* would discriminate against women, as feminist groups argued, or help them gain the treatment they desired, as Spitzer and the majority of the advisory committee members believed. After all, the ACPD reasoned, psychiatrists weren't telling them, as Caplan insisted, that they were crazy. No one was imposing a label on anyone; women who received the supposedly objectionable diagnosis were ones who voluntarily sought help for their distressing conditions.

In the end, the APA took a third position. It was less concerned with either rejecting a stigmatizing diagnosis or accepting a helpful one than with avoiding reputational damage to the psychiatric profession. In a surprising rebuke of Spitzer and its own advisory committee, the APA Board of Trustees voted to relegate SDPD to an appendix in the *DSM* called "proposed diagnostic categories needing further study." Sensitive to feminist objections, it balanced SDPD with a new category of sadistic personality disorder (SPD), which was "far more common in males than in females."[13] The stated goal was to allow more research data to accumulate that would either support or reject the inclusion of each condition in the main text of future manuals. In fact, placing these diagnoses in an appendix represented a political compromise between the ACPD and its feminist critics.

An unintended consequence of the SDPD and associated controversies was the ouster of Robert Spitzer from the leadership of the *DSM* process. The APA was disturbed by the negative publicity the debates with feminists generated and blamed Spitzer for allowing too many nonpsychiatrists into the process. The organization wanted to ensure that the next revision of the *DSM* would remain out of the public eye to avoid the embarrassing protests that marked the *DSM-III-R* discussions of the personality disorders.

The APA's attempt to escape further controversy failed. Indeed, antagonism to SDPD and other diagnoses perceived to discriminate against women intensified in the *DSM-IV* deliberations. Caplan was again the most visible opponent, appearing on an episode of *The Phil Donahue Show* and jointly with Spitzer on *The Today Show*. Numerous media reports in publications including in the *New York Times,* the *Washington Post,* the *Wall Street Journal,* and *Newsweek* covered this debate. The result was that SDPD (and SPD) were removed from the *DSM-IV.* The potential professional discomfiture from disorders that politically organized groups considered stigmatizing ultimately trumped the presumed scientific basis for these diagnoses. Task force member Theodore Millon concluded "that the true motive for this decision was essentially a political one, a decision to sweep under the rug what was difficult to sustain in the face of unrelenting criticisms by a small minority of mental health professionals."[14] Aside from feminist protests, however, little controversy accompanied the personality disorders in the construction of the three diagnostic manuals that followed the *DSM-III.*

The Divergent Impact of *DSM-III* on Researchers and Clinicians

Feminist protests notwithstanding, the *DSM-III* revolution successfully transformed the crumbling credibility of psychiatry in the 1960s and 1970s into a confident vision of the intellectual breakthroughs that the manual would produce. The *DSM-III* led to radical changes in the profession. One was the rise of biologically oriented psychiatrists to unchallenged dominance. In 1983, Gerald Klerman, the highest-ranking psychiatrist in the federal government, called the manual a "reaffirmation on the part of American psychiatry to its medical identity and its commitment to scientific medicine."[15] Conversely, the advent of the *DSM-III* heralded the demise of psychoanalysis within psychiatry: few psychiatrists who entered the field after 1980 became analysts.

At the same time, the number of patients receiving treatment for mental illness, especially in the general medical care sector, soared.[16] Rates of psychiatric care also grew rapidly, but this rise involved only drug therapies; the provision of psychotherapy among psychiatrists actually declined in this period.[17] The personality disorders, however, were exceptions. For one thing, no medications specifically targeted this class, which is more resistant to drug treatments than other categories of mental disorder. For another, psychiatrists were far more likely to use psychotherapy to treat personality disorders than to treat other types of mental illnesses.[18] Because psychotherapy was the preferred response to the personality disorders, the relatively small number of psychiatrists could not handle the demand for this modality. Consequently, much of their treatment spread to clinical psychologists, social workers, counselors, and other therapists who seemed equally adept as psychiatrists at providing talk therapies, and were cheaper to boot. The clinical handling of the personality disorders was diverging from that of other mental disorders, which were increasingly treated by psychiatrists and other physicians solely through drug therapies.

The clinicians who led the opposition to the formulation of the *DSM-III* had been concerned that the new manual would overturn decades of progress in understandings of mental disorder, devalue clinical expertise, and threaten the reimbursement of Axis II conditions. Yet after 1980 they quickly came not just to acquiesce but to embrace the new manual. For one thing, the *DSM's* medical-like diagnoses led to rising prestige among all mental health professionals. For another, the potential monetary damage from placing the personality disorders on a separate axis was not realized.

Third-party private and public payments for psychotherapy, which were available to nonmedical professionals as well as to psychiatrists, had become nearly universal. Some psychiatrists remained concerned about their ability to receive reimbursement for treating the kinds of problems associated with personality disorders: "Much of what we treat people for in intensive individual psychotherapy—gross dissatisfactions with the course of their life, difficulties in the area of interpersonal relationships or work adjustment . . . school or work inhibitions, and so on—are not considered by the third party pays to be formal diseases for which they should be expected to carry the treatment costs," Robert Wallerstein bemoaned in 1991.[19] Yet, although insurers sometimes balked at paying for the treatment of personality disorders, this did not turn out to be a serious handicap for most clinicians. Most people with a personality disorder, about 80 percent, also met criteria for some Axis I condition that therapists could bill for.[20] Anthropologist T. M. Luhrmann's ethnography of a psychiatric hospital found, "An Axis II diagnosis by itself commonly does not qualify for admission. Even if a clinician believes that a patient's borderline personality disorder is responsible for her suicidal rage, he will list a diagnosis like 'major depressive disorder' on Axis I."[21]

Clinicians did not need to believe that the manual's diagnostic entities for the personality disorders (or any other condition) were valid. In particular, they did not treat Axis I and Axis II disorders as separate groups. "These studies suggested a startling disconnect between how clinicians think of mental disorders and how they are organized in the current DSM," Blashfield and colleagues observe.[22] These manuals, though, sufficed as tools for them to bill for their services. Clinicians, therefore, were not unhappy with the *DSM-III* multiaxial system that persisted through the next three revisions.

The *DSM-III* did not have a straightforward impact on research about the personality disorders. After 1980 their trajectory depended on the particular condition. Most studies focused on BPD, which flourished in the decades following the *DSM-III*, and ASPD, which maintained a high level of visibility in psychiatric journals. The new schizotypal diagnosis also drew some interest among researchers. From 1998 to 2010, the most studied disorders in professional journals were ASPD (3,432), BPD (3,005), OCD (1,422), and schizotypal (1,249).[23] However, the dependent, narcissistic, paranoid, and passive-aggressive diagnoses averaged fewer than ten articles per year.[24] Overall, while researchers did not flock to study the personality disorders, most shed the stigmatizing attitudes they held toward this class in the pre-*DSM-III* era.

Dissatisfaction with the *DSM* Emerges

The two major revolutions in psychiatry after 1980—the ascendance of the *DSM*'s categorical system and the rise of neuroscience—developed on parallel tracks. During the 1980s and 1990s, the *DSM* remained immune to psychiatry's biological turn. However, the manual's clear-cut diagnostic criteria were turning out to hinder research: "We have searched for big, simple neuropathological explanations for psychiatric disorders and have not found them. We have hunted for big, simple neurochemical explanations for psychiatric disorders and have not found them. We have hunted for big, simple genetic explanations for psychiatric disorders and have not found them," psychiatrist Kenneth Kendler lamented.[25] Ironically, the researchers who led the charge to implement the *DSM-III* over strenuous clinical objections became the major advocates for a radical transformation of the manual's diagnostic system.

Researchers had many reasons for their discontent with the *DSM* classification. Far from the separable entities that Robins and Guze had envisioned, huge overlap existed among diagnoses. In fact, most people who received one diagnosis also qualified for one or more others. This widespread diagnostic comorbidity was especially true for the personality disorders, which nearly always overlapped with each other and with Axis I diagnoses.[26] For example, one study found that over half of patients with a diagnosis of obsessive-compulsive PD also received a diagnosis of avoidant PD.[27] In addition, the categorical nature of the *DSM-III* classification mandated a sharp division between those who met the criteria for some disorder and those who didn't. Researchers, however, had reached a consensus that categorical diagnostic cutoffs were arbitrary and empirically unjustified: "Disorders might merge into one another with no natural boundary in between."[28]

The extant categorical system was a particular handicap for the surging number of neuroscientific studies of mental disorders. Beginning in the late 1970s new technologies including positron emission tomography (PET), electroencephalography (EEG), and functional magnetic resonance imaging (fMRI) offered unprecedented opportunities for neuroscientists to observe brain-based activities. The two decades that followed the *DSM-III* were marked by a surge of research that strove to find the brain and genetic correlates of mental disorders, including personality disorders. Yet, because the *DSM-III*'s categorical system was so poor, the hunt for a neurogenetic basis for mental disorders almost completely failed. Research since 1980 did not identify a single biological marker for any mental disorder. Indeed, researchers singled out the *DSM* system itself as a major reason for their lack of success: no genetic correlates can possibly exist for conditions that themselves are contrived.

A report from an APA planning group in 2002 summarized the reasons for the widespread dissatisfaction with the *DSM-III* paradigm:

> In the more than 30 years since the introduction of the Feighner criteria by Robins and Guze, which eventually led to DSM-III, the goal of validating these syndromes and discovering common etiologies has remained elusive. Despite many proposed candidates, not one laboratory marker has been found to be specific in identifying any of the DSM-defined syndromes. Epidemiological and clinical studies have shown extremely high rates of comorbidities among the disorders, undermining the hypothesis that the syndromes represent distinct etiologies. Furthermore, epidemiological studies have shown a high degree of short-term diagnostic instability for many disorders. With regard to treatment, lack of treatment specificity is the rule rather than the exception.[29]

The problems of lack of validity, high rates of comorbidity, diagnostic instability, and treatment nonspecificity were particularly apparent for the personality disorders.

The extreme internal heterogeneity of many extant *DSM* diagnoses presented an additional difficulty; the symptoms of one person diagnosed with a disorder often barely resembled the symptoms of others who received the same diagnosis. Again, this was especially the case for the personality disorders.[30]

Another source of dissatisfaction for the personality disorders in particular was the extremely high occurrence of the diagnosis of personality disorder not otherwise specified (NOS). This label was applied when patients met the general criteria for a personality disorder and some, but not all, criteria for a specific personality disorder.[31] Extraordinarily, NOS was the single most common classification of the personality disorders.[32] One study that surveyed

238 psychiatrists and psychologists reported that "the majority of patients with personality pathology significant enough to warrant clinical psychotherapeutic attention (60.6%) are currently undiagnosable on Axis II."[33]

The same constituency of researchers that designed the *DSM-III* identified this system itself as the problem that the next revision of the manual must overcome: the *DSM* model was "*the* major factor in how little we yet know of the causes and cures of mental disorders."[34] By the end of the century researchers generally agreed that the extant *DSM-IV* criteria for the personality disorders were not empirically based, lacked theoretical justification, were not specific to personality conditions, and had arbitrary diagnostic thresholds.[35] Many researchers had also concluded that they could be better formulated as more chronic types of various Axis I disorders. Others were dissatisfied that the PDs continued to have a psychodynamic taint.[36] In short, the *DSM* diagnoses of personality disorders were a mess. "The personality disorders are not at all clearly distinct from normal functioning or from each other," Allen Frances summarized.[37] These defects led some participants at the first meeting of the *DSM-5* planning conference to suggest completely removing the class from the manual.

The researchers who led the revision process for the fifth edition anticipated that they would institute another paradigm shift that would eliminate the obstacles to a more valid system that the last diagnostic upheaval had created. Paradoxically, the forthcoming revolution would feature the personality disorders as the prototype for the projected new system.

A New Model Emerges

The psychoses had been at the heart of psychiatry's canon since the first mental illnesses were recognized in ancient times. The neuroses became preeminent in the late nineteenth century and maintained their significance through the *DSM-IV*. In contrast, personality disorders gained prominence during World War II and its aftermath, but their brief period in the limelight was already over by the time the *DSM-II* was published in 1968. The *DSM-III* recognized their distinct, although somewhat tarnished, nature when it placed them on a separate axis from other classes of mental disorder.

In an astonishing turnaround, the personality disorders became the major concern in the deliberations leading up to the *DSM-5*. Equally amazing, academic psychologists, who had little involvement in the construction of previous manuals, attained a central position in the *DSM-5* process. The creation of this manual featured a reconciliation of psychological and psychiatric researchers about the desirability of replacing the extant categorical paradigm with a dimensional portrayal of personality.

In one of the great ironies of psychiatric history, far from eliminating the personality disorders, the researchers who planned the new manual used them as the *model* for the projected overhaul of the *DSM-IV*. They viewed this class as providing the best opportunity for a new paradigm based on dimensional principles that they envisioned would eventually infuse the entire *DSM*. The continuous qualities of personality disorders that made them such a poor fit for the *DSM-III* categories would serve as the basis for a new form of measurement in the next edition of the manual. What came to be called the *DSM-5* would be built on the foundation of the personality disorders.

In a second great irony of psychiatric history, the body of evidence the DSM-5 Task Force would come to rely on was mainly research findings from psychologists, not psychiatrists. Based on studies in the general population, rather than among treated patients, it was personality psychologists who concluded that mental disorders were better conceived as continuous dimensions that involved a gradient of severity ranging from weak to strong as opposed to the arbitrary either/or thresholds that the *DSM* approach embraced. One prominent personality psychologist marveled, "Many clinicians and researchers continue to favor a categorical system of personality diagnosis. This is remarkable, given the deficiencies and limitations of DSM-IV Axis II. . . . Overwhelming evidence indicates that personality pathology is better conceptualized dimensionally."[38]

The Appeal of Dimensional Models

In 1999 the APA and the NIMH began preparations for what would eventually become the *DSM-5* in 2013. Even at this early stage, these institutions expected that a new dimensional system would replace the categorical *DSM-IV*. The very first work group in the planning process concerned dimensional approaches to the personality disorders. "As useful as the DSM-III paradigm was," the preface to a volume reporting on the conference asserted, "a new paradigm may be needed if we are to be successful in uncovering illness etiology in psychiatry."[39] The work group identified the major problem with the *DSM-III* revolution and its reliance on the Washington University categorical approach: "The single most important precondition for moving forward to improve the clinical and scientific utility of DSM-V will be the incorporation of simple dimensional measures for assessing syndromes within broad diagnostic categories and supraordinate dimensions that cross current diagnostic

boundaries. Thus, we have decided that one, if not the major, difference between DSM-IV and DSM-V will be the more prominent use of dimensional
measures in DSM-V."[40] Researchers had come to see the major psychiatric
disorders as continuous, ranging from generally healthy individuals on one
end, to mild and transient disturbances, to moderate symptoms, to severe and
prolonged distress on the other end.

Psychologists had developed sophisticated quantitative measures of personality traits that many researchers believed could provide the prototype for
a new way of conceiving mental disorders in general. Their models were
coming to influence psychiatric research. Psychologists Robert Krueger and
Jennifer Tackett observed, "Our field is currently enjoying a renaissance of
research linking personality and psychopathology. During much of the recent past, the personality and psychopathology literatures proceeded mostly
in parallel. . . . Current research might therefore be conceptualized as a rap-
prochement of the personality and psychopathology literature."[41] The initial
recommendations of the participants in the earliest efforts to develop a new
DSM indicated that a dimensional model of the personality disorders might
even serve as a basis for the entire manual: "If a dimensional system of personality performs well and is acceptable to clinicians, it might then be appropriate to explore dimensional approaches in other domains."[42]

In particular, research on the five-factor model (FFM) of personality (the
Big Five) had exploded after 1980.[43] It was the heir of the individual differences model that dominated US psychology since the early twentieth century.
The FFM views personality as composed of five major dimensions: openness
to experience through closedness, conscientiousness through negligence,
extraversion through introversion, agreeableness through antagonism, and
neuroticism through emotional stability. It uses the statistical technique of
factor analysis to calculate the quantitative relationships between large numbers of personality traits to find the correlations between the traits. It then
derives a smaller number of second-order factors that are believed to form
the major dimensions of personality. Like its predecessors, the FFM relies
on numerical differences between individuals rather than intraindividual dynamics, real-life situations, or cultural and historical processes to measure
personality traits.

From a tiny number of publications in 1980, about 300 articles about the
FFM had appeared by 1990 when the research literature exploded to more
than 1,500 pieces between 2005 and 2009.[44] By the turn of the century, it had
overshadowed its antecedents, such as Cattell's 16 Personality Factor model

and Eysenck's PEN (psychoticism, extraversion, and neuroticism). The FFM had become something of a cult among many personality psychologists, for whom the five factors it portrayed were not statistical constructions but real entities: "We believe it is an empirical fact, like the fact that there are seven continents on earth or eight American presidents from Virginia," proclaimed prominent boosters of the model.[45]

Although psychologists developed it to explain personality differences in normal populations, they also claimed that the FFM "is fully adequate to account for the dimensions of abnormal personality as well."[46] Adherents claimed that the *DSM* personality disorders were extremes of its five dimensional traits: "Variation across the range of personality disturbance is well encapsulated in four or five factors. These can have different names but cover aggression, confrontational and impulsive traits (antisocial, sociopathic and dissocial); withdrawn, isolated and suspicious traits (schizoid and paranoid); perfectionistic and rigid traits (obsessive-compulsive); and anxious, dependent and internalizing traits (anxious-dependent, avoidant)."[47]

Because every person received a score on all five dimensions, advocates touted how the FFM provided "precise, individualized descriptions of the personality structure of each patient."[48] In addition, they rejected the assumption that the categorical *DSM* disorders were distinct from normality, instead asserting that there was no sharp difference between abnormal and normal personalities. Personality disorders were simply extremes on a continuum that ranged from not present, to mild, to moderate, to severe traits. Finally, they touted the model's presumed universality: "There is every reason to think that the FFM characterized people in Homer's day as much as today."[49]

The planners of the *DSM-5* initially thought that the FFM, or a similar system, might apply not just to the personality disorders but could exemplify how to construct dimensional measures for *all* classes of mental disorder. The easily measurable, quantitative, and seemingly scientific nature of psychological research on personality might reintroduce the legitimacy that was starting to erode within psychiatry because of its failure to realize the goals of the *DSM-III* and neuroscientific revolutions. In particular, a dimensional model might help break the impasse in neuroscientific research about the biological underpinnings of personality. Many researchers optimistically predicted that a continuous view of personality traits could overcome the lack of compatibility between the *DSM* categories and neurogenetic findings. "There is clear evidence that much, perhaps most, of the variance in adult personality traits is genetic in origin," psychologists asserted.[50] Researchers reported that the heritability of *DSM-III-R* personality disorders ranged from 28 percent to 79 percent.[51] These genotype–phenotype correspondences for the personality disorders were generally higher than the weaker associations observed with many other classes of mental disorders.[52]

"Ultimately, as one builds toward DSM-V, what may emerge is a structured set not of categorical diagnoses but of component dimensions, a set of symptom-cluster building blocks from which the panoply of diagnoses could be constructed," two prominent psychologists wrote.[53] A new dimensional system might not merely patch up but even replace the extant *DSM* Axis II system.[54] "Having thus disposed of issues regarding content, coverage, and cutoffs, we can now proceed to Just Do It: Replace the 10 personality disorder categories in Axis II with the 10 diagnoses associated with the high and low poles of each of the five factors of the FFM," psychologist Paul Costa boldly proclaimed.[55]

The leaders of the *DSM* revision did not seem concerned that the researchers who designed and conducted studies using the FFM and similar models didn't deal with clinical populations or even with actual people.[56] They were confident that a model developed to explain differences in personality in the general population could with little difficulty become a tool for diagnosing patients in clinical settings: "The idea of replacing the DSM-IV PDs with an empirically based structured trait-dimensional model is fundamentally sound."[57] The clinicians who were the largest constituency of the APA—but who were barely represented on the DSM-5 Task Force—would prove to be far less impressed with these sophisticated quantitative studies.

Planning a New *DSM*

An early planning conference for the *DSM-5* in 2004 was devoted to dimensional models for the personality disorders.[58] Psychologists and a few psychiatrists had developed numerous dimensional models of personality disorders that had not yet penetrated the *DSM* definitions. Thomas Widiger, a prominent personality psychologist and member of the *DSM-IV* personality disorders work group, chaired the conference. Widiger, following common assumptions among psychologists, conceived of personality disorders as residing on continuous dimensions ranging from introversion to extraversion, constraint through impulsivity, emotional stability to instability, and compliance to antagonism. These dimensions applied to not just psychiatric patients but also everyone who has a personality, that is, everyone.[59]

A major issue for conference participants was the overabundance of possible dimensional models. Widiger and psychiatrist Erik Simonsen reviewed eighteen proposals for measuring personality.[60] On one extreme was renowned psychologist Raymond Cattell's 16 Personality Factor that used 171 groups to derive forty-two clusters that in turn were reduced to sixteen source traits. On the other extreme, psychiatrist Robert Cloninger's model linked just three dimensions of harm avoidance, novelty seeking, and reward dependence to three specific underlying neurochemical substrates.[61] The group that was charged to develop the personality disorders section for the *DSM-5* would have plenty of options for designing their criteria, although some variant of the FFM seemed likely to emerge.

The conference was not without dissenters. Some contributors raised questions about the usefulness of dimensional measurements. For starters, continuous models were not the only alternative to what everyone agreed were the deficiencies of the *DSM* categories. Psychologist Drew Westen observed how most researchers favored trait-oriented dimensional measures over person-centered categorical models that described particular kinds of people. In contrast, Westen and colleagues proposed a person-centered approach that would better correspond to clinicians' views of patients.[62] Instead of specific diagnostic criteria, prototypes presented brief narrative descriptions of a typical case of each personality disorder:

> A prototype consists of the most common features or properties of members of a category and thus describes a theoretical ideal or standard against which real people can be evaluated. All of the prototype's properties are assumed to characterize at least some members of the category, but no one property is necessary or sufficient for membership in the category. Therefore, it is possible that no actual person would match the theoretical prototype perfectly. Instead different people would approximate it to different degrees. The more closely a person approximates the ideal, the more closely the person typifies the concept.[63]

Clinicians would use a 5-point scale to indicate the degree to which a patient's presentation matches the prototype for each disorder: 1 = description does not apply; 2 = only minor features of prototype; 3 = significant features of prototype; 4 = strong match, patient has the disorder; and 5 = exemplifies the disorder, prototypic case (figure 2).[64]

Westen and other proponents of the prototypical method touted its benefits for integrating categorical and dimensional approaches. Patients with ratings of 4 or 5 would receive a categorical diagnosis comparable to the extant

Patients who match this prototype tend to be deceitful and to lie and mislead others. They take advantage of others, have minimal investment in moral values, and appear to experience no remorse for harm or injury caused to others. They tend to manipulate others' emotions to get what they want; to be unconcerned with the consequences of their actions, appearing to feel immune or invulnerable; and to show reckless disregard for the rights, property, or safety of others. They have little empathy and seem unable to understand or respond to others' needs and feelings unless they coincide with their own. Individuals who match this prototype tend to act impulsively, without regard for consequences; to be unreliable and irresponsible (e.g., failing to meet work obligations or honor financial commitments); to engage in unlawful or criminal behavior; and to abuse alcohol. They tend to be angry or hostile; to get into power struggles; and to gain pleasure or satisfaction by being sadistic or aggressive toward others. They tend to blame others for their own failures or shortcomings and believe that their problems are caused entirely by external factors. They have little insight into their own motives, behavior, etc. They may repeatedly convince others of their commitment to change but then revert to previous maladaptive behavior, often convincing others that "this time is really different."

5	Very good match (patient *exemplifies* this disorder; prototypical case)	Diagnosis
4	Good match (patient *has* this disorder; diagnosis applies)	
3	Significant match (patient has *significant features* of this disorder)	Features
2	Slight match (patient has minor features of this disorder)	
1	Little or no match (description does not apply to this patient)	

Figure 2. Proposal for a prototype of antisocial personality disorder in the *DSM-5*. Reprinted from Westen, Shedler & Bradley with permission from *FOCUS* (© 2013). American Psychiatric Association. All rights reserved.

DSM criteria. They would also have a dimensional score ranging from 1 to 5. Thus, this method captured both systems of measurement.[65] In many ways, however, the use of prototypes seemed to be a return to the kind of idiosyncratic procedures that prevailed in the *DSM-I* and *-II*, which allowed clinicians to focus on whatever aspects of diagnostic portrayals best suited their subjective preferences.[66] Some participants claimed that this process would lead the *DSM-5* diagnoses to have lower reliability than even the *DSM-II* personality conditions.[67]

Other conference members raised questions about the adequacy of the FFM and its siblings as models for diagnostic criteria. They claimed that the reductionist framework of such techniques could not provide the types of understandings that complex phenomena such as the personality disorders required. Psychiatrist Joel Paris assailed FFM-like methods because their easily measured descriptive factors could not uncover any underlying dynamics that led to these conditions. They were also unable to assess concepts such as rigidity that are essential to definitions of personality disorders, failed to distinguish stable personality traits from symptoms that vary over time, and lacked procedures to separate high levels of a trait from the presence of a disorder. Paris also expressed doubts that dimensionalization was possible at the time: "It may well be that our understanding of brain mechanisms is at too early a stage to conduct this research program successfully. Until we know more about the neuroscience of emotions and behaviors, attempts to develop a neurobiological model linked to personality dimensions are premature." Further, he noted that "there is little evidence that personality dimensions correspond in any predictable way to brain systems. Instead, traits can be thought of as complex outcomes of interactions between many systems."[68]

Psychiatrist Erik Simonsen also critiqued the majority view as simplistic and lacking in clinical applicability: "Any dimensional approach has limitations. Because some of the models are based on factor analytic techniques, which are designed to extract independent factors, the dimensional approach tends to fractionate the intrinsic unity of personality into separate rows and columns of uncoordinated traits. But human nature and behavior do not work that way. They behave and react as highly interrelated and coordinated dynamic systems. And some kind of grouping in categories articulated in domains will probably always be needed, when clinicians communicate short information about their patients."[69]

Conference participants also raised the issue of how to handle the *DSM*'s multiaxial system that placed disorders involving symptoms on Axis I and those concerning personality traits on Axis II. This procedure assumed that there was a basic distinction between symptoms that arose in circumscribed episodes and the pervasive and enduring qualities that characterized the personality disorders. While Axis I symptoms indicated an underlying disorder that seemingly was not a fundamental part of personality, the Axis II conditions arose from stable propensities to show characteristic patterns of behaviors, attitudes, or feelings. Yet, research conducted after 1980 indicated that many symptom-defined disorders, especially anxiety and affective conditions, were often chronic and persistent. Conversely, many traits of the personality disorders fluctuated over time to a greater degree than their placement on Axis II would warrant.[70] For example, less than half of those diagnosed with some personality disorder retained their diagnosis in follow-up studies.[71]

Because diagnoses on both axes combined symptom- and trait-related criteria, the placement of the personality disorders on a separate axis seemed unwarranted.[72] The initial plan was to move all the personality disorders to Axis I and reserve Axis II for ratings of personality traits among all patients, whether or not they received a diagnosis of some personality disorder.[73] This change would at the same time grant the personality disorders an equivalent status to other mental disorders and facilitate third-party payment for treating them.

Despite the recognition of fundamental problems in conceptions of the personality disorders at this early planning stage, dimensional measures became the ideal for measuring *all* types of *DSM* disorders. The leaders of the *DSM-5* revision process proposed a "paradigm shift" that would replace the either/or categorical *DSM-III* diagnoses with a classification that viewed mental disorders as ranging along a variety of dimensions, each of which ranged from mild to moderate to severe. The *DSM-5* that they envisioned would incorporate dimensions in addition to, or even instead of, the extant categorical conditions.[74] At minimum, they expected that the personality disorders would be incorporated with the other Axis I mental disorders. The advent of a more dimensional system could help remove the main obstacle to progress in finding the etiology, prognoses, and most effective treatments for psychiatric disorders: the *DSM*'s categorical model. A second conference, convened in 2006, examined how dimensional measures could apply not just to the personality disorders but to all *DSM* conditions.[75]

The original proposal for the personality disorders that emerged from these conferences most closely resembled psychiatrist John Livesley's Dimensional Assessment of Personality Pathology.[76] This model focused on how personality disorders featured a failure to develop a coherent sense of self as well as persistent interpersonal dysfunctions. It listed thirty pathological personality traits, other lists of traits associated with particular personality disorders, and general criteria for personality impairment.[77] These were arranged into four broad groups of emotional dysregulation, dissocial behavior, inhibitedness, and compulsivity that described the personality of every patient, regardless of whether they had a personality disorder diagnosis.[78] This procedure would eliminate the problem of NOS diagnosis because every patient would receive a distinct score on each scale. In addition, because all patients had scores on the four broad trait domains, comorbidity would be reduced or eliminated. It appeared that the personality disorders were ready to initiate the paradigm shift envisioned for the *DSM-5*.

The Task Force Begins

In 2006 the APA selected David Kupfer, a leading academic authority on mood disorders, to chair the DSM-5 Task Force. Kupfer teamed with Vice Chair Darrel Regier, the APA's research director and a notable epidemiologist, to oversee the revision. Both Kupfer and Regier were committed to fundamentally changing the manual by introducing dimensional measures into diagnostic criteria. Regier, for example, stated that the categorical structure of the *DSM* was "a root cause of many of the problems with current psychiatric diagnostic classifications."[79] Kupfer and Regier assembled a task force of about thirty members to oversee the procedure, thirteen work groups to revise the major *DSM-IV* categories, and well over a hundred consultants.

The following year, Kupfer and Regier chose psychiatrist Andrew Skodol to chair the Personality and Personality Disorders work group (PPDWG). Unique among the various *DSM-5* work groups, six of the eleven members Skodol selected for the PPDWG held PhDs in psychology. This signaled the task force's determination to overthrow the manual's categorical measures of disorder and reformulate the personality disorders through the quantitative, dimensional formulations that typified psychological research in the area. Surprisingly, the members did not include either Thomas Widiger or Michael First, who had played key roles in the *DSM-IV* developmental process. "Nobody on the work group ever asked for my input or informed me about what was going on," Widiger told Gary Greenberg.[80] Only one member of the PPDWG, psychiatrist Larry Siever, was retained from the *DSM-IV* committee. The abandonment of key participants in previous work groups signaled the task force's resolve to develop an entirely new paradigm for the personality disorders.

When the PPDWG began its deliberations, there was little doubt that it would implement revolutionary changes. A survey of personality experts at the time found about three-quarters wanted to replace the *DSM-IV* categories, and nearly 90 percent wanted some sort of dimensional system.[81] Skodol

argued that "our field has been clamoring for more than 30 years" for dimensional representations of personality.[82] Indeed, in 1993 Allen Frances had de-
clared that a dimensional system for the personality disorders was inevitable:
"not whether, but when and which."[83] In the five-year interval between the
appointment of the committee in 2007 and the acceptance of the *DSM-5* in
2012, however, the deliberations went seriously awry.

A Chaotic Process

The process surrounding the design of the *DSM-5* thoroughly differed from
previous revisions of the manual. Robert Spitzer carefully controlled every
aspect of the development of the *DSM-III* and *-III-R*. Allen Frances, the head
of the *DSM-IV* process, was less directive than Spitzer but set out clear guide-
lines for all work groups to follow. In contrast, Kupfer and Regier deliberately
created a bottom-up structure where the various committees would develop
their own proposals. The PPDWG, like the others, had almost complete autonomy to cultivate radical changes.

Initially, all members of the PPDWG agreed on five goals. The criteria for
the personality disorders would (1) be congruent with research about the structure of personality in general, (2) eliminate strict categorical cutoffs, (3) abandon the NOS category, (4) reduce diagnostic comorbidity, and (5) decrease
the internal heterogeneity of each personality disorder.[84] The resulting diagnoses would be empirically derived, dimensional, and a significant departure
from the *DSM-III/IV* categories. Had the PPDWG realized these intentions,
the personality disorders would indeed have embodied a true paradigm change
in psychiatric diagnosis.

Despite the consensus about what general form diagnostic criteria should
take, problems quickly developed within the PPDWG. Intense disagreements
arose over several issues. One was that, although all members advocated some
sort of dimensional model, they could not agree on what was the best particular method. Some were committed to the dominant FFM that used several
(typically five) dimensions of personality traits. Others, however, advocated
for prototypes that presented clinicians with ideal typical portrayals of each
personality disorder and asked them to rate the degree to which a patient resembled them. This group maintained that a person-centered method would
be more in tune with traditional clinical thought than the psychologists' statistical portrayals. The PPDWG could not agree on whether prototypes should
be part of the proposal and, if so, what their relationship to other aspects of
the model should be.

A second controversy arose over the extent to which diagnostic criteria should be based on the body of empirical evidence from community studies or on clinical usefulness. The empiricists argued that only published research could provide a scientifically valid foundation for any type of mental disorder, including personality disorders. Others, however, countered that much of the research base about personality traits stemmed from nonclinical populations. They questioned its relevance for characterizing treated patients, especially because it lacked criteria that could separate disordered from non-disordered groups. Moreover, critics contended that "there is virtually no empirical support for the specific proposals of DSM-5."[85]

Intense differences also arose over which particular *DSM-IV* personality disorders should be maintained or eliminated. The committee could not reach consensus on the criteria to use to make this decision. Exacerbating this problem was that those conditions that had the largest research base were often not ones commonly found in clinical treatment. For example, the widely studied ASPD diagnosis was rarely found outside of forensic settings. Conversely, highly prevalent clinical conditions such as narcissism did not have a strong research base. Initially, the PPDWG concluded that half of the personality disorders recognized and treated over the previous thirty years lacked validity or utility.[86] It recommended that the next manual should retain only five conditions—borderline, obsessive-compulsive, avoidant, antisocial, and schizotypal—and eliminate the remaining five—paranoid, schizoid, histrionic, narcissistic, and dependent. However, their reasoning for why some disorders should be kept and others excised was opaque and contradicted other empirical studies.[87] "Well-studied conditions that represent important clinical presentations, such as dependent and narcissistic PDs, are slated for elimination, whereas obsessive-compulsive PD, which is often associated with less serious pathology, will be retained," Livesley observed.[88] A rare point of agreement among all sides was that the choice of which conditions to maintain or eliminate was essentially arbitrary rather than empirically based.

The status of narcissism generated a major dispute. Initially, the PPDWG unanimously eliminated narcissistic personality with what it considered to be an "evidence-based" decision. One of the committee members, psychiatrist Renato Alarcón, later found that NPD had generated a relatively small literature of 322 articles between 1998 and 2010.[89] In addition, no long-term outcome or comparative treatment studies existed for NPD. Like other personality disorders, narcissism overlapped with a number of other conditions, especially ASPD. The PPDWG saw no scientific reason to maintain NPD in the *DSM-5*.

Debates over the *DSM-III* had been mostly confined to research psychia-trists and their analytic adversaries. While its subsequent revisions generated more public controversies, the advent of the internet subjected the *DSM-5* proposals from the various work groups to far more scrutiny than their pre-decessors. Not just every type of mental health professional but also patients and their advocates as well as media outlets intently dissected all aspects of *DSM-5* plans.

A firestorm of criticism followed the posting of the PPDWG's recommen-dations on the *DSM-5* website. Many of the denunciations regarded the elim-ination of NPD. Narcissism had become both an important theoretical con-struct and a major diagnostic resource for clinicians. Most practitioners were appalled that the work group proposed to eliminate such a prominent clinical diagnosis. Others objected that the proposal vastly oversimplified the basic aspects of narcissism and other personality disorders. Psychologists Patrick Luyten and Sidney Blatt objected, "Patients with narcissistic personality dis-order typically present with high self-esteem as a defense against underlying feelings of inferiority and emptiness. Hence, these individuals appear to si-multaneously have 'high' and 'low' levels of self-esteem, which is difficult to explain in a trait model that views traits as relatively stable dimensions."[90] Despite the consensus within the PPDWG, the committee responded to the public outcry by quietly reintroducing narcissism as one of six personality conditions for inclusion in the *DSM-5*. The kerfuffle over NPD would foretell the response the work group's final recommendations would receive when they were submitted for the APA's approval.

The PPDWG also struggled with how to derive notions of "disorder" from dimensional models. Its proposal defined just one pole but not the other as disordered (negative affectivity vs. emotional stability, detachment vs. extra-version, antagonism vs. agreeableness, disinhibition vs. conscientiousness, and psychoticism vs. lucidity). This meant that its dimensional model was un-able to capture conditions such as low levels of negative affectivity (e.g., psy-chopathic fearlessness) or of maladaptive agreeableness.[91]

The proposal that the PPDWG eventually settled on replaced the *DSM-IV* conditions with an entirely new dimensional system that was a steep depar-ture from earlier classifications.[92] It was incredibly complex, incorporating an eight-step process. Clinicians would first use seven criteria such as the degree of identity integration and interpersonal cooperativeness to establish the pres-ence of a personality disorder. Next, they would diagnose which particular personality disorder someone had. This step involved a new procedure where, instead of using diagnostic criteria, clinicians would establish the fit between a particular patient and prototypical descriptions of each disorder. They would then match the patient to thirty-seven personality traits from six different trait domains (negative emotionality, introversion, antagonism, disinhibition, compulsivity, and schizotypy).[93] Finally, they would rate the severity of the patient's condition on a scale of one to three on four dimensions involving two different areas of functioning.

The work group's awkward combination of dimensions and prototypes garnered almost no support. Unsurprisingly, responses to the proposal involved a mix of astonishment and derision. "The assessment of personality pathology using the DSM-5 model has eight components that together cannot be described as user-friendly, inherently logical in its progression or quick to complete," British personality expert Peter Tyrer complained."[94] Others argued that clinicians would find the proposal unworkable: "The new model will require clinicians to rate patients for the presence or absence of a personality disorder, the degree of impairment they experience as a result of the personality pathology, their degree of match to each of the five prototypes, and the degree to which the given traits are extremely and moderately descriptive of each patient."[95]

The model's complexity came under sustained critique. "It is way too complicated and time-consuming for anyone to actually use," Gary Greenberg observed of the proposed procedure.[96] Psychiatrist James Phillips provided a scalding assessment: "For all their scholastic erudition, the work group have created a monster—a bloated, pedantic, cumbersome diagnostic instrument that will never be used by anyone working in the hurly-burly of clinical practice."[97] Some objected that matching patients to narrative prototypes was an unfamiliar procedure to the clinicians who were the intended audience. Livesley, whose scale had been at the center of the original personality disorders conference, called the committee's proposal a "disaster" and resigned from the work group in 2011. Even strong proponents of dimensional measurement such as Thomas Widiger found the PPDWG proposal far too unwieldy to have any clinical usefulness.[98] Widiger claimed that the proposal was "invented out of thin air" and ignored the long history of research on the personality disorders.[99] The chair of the *DSM-IV* personality disorders committee John Gunderson's appraisal, too, was harsh: "The resulting amalgam of two systems with categories and traits and dimensions that were all newly conceived within this particular DSM-5 WG was too radical to offer continuity with the past, too conceptually incoherent, and too complex to be used clinically."[100]

Others targeted the seemingly capricious presence of just five (later six) of the ten *DSM-IV* specific personality disorders. A ranking of the *DSM-IV* conditions based on the validity of research findings about them found that the most valid condition—dependent personality disorder (DPD)—was not kept while the least valid—obsessive-compulsive personality disorder—was retained. The other personality disorders proposed for retention were avoidant and schizotypal (tied for second), borderline (5), and antisocial (7). In addition to DPD, those recommended for elimination were paranoid (4), schizoid (5), narcissistic (8), histrionic (9), and passive-aggressive (10).[101] Although reverence for empirical findings was supposedly the guiding principle of all *DSMs* since 1980, even three decades later choices for retention or excision seemed to be more arbitrary than evidence based.

The vigorous objections to the PPDWG proposal quickly went public. Eight prominent personality psychiatrists and psychologists, including Aaron Beck, Otto Kernberg, and John Gunderson, published a letter in the *American Journal of Psychiatry* that accused the work group of recommending an untested instrument that ignored decades of empirical research. They insisted that any adequate system for diagnosing personality disorders must focus on types of people, not types of rating scales: "Regrettably, the proposed system for classifying personality disorders is too complicated, includes a trait based approach to diagnosis without an adequate clinical rationale, and omits personality syndromes that have significant clinical utility." They went on to say that the proposal failed to take into account the differences between the study of personality in normal populations and in clinical treatment. A dimensional system that might be appropriate for studies of untreated populations was inappropriate for classifying individuals who were in treatment. They concluded that the work group's proposal was "unworkable" and "needlessly complicated."[102]

In another public attack, thirty-one prominent researchers and clinicians detailed the shortcomings of the PPDWG proposal. Their conclusion was harsh: "It is too complicated, it is unfamiliar to the clinicians who will be expected to use it, it will aggravate (not alleviate) the problems with clinical utility, it lacks a scientific rationale." They went on, "In retrospect, the members selected for the PD WG were too adversarial, too ideologically inflexible, and lacked a strong clinical presence. As noted, the voice of psychotherapists was in particular hard to discern." Moreover, the proposal "undermines psychiatry's professional and public integrity and worse, it undermines our credibility with the patients we are dedicated to serve."[103]

From a different perspective, Livesley argued that the PPDWG proposal valued the political needs of clinicians over the scientific concerns of researchers. It embodied the view that "clinical tradition outweighs evidence" in a way that encompassed the worst features of the categorical *DSM-IV* and of the proposed dimensions for *DSM-5*. Livesley insisted that any adequate model must recognize that there is no sharp distinction between normal personalities and personality disorders. In contrast, he touted the FFM as an empirically supported, valid model of personality.[104]

In response to the torrent of criticism, in 2010 the PPDWG proposed a slightly less cumbersome proposal that lowered the number of trait domains from six to five, reduced the number of facets from thirty-seven to thirty-one, and restored narcissistic personality disorder. The task force's intention to use the personality disorders as a model for the entire *DSM-5* was coming to a disappointing close.

A Messy Ending

The debates over the personality disorders illustrated the steep divisions among various branches of personality inquiry. Many researchers argued that the extant *DSM* diagnoses of personality disorders were so fundamentally flawed that they did more harm than good and had to be thrown out.[105] They took for granted the many advantages that dimensional measures had over categorical ones: maximizing the amount of information available about each patient; not making a sharp cutoff between people who had some disorder and those who didn't; and helping to resolve the problems of internal heterogeneity, comorbidity, and NOS diagnoses that plagued the extant categorical system.[106] Yet others argued that the sharp break of the PPDWG proposal from the *DSM-IV* categories would both disrupt empirical research and impair clinical utility.[107] The dimensional approach threatened not just clinical practice but also could profoundly unsettle the many institutions that depended on the *DSM* edifice. "Adopting a dimensional approach would likely complicate medical record keeping, create administrative and clinical barriers between mental disorders and medical conditions, require a massive retreating effort, disrupt research efforts (e.g., meta-analyses), and complicate clinicians' efforts to integrate prior clinical research using *DSM* categories into clinical practice," psychiatrist Michael First summarized.[108]

The chaotic process that marked the PPDWG was not unique. The great amount of internal dissensus within many work groups and criticism from outside of them led the APA to establish a Scientific Review Committee (SRC) in 2009 to oversee all of the groups. At odds with Kupfer and Regier's intentions, the SRC was committed to the *DSM-IV* principle that a well-accepted body of research must justify any radical changes in diagnostic criteria. This oversight body concluded that the PPDWG proposal had little empirical support and should not be implemented. A year later, the APA Assembly DSM-5 Review Committee also rejected the dimensional model for the personality disorders. An additional oversight group, the Clinical and Public Health Committee, overruled the PPDWG proposal because of its lack of clinical utility. Still another oversight committee, the Summit Group, which was established in 2012, also rejected the PPDWG proposal. Finally, in May 2012, the APA Assembly, a body mostly composed of practicing psychiatrists from all regions of the country, strongly opposed dimensionalizing the personality disorders.[109]

The *DSM-5* did implement the PPDWG recommendation to abolish Axis II, which most considered "arbitrary and counterproductive," and incorporate the personality disorders into Axis I.[110] This recognized that the defining characteristics of "stability" and "endurance" of the personality disorders were often no greater than they were for conditions such as anxiety or depression. Other prominent psychiatrists, however, believed that separating the personality disorders from other conditions abolished a valuable distinction and lamented the loss of Axis II.[111]

The remarkable result was that the main body of the *DSM-5* maintained, word for word, the personality disorders section from *DSM-IV*. As a sop to the work group, the APA placed the PPDWG proposal in a separate Section III on "emerging measures and models" that was not part of the regular diagnostic criteria but that might warrant further study.[112] Ominously for the organization, the NIMH began an effort to displace the *DSM* itself with a new diagnostic system for researchers, the Research Domain Criteria. The fiasco was "a story of shifting expectations, conflicting goals, and fractured alliances," a history of the process observed.[113] "This debacle," psychiatrist Joel Paris concluded, "was well-deserved."[114]

Conclusion

The debates over the *DSM-5* personality disorders illustrate some of the central problems in the study of mental disorders. As with all recent *DSMs*, researchers dominated the making of the *DSM-5*. They bet that a quantitative system that had been fruitful in illuminating various personality traits in the general population could also be utilized in clinical settings. Researchers ignored the sharp division between how they and clinicians justify their decisions and their deeply divergent interests.

Participants in the *DSM-5* debates intensely disagreed about what type of evidence warranted diagnostic changes in the personality disorders. Most PPDWG members relied on the strength of empirical data from large community studies to validate their decisions. They regarded this quantitative research base as providing a solid foundation for a new dimensional system. Conversely, they dismissed clinicians' objections to the proposed changes as a case where "clinical tradition outweighs evidence."[115] It seemed self-evident to the group advocating for dimensional measurement that empirical data should override clinical opinion and political wrangling. Others, however, rejected this portrayal, noting how the bulk of research that stemmed from community samples had little relevance for diagnoses among treated patients. Clinical psychologist Roel Verheul, who resigned from the PPDWG in 2012, charged that the proposed changes had "little or even no evidence."[116] Similarly, Michael First cautioned against making such radical changes without the presence of more convincing research.[117] Instead, most opponents of the proposal claimed that clinical utility must be the foremost consideration.

Perhaps most fundamentally, the failure of the *DSM-5* to implement dimensional measures of the personality disorders illustrates the deep divide between researchers and clinicians. Researchers can be taken seriously only when they place themselves on the natural side of the Kantian divide. They must measure observable entities that follow lawlike processes. Therefore, they deal with aggregated numbers but do not interpret individual experiences. However valid their research might be for investigating large populations of community members, they had little relevance for clinicians who treated patients with personality disorders.

Clinicians faced a profoundly different situation. They found the PPDWG proposal to be a Frankenstein's monster that could never work in therapeutic situations. "Thus far, dialogue about the future format of DSM has been almost exclusively by and between laboratory researchers; the voice of the clinician has gone largely unheard," Spitzer and colleagues noted.[118] Clinical work, where clinicians must make judgments about individual patients, is intrinsically what Kant considered to be an intuitive practice. Clinicians' goal is to understand the problems of particular people, not to make scientific generalizations. They thus deal in idiosyncrasies more than uniformities. The differing demands of clinical and research practices are fundamentally irreconcilable.

Advocates for a dimensional approach were not discouraged after their crushing defeat. "The PD field is arguably the most forward-thinking area in contemporary psychopathology," PDAC member Robert Krueger wrote in 2013. "This is because many PD scholars do not accept the inadequate polythetic-categorical approach to psychopathology classification of DSM-IV (which, owing to conservative political forces, also frames Section III of DSM-5). PD research is therefore at the vanguard in conceptualizing, studying, and treating psychopathology because it is not slavishly tethered to the DSM, and its approach to defining mental disorder through political processes."[119]

The *DSM-5* deliberations cast a bright light on the fundamental dilemma of psychiatry's competing commitments to natural science and therapeutic practices that straddle both sides of the Kantian divide. Whether some settlement of this division will be possible in the future remains an open, but unlikely, outcome.

CHAPTER SEVEN

Mental Disorders or Problems in Living?

The questions this book opened with, raised by the ancient Greeks, continue to animate present debates: Does each person have a characteristic style of personality, or can personality be broken down into its component traits? Are personalities inborn or learned? To what extent are personalities separable from situations and social roles? Is personality an individual quality or a result of societal influences? Finally, and perhaps most challenging, are personality disorders extremes of traits that everyone shares to some degree, or do they have some essential nature? As the *DSM-5* deliberations indicated, students of personality have yet to establish consensus on these questions. Perhaps they never will.

Defining Personality Disorders

The ancient meditations on personality did not rise to major societal concern before the end of the nineteenth century. At the same time that personality was replacing character as the major way of understanding individuals, the natural sciences were rapidly gaining prestige. Models of human action, as well as physical phenomena, had to be seen as the result of scientific procedures in order to have social credibility. This atmosphere pushed students of mental disorders to define them as objective entities grounded in observable mechanisms. Realizing this goal has proven particularly elusive for the personality disorders. Three major factors account for the difficulties of integrating the personality disorders into the same framework as other mental and medical disorders: the nature of diseases, the variety of disciplines concerned with personality, and the disparate perspectives of researchers and clinicians.

Diseases or Problems in Living?

Modern psychiatric diagnoses originated in attempts to replicate nineteenth-century medicine's embrace of germ theory. According to this then-new conception, prototypical diseases arose from invasions by outside pathogens that produced distinct symptoms with predictable courses and outcomes. This view of disease extracts symptoms from the personal characteristics of those they afflict to produce diagnoses that are more objective, technical, and mechanistic.[1] Kraepelin famously applied this model to the study of mental disorders, which he argued could be specific diseases of the same type as physical ailments.

Debatably, the disease model is congruent with many common mental symptoms—invasive thoughts, uncontrollable compulsions, melancholic depression, post-traumatic flashbacks—because they intrude on someone's sense of self and so can be studied apart from personality dynamics. Indeed, the original term for psychiatrists—"alienists"—captures this critical feature of such symptoms. In contrast, personality difficulties seem to involve who a person *is*, not what condition they *have*. They encompass a total way of interacting with the social world that cannot be reduced to particular symptoms. Their essence involves, as Gordon Allport's definition indicated, a person's "characteristic behavior and thought."[2] The dysfunctional self-definitions and interpersonal relationships that are at the heart of personality disorders are problems in living that appear to be inseparable from their bearers. "What we call the 'disease,'" Karl Menninger explained, "is the logical outgrowth of the particular personality in its efforts to solve a particular problem. The disease is a part of him, not an intruder or an invasion from without."[3] The history of the personality disorders illustrates the difficulties of shaping them into the sorts of objects that can be regarded as disease entities.

The resistance of personality disorders to medical conceptions accounts for their neglect in early psychiatric classifications. Kraepelin, for example, ignored the personality disorders until late in his career and even then considered them to be a subset of mood disorders rather than an independent category. The *Statistical Manual* that guided US classifications from 1920 to 1950 almost completely disregarded them. The influential Feighner criteria that were the basis for the *DSM-III* in 1980 contained just one personality disorder, antisocial personality disorder.

The diagnostic classifications that emerged after World War II featured the personality disorders but did not tie them to a disease model. The analytically inflected *DSM-I* explicitly detached its definition of personality disorders from medical conceptions: "Grouped as Personality Disorders are those cases in which the personality utilizes primarily a pattern of action or behavior in its adjustment struggle, rather than symptoms in the mental, somatic, or emotional spheres."[4] This manual's first listed type is exemplary: those with inadequate personalities "are neither physically nor mentally grossly deficient on examination, but they do show inadaptability, ineptness, poor judgment, lack of physical and emotional stamina, and social incompatibility."[5]

The developers of the *DSM-III* were determined to overthrow such overtly evaluative conceptions and to make psychiatry's diagnostic system conform to a medical model. To this end, they sought to develop definitions that were free from nonobjective, value-laden criteria and so could be diagnosed more reliably. This posed a quandary in regard to the personality disorders. Their subjective aspects and psychodynamic taint were difficult to reconcile with the *DSM-III*'s medically minded perspective. The developers of this manual faced the dilemma that the extant definitions of personality disorders resembled problems in living far more than any medical notion of disease, were infused with evaluative notions, and resisted empirical verification. Robert Spitzer, the mastermind of this revolutionary manual, well aware of their incompatibility with his proposal for a medically oriented *DSM-III*, asked, "How do we deal with the fact that personality disorders are 'fuzzy at the edges?' Pathology shades into normal problems of everyday life. . . . Of course, the spectrum concept does not easily lend itself to diagnoses based on discrete subdivisions, which were being espoused for DSM-III."[6] Spitzer and his task force tried to resolve the mismatch between the *DSM-III*'s categorical, disease-like diagnoses and the possibly dimensional nature of the personality disorders by placing them on a separate axis from the other classes of mental disorder. Spitzer shrewdly bridged the gap between the personality disorders and the *DSM-III* system through creating a multiaxial system that separated the twelve personality disorders from other classes of disorder.

That personality disorders are intrinsically value laden also accounts for their resistance to disease conceptions. The earliest attempts to subject personality to a medical worldview in the nineteenth century overtly used moralistic terms such as "decency," "depraved," "perverted," and "propriety."[7] Kraepelin, too, struggled to mold the personality disorders into his seemingly objective system. While his definitions of schizophrenia and manic depression could be assimilated to disease conceptions, his formulations of the personality disorders encompassed born criminals, pathological liars, querulous persons,

vagabonds, spendthrifts, and dipsomaniacs.[8] The ASPD diagnosis in the Feighner criteria and, later, the *DSM-III* relied on socially devalued behaviors such
as difficulties in school, running away from home, troubles with the police,
poor work histories, marital worries, sexual promiscuity, and vagrancy that
were thoroughly distinct from disease-like symptoms of mental disorder such
as panic attacks, persistent low mood, or hallucinations. The history of this
diagnosis from its earliest formulations as psychopathic personality through
the *DSM-III* criteria resembles an accusatory judgment more than a clinical
assessment. Renegade psychiatrist Thomas Szasz famously asserted that mental illnesses were "myths" because they were actually ethical judgments of disliked behaviors that did not display the physical lesions that genuine diseases
featured. Szasz's claims, which were targeted at conditions such as schizophrenia, met with fierce criticism. They might, however, accurately characterize the kinds of problems of living that mark the personality disorders.[9]

Psychology, too, could not escape the same issues. Sociologist William
Whyte provided perhaps the most incisive critique of the way that the statistical approaches psychologist use disguised underlying evaluative criteria:
"The mathematics is impeccable—and thus entrapping. Because 'percentiles'
and 'coefficients' and 'standard deviations' are of themselves neutral, the sheer
methodology of using them can convince people that they are translating
uncertainty into certainty, the subjective into the objective, and eliminating
utterly the bugbear of value judgments. But the mathematics does not eliminate values; it only obscures them."[10] Psychology's current techniques are far
more sophisticated than percentiles, coefficients, and standard deviations but
unavoidably continue to conceal value judgments.

Notions of "adaptation" and "maladaptation," which have been central to
definitions of personality disorders since Adolf Meyer's view of what constituted personality (and all other) disorders, are themselves value judgments.
All theories of personality disorders, whether biological, psychological, or
social, incorporate "maladaptation" into their definitions, a term that is intrinsically evaluative. Depending on the environment, adaptation to it can
be healthy or morbid: "Here value judgments must be made, and adaptation
is distinguished from maladaptation according as a particular valued state is
favoured or jeopardized," psychiatrist Aubrey Lewis observed.[11]

Although the current *DSM-5* no longer places the personality disorders on
a separate axis, values continue to infuse its definitions. Antisocial personalities show a "pervasive pattern of disregard for and violation of the rights of
others," "failure to conform to social norms," "deceitfulness," and "irresponsi-

bility." Narcissistic personalities are "arrogant," "lack empathy," and are "interpersonally exploitative." Those with histrionic personalities show "excessive attention seeking," "inappropriate sexually seductive and provocative behavior," and "shallow expression of emotions." People with borderline personality disorder show "inappropriate, intense anger."[12]

The diagnostic criteria for the personality disorders evaluate behavior according to culturally specific norms. "Borderline and narcissistic personalities are rarely seen in Iowa City or in Mobile; certainly, they are not recognized in Tangiers or Bucharest," psychiatrist George Vaillant noted.[13] Traditional kin-based societies reject narcissists, but they flourish in market-driven capitalist ones.[14] Asian cultures often promote values that submit individual welfare to group goals, limit autonomy, and promote low levels of self-assertion, which might qualify for a diagnosis of dependent personality disorder in Western societies.[15] Yet the *DSM* does not contain a counterpart condition of "independent personality disorder." Psychiatrist Jerome Frank suggested that members of closely knit societies might consider a US teenager who travels thousands of miles away from his family to attend college as having such a disorder.[16] Similarly, anthropologist Ruth Benedict asserted that the Dobuans of Micronesia cultivated traits associated with what our society calls "paranoid disorders."[17] Cultural values inevitably influence which behaviors indicate pathological or normal personalities.

The perennial use of evaluative criteria for the personality disorders is unavoidable. Their diagnoses inevitably rely on cultural norms of what are suitable or unsuitable levels of, for example, anger, attention seeking, empathy, and respect for the rights of others. These characteristics, in turn, depend on sociohistorical and group-specific values. The herculean efforts to formulate personality deviations as objective, disease-like entities have consistently failed, a situation that is unlikely to ever be remedied.[18]

A Plethora of Disciplines

A second factor preventing the consensus on definitions of personality disorders has been the variety of disciplines sharing jurisdiction over them. At various times, psychology, psychiatry, psychoanalysis, and the social sciences all gave personality pride of place in their theories, research, and practices, although each field developed very different conceptions of its object. Distinct disciplinary assumptions hamper the development of uniform characterizations.

The emergence of personality as a topic of interest in nineteenth-century

Europe occurred within a context dominated by Immanuel Kant's influential division of the appropriate ways to study natural and cultural phenomena. Kant posited that the sorts of quantitative, lawlike propositions that characterized the physical and natural sciences were inappropriate for the study of inner, psychological experiences that required introspective—and therefore idiosyncratic—understandings. Yet by the end of the century such intuitive approaches were seen as unscientific and, therefore, to be avoided. This atmosphere was especially influential in shaping psychological conceptions of personality.

Psychologists developed the earliest scientific notions of personality. The discipline of psychology emerged at the same time that personality was becoming a topic of interest in Western societies. Because no other field had yet captured its study, psychologists featured personality in their early efforts to build a new discipline. Since medical fields already owned notions of "disease," psychologists used "quantification" as their passport to scientific respectability. From its origins, psychology's métier has been developing and applying sophisticated statistical methods to assess individual differences in personality traits. Striving to achieve the goals of early pioneers Wundt, Fechner, and Galton, psychologists formulated personality traits through mathematical equations. The type of knowledge that psychology brought to the study of personality embodied the qualities of rationality and logic that have the highest value in scientific culture.[19]

The founders of the field understood the power of science to justify their endeavors. A book published in 1931, *Psychology: Science or Superstition*, observed, "Do psychologists want to be scientists? All of their protestations, all their laboratories, their tedious researches, their technical treatises, seem to answer that they do. Science is a magic word today, and every single psychologist, no matter what his private beliefs, has profited enormously through the circumstance that Wilhelm Wundt proclaimed, and to a certain extent proved, that psychology could be as exact as any natural science."[20] The field's well-defined variables and verifiable propositions make it the most scientific-seeming of the various disciplines concerned with personality research.

In contrast to psychology, psychiatry was not centrally concerned with personality disorders before World War II. Instead, the field focused on the kinds of conditions—psychoses, alcoholism, syphilis—that were found in their asylum-based practices. Psychopaths, who occasionally entered mental hospitals, were the sole exception. The research psychiatrists who came to dominate the profession in the 1970s cast an especially wary eye on the personality disorders. For them, as Aaron Beck's appraisal indicated, the very concept of personality disorder was a "construct so artificial and removed from observables, that it is probably of little utility and, even worse, it is probably a misleading fiction."[21] Moreover, as the trend to treat mental disorders with drugs emerged in the 1950s, biologically oriented psychiatrists had little interest in disorders that had no pharmaceutical treatment.[22] After 1980 psychiatry staked its relevance on the categorical *DSM* diagnoses that, in the case of the personality disorders, presented roadblocks to understanding. They were highly overlapping, internally heterogeneous, and hard to operationalize. While psychiatric researchers came to recognize these flaws, they could not develop professionally suitable replacements.

Psychoanalysis, too, was a relative latecomer to the personality disorders. After an initial period of interest in how neurotic symptoms arose from instinctual drives, over the course of the 1930s Freud and his followers turned their attention to ego psychology and character disorders. They developed theories and methods that could hardly be more distinct from those found among psychologists and medically minded psychiatrists. Analysts studied hidden, not manifest, processes, used intuitive rather than quantitative and testable assertions, and constructed narratives about particular individuals instead of examining differences between them. They assumed that personality traits (or any other psychological process) could not be understood in isolation but were dynamic constellations of interacting intrapsychic forces. Analytic influence reached its zenith in the post–World War II United States, shaping therapy, child rearing, education, the arts, and the social sciences among other areas.[23]

Many analytic clients sought help to deal with problematic interpersonal patterns, such as difficulties with emotional intimacy or repeatedly seeking intimacy with the wrong kind of person.[24] Yet, like psychologists and psychiatrists, analysts did not develop clear definitions of when personality was "disordered" as opposed to distressing, disliked, or disruptive. Orthodox psychoanalysts also never adequately integrated historical and social processes, instead viewing the psyche as universal and timeless: "I perceived ever more clearly that the events of human history, the interactions between human nature, cultural development . . . are no more than a reflection of the dynamic conflicts between the ego, the id and the super-ego," Freud recollected.[25]

The social sciences, particularly anthropology and sociology, were major influences on understandings of personality disorders from the 1930s through the 1960s. Their approaches inverted the intraindividual focus found in psychology, psychiatry, and psychoanalysis. They viewed personality types and disorders as products of historical, socioeconomic, and cultural forces. The studies of anthropologists and sociologists such as Ruth Benedict, Margaret Mead, and David Riesman, which promoted fully social views of personality, were cultural sensations. For them, people who deviated from conventional social norms were more likely to be nonconformists than to have personality disorders. This assumption was difficult to integrate with research from other disciplines. Moreover, psychiatry's turn away from socially oriented work after 1980 marginalized the once-prominent social-scientific studies of personality.

The distinct perspectives of psychologists, psychiatrists, psychoanalysts, and social scientists have precluded the development of consensus regarding personality disorders. A third chasm, this one between the approaches of researchers and clinicians, led to the failure to reconcile psychological and psychiatric views in the *DSM-5* proceedings.

Researchers and Clinicians

The efforts of researchers to bring a scientific approach to the study of personality disorders created an additional divide: they required empirical, observable, and fact-based approaches that uncover truths independent of particular observers or subjects. Unique qualities of individuals are extraneous to their search for commonalties across people. Their focus on applying explicit rules led researchers to scorn clinical intuition. "The clinical interpreter is a costly middleman who might better be eliminated," psychologist Paul Meehl disdainfully concluded.[26]

Clinical approaches could hardly be more distinct. Karl Menninger's derisive view of researchers mirrors Meehl's contempt for clinical insight: "Now, no human mind is ever shut up in a laboratory; at least no mind lives so."[27] Clinical work is more akin to the interpretative understandings of the humanities than to the rationality of the sciences. Practitioners confront the problems of particular people, not the individual differences that researchers attend to. They form intense interpersonal relationships with patients that in many ways are unique to each interaction.[28] The qualities that are most important for therapeutic success—establishing an effective alliance with clients, empathy, and warmth—dramatically contrast with the objectivity, abstraction, and rigor that mark research perspectives.[29] Clinical decision making also relies on a wider variety of indicators than standardized research protocols. "Mental health professionals train their attention on patients' appearance, habits, and demeanor, noting any peculiarities in dress, attitude, or speaking style. Patients may speak with unusual speed or determination, may avoid eye contact, or may assume a defensive tone—all characteristics that shed light on their personalities and color what they say," psychiatrist Donald Black observes.[30]

The abyss between the approaches of researchers and clinicians was particularly apparent in the *DSM-5* deliberations that "emphasized factor structure over clinical relevance."[31] Researchers identified the extant *DSM*'s major problem as its clear-cut criteria that required either/or diagnostic decisions. They insisted that only dimensional gradients could accurately capture the essence of personality disorders. Yet they underestimated the extent to which clinical treatment involves categorical decisions, however arbitrary the *DSM* measures might be. Insurers, schools, courts, the military, and other institutions require some diagnosis before patients are eligible for treatment and resources. Therefore, the most common use of diagnoses in clinical practice is for administration and billing.[32]Clinicians who rely on third-party payments have no choice but to classify patients as having some *DSM* disorder, regardless of whether they believe in the validity of any diagnosis. Unsurprisingly, most prefer the *DSM*'s categorical approach to a dimensional alternative.[33] The different worldviews of clinicians and researchers ensure that basic conflicts in portrayals of personality disorders will persist.

Unresolved Issues

The history of personality disorders shows the difficulties of separating medical from value-laden components, reconciling the variety of disciplinary perspectives that apply to them, and integrating clinical and research perspectives. These problems lead to the marked lack of progress in resolving the various questions the ancient Greeks initially raised.

What Is a Disordered Personality?

The writings of the Hippocratics and Galen provided the earliest attempts to define personality disorders. Analogous to current dimensional measures, these traditions regarded personality pathologies as excesses or deficits of the same traits that everyone possessed. All humans contained mixtures of yellow bile, black bile, blood, and phlegm, but excessive amounts of a humor could cause choleric, melancholic, sanguine, or phlegmatic disorders. Aristotle developed a contrasting view that some character traits are intrinsically good and others, such as envy or spite, were inherently "themselves bad, and not the excesses or deficiencies of them. It is not possible, then, ever to be right with regard to them; one must always be wrong."[34] Theophrastus, too, emphasized the dislikable, unpleasant, and obnoxious qualities inherent in various personality types. The contrast between dimensional and essentialist views remains unresolved.

Early definitions from Prichard through Kraepelin characterized personality disorders in value-laden terms that were indistinguishable from crime, delinquency, and deviance. The initial efforts of psychoanalysts and, in the United States, the mental hygiene movement and Meyer's psychobiology showed little concern for developing definitions of personality *disorder*. Freud, for example, did not have a distinct theory of personality pathology but considered character disorders to be variations of traits in degree, not in kind. Second-generation analysts such as Karl Abraham, Wilhelm Reich, and Otto Fenichel elaborated this notion: those with personality disorders had inflexible and enduring character patterns that limited the ego's ability to respond to instinctual impulses, on the one hand, and environmental demands, on the other hand.

The current *DSM-5* definition states, "A *personality disorder* is an enduring pattern of inner experience and behavior that deviates markedly from the expectations of the individual's culture, is pervasive and inflexible, has an onset in adolescence or early adulthood, is stable over time, and leads to distress or impairment."[35] As chapter 1 noted, the major features of this definition— "enduring pattern of inner experience and behavior," "pervasive," "onset in adolescence or early adulthood," "stable over time"—also characterize *normal* personality types. The stipulation that the condition "deviates markedly from the expectations of the individual's culture" does not demarcate personality disorders from nonconformity, eccentricity, or social deviance and conflicts between the individual and society that the *DSM*'s general definition of mental disorder explicitly disqualifies as mental disorders. "Inflexible" is the definition's only element that distinguishes disordered from normal personalities.

From this point of view, as early formulations such as those of Abraham, Reich, and Fenichel recognized, the essential aspect of a personality disorder is the inability to adapt to social and psychological situations and relationships. In contrast, depending on the particular circumstances, healthy personalities are able to use a variety of defenses and adaptations. Determining whether a personality is "rigid" or "flexible" requires judging it within a variety of contexts that require various expressions of personality. Consider Mary Trump's characterization of her uncle: "Donald today is much as he was at three years old: incapable of growing, learning, or evolving, unable to regulate his emotions, moderate his responses, or take in and synthesize information."[36] Other examples include a paranoid's pervasive suspiciousness, schizoid and schizotypal types who are so isolated that they cannot engage in interpersonal interactions, or those with ASPD who are not capable of forming mutual bonds.[37]

Because they intrinsically involve judgments about when personalities are rigid or flexible and adaptive or maladaptive, personality disorders remain recalcitrant to conceptions of disease that might be suitable for other kinds of mental disorders. Accordingly, their definitions remain as indistinct, unclear, and evaluative as those initially proposed a century ago.

Traits or Organization?

From Theophrastus through the *DSM-5*, a continuing issue has been whether personality is best viewed as a collection of separable characteristics or as an interrelated organization.[38] Two distinct portrayals have dominated studies of this question.

Personality psychologists traditionally assumed that people have a variety of independent personality traits rather than holistic selves. Each trait is "a tendency to feel, perceive, behave, and think in relatively consistent ways across time and across situations in which the trait may be manifested."[39] Their models assign individuals separate scores on qualities such as openness to experience, conscientiousness, extraversion, agreeableness, and neuroticism. The score on one trait has no implication for the scores on others.

Soon after psychologists established the trait approach, Gordon Allport countered that people had holistic selves, not fragmented traits: "Personality is the dynamic organization within the individual of those psychophysical systems that determine his unique adjustments to his environment."[40] Psychological research, he emphasized, ought to focus on how each individual had a "dynamic organization" of personality that created a "unique" self. Allport also postulated that all personality traits had two aspects, which were both observed tendencies to behave in particular ways and underlying dispositions that might or might not correspond to overt behaviors. An example would be a person who acts in socially valued extraverted ways but inwardly feels withdrawn from situations, as in Smokey Robinson and the Miracles "Tears of a Clown": "Now if I appear to be carefree / It's only to camouflage my sadness."[41]

Freud, too, stressed the dynamic aspects of personality. His writings emphasized the types of defenses, conflicts, and relatedness that holistic personalities use to deal with their environments. Freud's exploration of the anal character stressed the intrinsic interrelation of the three characteristics of orderliness, parsimony and obstinacy that made this personality type not just a constellation of separable traits but a general way of being.[42]

The issues that Allport and Freud raised resurfaced in 1968 in psychologist Walter Mischel's famous critique of the trait method.[43] Personality, Mischel argued, was not a collection of static traits but dynamically shaped the ways that people responded to the social world. The question of whether personality is best formulated as separable traits or a dynamic organization again reappeared in the contentious *DSM-5* deliberations. Personality psychologists continued to insist that distinct, quantifiable qualities provide precise and individualized descriptions of each patient.[44] Their opponents objected that more person-centered, holistic portrayals were essential for capturing the nature of personality.

Dimensions or Prototypes?

Aristotle provided an early dimensional model of personality disorders when he posited that although some traits were inherently good or bad, others such as cowardice and courage or congeniality were better seen as gradients that resembled continuous distributions. Over two millennia later, Galton developed statistical depictions that placed individual traits along the spread of the bell curve. Early personality psychologists used Galton's formulations to develop dimensional views that sharply contrasted with dichotomous medical conceptions of health and disease. For them, what are called "personality disorders" were extreme variants of normal personality traits: "There are no essential differences between the personality structure of those with and without personality disorder, and so a good classification of pathological personality should cross the range from normal to severe disturbance."[45]

The question of whether diagnostic criteria should use continuous or categorical models became the primary issue in the *DSM-5* deliberations. Proponents of dimensional approaches emphasized that no sharp distinctions existed between normal and abnormal personalities; instead, everyone was on a spectrum that ranged from no personality disturbance through mild, moderate, and severe pathology. They urged abandoning the categorical *DSM* conditions and replacing them with continuous scores. According to personality psychologist Paul Costa, "This FFM reformulation of personality disorders dispenses with the problem of defining trait thresholds or cutoffs. As personality traits are continuously graded and there is no optimal cutoff point, no single value or range of values can infallibly identify disordered personality. This is why trying to define exact cutoff points, as is currently the case, is misleading and likely to be fruitless."[46] Costa and many other personality psychologists point to a robust body of empirical evidence that supports this conclusion.[47]

Dimensional measures provide each individual a single score that defines their position on a continuum. People cannot simultaneously be high and low on any particular trait. Opponents of this method argue that the essence of many personality disorders involves just such dynamics. Dependent personalities self-report very low amounts of aggression but nevertheless harbor strong aggressive feelings. Avoidant personalities both desire and fear intimacy.[48] The rigidity of the paranoid personality can be a defense against a fragile self-concept.[49] Scales that provide a single dimensional score for each person cannot identify such dynamics.

Critics of dimensional models also emphasize their potential to generate many false positives, where non-disordered people are classified as disordered.[50] Although people with personality disorders are likely to fall on at least one extreme of trait distributions, most people on these tails are not disordered. Cutoffs that use extremes of statistical distributions to define disorder can thus conflate personality oddities with mental disorders. Prominent diagnostician Robert Kendell observed that statistical models fail "to distinguish between deviations from the norm which are harmful, like hypertension, those which are neutral, like great height, and those which are positively beneficial, like superior intelligence."[51] Highly creative persons, geniuses, and eccentrics have traits that fall on statistical tails without having personality disorders. Depending on where cutoffs on the various dimensions are set, huge proportions of the population can be seen as having personality disorders. Finally, any notion of a personality "disorder" must contain some criteria for what distinguishes dysfunction from normal variation. These boundaries might be fuzzy, but—like distinctions between infants, toddlers, children, and adolescents—they are not arbitrary.[52]

Person-centered conceptions of personality, in contrast, focus on types of people rather than traits abstracted from particular individuals. They dominate among clinicians, who inherently confront holistic characters. In addition, a dimensional system does not meet the requirements in medical settings for categorical treatment decisions.[53]

A third possibility, which Aristotle might have approved, is to apply the prototypical model to the personality disorders it best fits, while using dimensions on those it better captures. Psychiatrist Joel Paris suggests that BPD and ASPD are more amenable to categorical than to continuous assessments but that other personality disorders are more compatible with dimensional models.[54] In this view, the choice of prototypical or dimensional models need not be universal but should be made on a type by type basis.

Stable or Situational?

Two notions of personality have competed since the earliest writings. The Theophrastian depiction viewed personalities as relatively stable inner traits that persist across various situations. Contrasting Aristotelian portrayals regarded humans as essentially social animals with personal qualities that are designed to adapt to a variety of roles and relationships. The extent to which personality is mainly a consistent inner feature or a situationally adaptive quality persists through the present.

Since the late nineteenth century, psychological researchers have assumed that personality traits are individual qualities that can be abstracted from the contexts in which people operate, because they assume that personality traits are universal aspects of the human species. Their belief echoes the certainty of the founder of factor analysis, Raymond Cattell, who proclaimed that the technique was "to psychology as the microscope was to biology."[55] Psychoanalysts, too, assert that personality types among adults emerge in infancy and early childhood while geneticists place the starting point of personality at conception. All of these fields regard personality as isolatable from cultural and historical particularities.

The link between internal qualities and outer behaviors, however, remains elusive. Mischel's notable 1968 assessment found only a relatively weak overall relationship between scores on personality tests and actual conduct. "It is as if we live in two independent worlds," he noted: "the abstractions and artificial situations of the laboratory and the realities of life."[56] Mischel observed that extraverts did not make friends more easily than introverts and conscientious people were little better at meeting deadlines than unconscientious ones. He concluded that situations were more powerful influences than internal personality differences on how people actually acted.

Adequate conceptions of personality disorder must confront the issue that Allport and Mischel raised of how individuals present their selves in various kinds of situations: "what people actually do, think, and feel in the various contexts of their lives."[57] Everyone deploys their personalities in interactional situations that involve role expectations, attributions of motives, and audience interpretations. Many criteria for the various personality disorders—dependence, dominance, manipulation, and so on—can be determined only through examining social interactions. For example, people with dependent personality disorders are submissive when they believe that passivity and compliance can bring about positive responses from potential caregivers but are aggressive in other contexts when they perceive that important relationships are threatened.[58]

Sociologist Erving Goffman's situational view that selves are products of social arrangements starkly contrasts with the stability model.[59] His studies show how personality can be seen as a performance where individuals choose to accentuate or conceal aspects of their selves that are compatible or incompatible with situational demands. For him, the social roles that people play at any given time more than any inherent traits they possess determine what personality characteristics they display. Residents of mental asylums, Goffman notes, create an image that "selects, abstracts, and distorts in such a way as to provide the patient with a view of himself that he or she can usefully expound in current situations."[60] He concludes about the performed self:

> While this image is entertained *concerning* the individual, so that a self is imputed to him, this self itself does not derive from its possessor, but from the whole scene of his action, being generated by that attribute of local events which renders them interpretable by witnesses. A correctly staged and performed scene leads the audience to impute a self to a performed character, but this imputation—this self—is a *product* of a scene that comes off, and is not a *cause* of it. The self, then, as a performed character, is not an organic thing that has a specific location, whose fundamental fate is to be born, to mature, and to die; it is a dramatic effect arising diffusely from a scene that is presented, and the characteristic issue, the crucial concern, is whether it will be credited or discredited.[61]

This analysis brings to mind Dollard's characterization of Southern descendants of formerly enslaved people as playing submissive roles that were not genuine aspects of their personalities but that their situations demanded when interacting with whites.[62] As Goffman indicates, individuals can deliberately present one personality to some people and another to others.

Another problematic aspect of models that focus on stable, inner traits stems from the differences between self- and other conceptions of personality. Psychologist Timothy Wilson illustrates this dynamic with a line from George Bernard Shaw's *Pygmalion*, when Henry Higgins tells his friend Colonel Pickering, "That woman has the most extraordinary ideas about me. Here I am, a shy, diffident sort of man. . . . And yet she's firmly persuaded that I'm an arbitrary overbearing bossy kind of person. I can't account for it."[63] Wilson observes that the correspondence between self- and other-rated personality traits "is not very high."[64] Indeed, other people's ratings of someone's personality are often better predictors of behavior than self-reports. Adding to this quandary, as Allport noted in the 1920s, observers who hold different relationships to someone often have varying evaluations of their personalities: an individual's coworkers might see him as cheerful, his children as despotic, his wife as neurotic, and his neighbors as stubborn.[65]

Allport in the 1920s or Mischel in 1968 could have written Jerome Kagan's 2012 appraisal of the field of personality psychology: "The evidence reflects an emerging consensus that there is a minimal, or at best a very modest relation between what people say about themselves, on the one hand, and descriptions of them by friends or, better yet, direct observations of behaviors or biological processes that should correspond with the verbal replies on the other."[66] Even Andrew Skodol, the head of the *DSM-5* PPDWG, acknowledged that "the correspondence between patient self-assessments of PD psychopathology and informant assessments has generally been found to be modest at best."[67]

The stability model of personality abstracts traits not only from relationships and situations but also from societal, historical, and cultural factors. It mistakes "the transient conditions of a certain historical age for the permanent conditions of human life."[68] The meanings of items change as cultural evaluations of traits change so that the "same" item means quite different things at different points in time. For example, only 9 percent of the modest Minnesotans who made up the original MMPI sample in the 1930s endorsed the statement "I am an important person." This item was, therefore, considered to be a sign of grandiosity and narcissism. After the test was revised in the 1990s, however, a majority of test takers who lived in a culture that by that time promoted human potential and self-esteem endorsed it.[69]

Nature or Nurture?

The earliest Greek writers were sharply divided over whether personality differences were organic and innate, on the one hand, or cultural and learned, on the other. On one side, the Hippocratics posited that personalities involved biologically grounded temperaments that interacted with environments.[70] On the other side, Aristotle theorized that social learning shaped the development of personality. The question of how nature and nurture combine to influence personality continues through the present.

For most of history either the nature or the nurture model guided research about the personality disorders. When personality first emerged as a research topic in the nineteenth century, interest focused on its anatomical and physiological roots. Approaches as divergent as Prichard's and Gall's agreed that personalities were grounded in brain-based qualities. This organic thrust continued through the first two decades of the twentieth century when most observers viewed personality disorders as resulting from degenerative hereditary processes that worsened over the course of successive generations. Many current students of personality also believe that many essential aspects of personality are genetic and so are apparent by early childhood.[71]

Personality traits have long been viewed as rooted in socially shared processes. Herodotus tied specific character traits to particular cultures, and Aristotle to the influence of social roles and life course stages. When social approaches emerged in psychoanalysis and the social sciences in the 1930s, the understanding of personality disorders underwent a 180-degree turn. Sociologists strove to liberate their field from biological influences. Likewise, John Watson and B. F. Skinner, the leading figures of behavioral psychology, were extreme proponents of the nurture view who denied the relevance of innate factors and firmly believed people displayed whatever behaviors their environments reinforced. Anthropologists, too, repudiated the importance of inborn human traits. "We are forced to conclude," Margaret Mead wrote, "that human nature is almost unbelievably malleable, responding accurately and contrastingly to contrasting cultural conditions."[72] The neo-Freudians, as well, focused almost exclusively on social forces. Moreover, the rise of Nazism and the accompanying identification of genetic forces with eugenics and racism dampened interest in biological causes of personality for several decades.

Developments since 1980 provide the mirror image of the social emphasis during the previous half century. Aside from feminist protests, socially focused attention largely disappeared after the *DSM-III* revolution. When studies of neurobiological influences on personality returned, they came with a vengeance. Armed with new technologies that allowed them to view brain activity, researchers strove, in phrenological fashion, to link various personality traits to specific cerebral regions. Attention turned to the neurotransmitters, synaptic connections, and genes that were responsible for particular types of personalities. As of yet, such efforts have disappointed. The multiplicity and complexity of brain systems have not yielded robust correlations between any neurological trait and any personality style.[73] In 2002, neuroscientist Joseph LeDoux asked how much his colleagues would say we know about the brain mechanisms of the self and personality and said the predominant response would be, not much.[74] Twenty years later, little has changed.

The current literature generally neglects how personality disorders relate to social class, race, and ethnicity, not to mention broader historical and social forces. Psychologists rely on what evolutionary anthropologist Joseph Henrich calls "massively biased samples."[75] Over two-thirds of participants in studies published in the six major American psychological journals between 2003 and 2007 were American college students between ages seventeen and twenty-five.[76] When compared to the small number of studies from non-Western settings, Western samples were on the extreme end of personality trait distributions.

Henrich argues that modern Western societies deviate widely from the prevailing personality patterns that persisted until the rise of Protestantism in sixteenth-century Europe. Unlike most of human history, when people saw their fundamental natures connected to deeply interrelated social networks, what he calls "WEIRD" (Western, educated, industrialized, rich, and democratic) personalities characterize individualist societies. These bounded and unique conceptions thoroughly contrast with the socially based selves that predominated before the modern period.[77] Westerners accordingly respond to questions about their personalities with answers about personal attributes as opposed to the roles and relationships that such questions elicit in traditional groups. For example, one Hong Kong study of children who were bilingual in English and Chinese found that they described themselves as more autonomous in English and as more interdependent in Chinese.[78] Current research, though, pays far less attention to the different meanings of personality traits across varying cultural settings than did studies from the 1930s through the 1960s. What many students of personality assume is universal about the human psyche might be a particular result of sociohistorical forces.

The Future of Personality Disorders

Coming decades are likely to see major changes in views of personality and its disorders. These might include greater attention to the connections between innate and external determinants of personality, a thorough revamping of personality disorder diagnoses, and changing attitudes toward the treatability of personality disturbances.

Integrating Biology and Culture

While neuroscientific studies initially attempted to ground particular types of mental disorders, including personality disorders, in specific brain regions or neurochemical systems, recent work has adopted more sophisticated portrayals integrating inborn temperament, biography, and social environments.[79] Studies of these interactions resemble earlier efforts, such as Meyer's psychobiology or Engel's biopsychosocial model, but go beyond these approaches through providing more specific definitions of both innate and environmental influences on personality.[80]

Many neuroscientists now view mental disorders as products of multifactorial combinations of biological, personal, and social characteristics of individuals and their exposure to environmental stressors. This conception fits the study of personality disorders far better than the disease and trait models. The interactive view can incorporate the dynamic aspects of personality, qualities of rigidity that produce personality disorders, and the interactions between inborn tendencies and learned environmental dispositions. Caspi and colleagues' longitudinal study of antisocial behavior among a cohort of men from New Zealand provides an example. It found no direct relationship between any genetic factor and antisocial behavior. However, a large association emerged among those with the *MAOA* genotype who also had suffered maltreatment in childhood: only maltreated youth with this genotype showed high levels of antisocial or aggressive behavior by age twenty-six.[81] Had the investigators limited their study to genetic or to environmental impacts they would have come up empty.[82]

A fully developed theory would root personality disorder in culture and society, add a developmental dimension, and establish valid character prototypes. Anthropologist and psychiatrist Horacio Fabrega puts this well:

> In deciding on a diagnosis of PD, the examiner needs to keep separate the following sorts of issues: (1) whether the personality traits or behaviors are manifest in a prominent way and are long-standing in the life of the individual, (2) whether they are part of the "normal" accepted patterns in the individual's cultural and social group, (3) whether they are judged as pathological by the individual and especially by his or her reference group, (4) whether they constitute requirements of a role the individual "has" to perform, and (5) whether they are part of a reaction pattern to a new or changed social situation of the individual. A crucial issue is whether the meanings of the personality traits or

behaviors of the individual are consistent with the body of theory pertaining to the PD, constituting maladaptive patterns that are prominent and long-standing, and have given rise to personal distress or interpersonal frictions.[83]

Any comprehensive theory of personality and personality disorders must integrate biological, psychological, and sociohistorical factors that together explain how people behave in various situations and when their behavior constitutes a mental disorder.[84]

A New Dimensional Era?

Over the course of the past century, US psychiatry has used numerous strategies to study personality and its disorders. First, Meyer's psychobiology examined the total personality and its relationship to inborn temperament and the social environment. Next, psychoanalysts posited that knowledge about personality (or character) structures was key to understanding the emergence of neurotic symptoms. After this approach became professionally unsustainable, psychiatry turned to a categorical, medical-like classification schema that gave the personality disorders a special status. Once the failings of diagnostically oriented psychiatry emerged, the field became enamored of the dimensional approach that psychologists had constructed over the past century. While researchers were highly attracted to this model, clinicians adamantly opposed it. In the third decade of the twenty-first century, the field finds itself at another impasse concerning how to best formulate the personality disorders. Researchers have discredited the extant *DSM*, but it remains at the heart of clinical classification. The result is, as Allen Frances has observed, a "gaping disconnect between a basic science enterprise that is remarkably dynamic and a clinical practice that is relatively static."[85]

One possibility is a complete rupture between researchers who study the personality disorders and clinicians who treat them. The NIMH's promotion of a new classification system, the Research Domain Criteria (RDoC), might herald such a thoroughgoing separation in research and clinical formulations of mental disorders, including personality disorders. The RDoC, which is meant for use in research, not treatment, is a biologically based system that is not bound by discrete diagnoses. Its goal is to identify the organic dimensions of mental functioning without reference to the *DSM*. The RDoC might portend an end to the era of a single diagnostic system for clinicians and researchers.[86]

The latest edition of the *International Classification of Disease*, eleventh revision (*ICD-11*) is a second indicator that diagnoses of personality disorders will undergo radical changes. In 2018, the *ICD* implemented a sweeping reformulation of these conditions that its major creator, British psychiatrist Peter Tyrer, calls the "most radical change in the classification history of personality disorders." Tyrer and colleagues enthusiastically embrace dimensional and disparage categorical models: "The science of personality, with its well-developed hypotheses founded on trait-based theory, unequivocally requires dimensional classification, and even more importantly, abhors adherence to independent and unvalidated categories."[87] The *ICD-11* contains a single dimension with five levels of severity: 1 = no personality disturbance, 2 = personality difficulty without disorder, 3 = mild personality disorder, 4 = moderately severe personality disorder, and 5 = severe personality disorder. It uses five trait domains—negative affectivity, detachment, dissociality, disinhibition, and anankastia (obsessive-compulsive)—to specify disorders.[88]

This system marks a revolutionary change from previous *ICDs* and the *DSM*. First, it conceives of personality disorders as continuous with, not divergent from, normal personality styles. Second, it relies on the degree of severity in self-conceptions and interpersonal relationships across all personality domains, rather than on categorical entities, to classify disorder. Third, aside from one type, it abolishes particular categories of personality disorder (e.g., NPD, ASPD, OCPD), instead using dimensional ratings of psychological traits to indicate personality pathology. The sole exception is that—to placate clinical objections—it includes a "borderline" qualifier.

The Section III model in the *DSM-5* is a third harbinger of a possible future upheaval for classifications of personality disorders. Its basic principle—"generalized severity is the most important single predictor of concurrent and prospective dysfunction"—mirrors the central *ICD-11* assumption.[89] Like the *ICD*, the Section III model downplays particular categories and focuses on how all types of PDs feature disturbances in self and interpersonal functioning:[90]

> Like most human tendencies, personality functioning is distributed across a continuum. An optimally functioning person has a complex, fully elaborated, and well-integrated psychological world that includes a mostly positive, volitional, and effective self-concept; a rich, broad, and appropriately regulated emotional life; and the capacity to behave as a well-related, productive member of a society. At the opposite end of the continuum, an individual with severe personality pathology has an impoverished, disorganized, and/or conflicted psychological world that includes a weak, unclear, and ineffective self-concept;

a propensity to negative, dysregulated emotions; and a deficient capacity for adaptive interpersonal functioning and social behavior.[91]

The Section III focus on identity and self-direction along with interpersonal empathy and intimacy cuts across all of the extant *DSM-5* Section II categories.

Proponents of a new dimensional system continue to make vigorous efforts to replace the *DSM*'s categories. In 2017 a group mostly composed of psychologists along with some prominent psychiatrists mobilized to form the Hierarchical Taxonomy of Psychopathology (HiTOP) consortium.[92] One article from HiTOP boosters aggressively opens with lines from a Bob Dylan song:

> And you better start swimmin'
> Or you'll sink like a stone
> For the times they are a-changin'.[93]

The HiTOP model is grounded in psychological research that uses the statistical technique of factor analysis to derive quantitative dimensions, such as internalizing and externalizing, that participants believe can overcome the problems of the current *DSM* categories. Its advocates contend that the results of their factor analyses provide a "true" portrayal of personality disorders: "Rather than forcing these phenomena into committee-derived categories, they are modeled as they are in nature." Their ultimate goal is to develop, in their preferred language, "multivariate models of the joint distribution of etiologic (e.g., genomic polymorphisms) and continuous phenotypic observations in larger samples."[94]

The *ICD-11*, *DSM-5* Section III, and HiTOP promise to eliminate some of the problems that plague the current categorical system, including the rampant co-occurrence of multiple types of personality disorders, the overuse of the NOS category, and the internal heterogeneity of many PDs. They also, however, pose their own serious difficulties. Each model is ultimately grounded on self-reported symptoms; they do nothing to overcome the inherent problems of descriptive, symptom-based approaches. They are unable to examine underlying personality dynamics, to characterize holistic personalities, or to distinguish personality disorders from statistical extremes.[95] In addition, they have the potential to pathologize a vast range of problems in living. For example, studies that use the *ICD-11* classify only a third of respondents with no personality disturbance; about half have some personality difficulty, and nearly 20 percent a mild, moderate, or severe condition.[96] Among the *ICD-11* criteria for "mild personality disorder" are such ubiquitous situations as "conflicts with supervisors and co-workers," "difficulties in developing close and mutually satisfying relationships," and "intermittent or frequent minor conflicts [in social relationships] that are not so severe that they cause serious and long-standing disruption."[97] This is especially troublesome because the *ICD-11* strives to incorporate its broad ratings into primary care, as well as specialty psychiatric settings, so that personality assessments would become a routine part of medical practice. Its advocates encourage primary care doctors to make personality assessments of "every person seen for the first time."[98]

The *DSM-5* Section III also loosens the criteria for a personality disorder, which needs to feature only "moderate or greater impairment" and be "relatively inflexible" and "relatively stable across time," considerably broadening the range of disorder.[99] Likewise, HiTOP encompasses a vast array of problems ranging from "full recovery" to "subthreshold symptoms" to "severe impairment."[100] While their promulgators welcome these expansions because the presence of undesirable personality traits predict negative treatment outcomes, are associated with premature mortality, and can have costly social consequences, others find this prospect a frighteningly immense expansion of social control.[101]

In addition, these recent efforts to dimensionalize the personality disorders do not overcome Whyte's earlier critique that "the mathematics does not eliminate values; it only obscures them."[102] The essential content of a personality disorder—some distortion in experiencing and thinking about the self, others, and the world—is unavoidably connected to social norms and values. For example, the *DSM-5* Section III definitions incorporate terms such as "hostility," "submissiveness," "suspiciousness," "intimacy avoidance," "callousness," "deceitfulness," "manipulativeness," "irresponsibility," and many others that cannot be separated from negative evaluations.[103] Dimensional and categorical classifications alike inevitably rely on judgments of what constitute good or bad personality qualities.

The recent movements to dimensionalize and quantify the personality disorders evoke the efforts of Galton and early personality psychologists to abstract personality traits from actual situations, culture, and history. None of these efforts incorporate the insights of the neo-Freudian and culture and personality schools that societal factors always influence personality styles. In addition, as the *DSM-5* deliberations and the successful lobbying to insert a borderline qualifier into the *ICD-11* indicate, efforts to dimensionalize the personality disorders are unlikely to convince either clinicians, who face real people in real situations, or the administrative entities who reimburse treatment. The current awkward situation where clinicians rely on a manual that researchers have discredited while researchers use a dimensional system that clinicians resist is not feasible in the long run. This impasse seems unsustainable but as yet no mutually acceptable solution has emerged.

Changing Attitudes toward Treatment

Clinicians traditionally assumed that personality disorders were the most difficult class of mental illnesses to treat. One reason was their belief that these conditions emerged in the earliest stages of development and were basically fixed in early childhood. Another was that, while patients with symptom-based disorders generally welcomed attempts to rid them of their distress, those with personality problems firmly resisted efforts to alter their basic characters.[104] Reich's influential notion of character armor described their defense mechanism against efforts at transformation. The *DSM-I* stated that many personality disorders "can rarely if ever be altered in their inherent structures by any form of therapy."[105] Even when psychoanalysts placed the personality disorders at the heart of their theories in the 1960s and 1970s, they regarded their treatment as more difficult and less likely to lead to good prognoses than other nonpsychotic conditions. They viewed patients with personality disorders as the least likely to establish therapeutic alliances, a robust predictor of successful treatment outcomes. As anthropologist Tanya Luhrmann noted from her fieldwork in the 1990s, "Personality disorder patients are the patients you don't like, don't trust, don't want."[106] Conversely, the vast majority of people—about 85 percent—who could be diagnosed with a personality disorder don't want to enter treatment in the first place.[107]

The persistent attitudes regarding the intractability of the personality disorders are beginning to change. Stern's initial observation that patients with borderline conditions were "extremely difficult to handle effectively by any psychotherapeutic method" shaped subsequent attitudes about the treatability of these conditions.[108] One prominent trend over the past thirty years has been the emergence of treatments specifically aimed at the personality disorders, especially BPD. Psychologist Marsha Linehan's dialectical behavior therapy (DBT) in the 1990s heralded a new optimism about treatments for personality disorders. DBT involves teaching people how to focus on the present and develop positive ways to cope with stress, regulate emotions, and improve relationships with others.[109]

Although DBT is effective in clinical trials, it faces formidable challenges in actual practice. One is that the technique requires clinicians to undergo lengthy and intensive training. Another is that DBT can be difficult to implement in real-life settings marked by high time demands, low levels of funding, and frequent staff turnover. Finally, the vast majority of people with personality disorders never seek help for their conditions and so will never have the opportunity to engage in DBT (or any other therapy). Other less complicated techniques have subsequently emerged, including forms of cognitive behavioral therapy adapted for the personality disorders, general psychiatric management, and stepped models of care.[110] Peter Tyrer's nidotherapy, which helps patients change their environments to minimize the impact of their personality disorders, is another promising development.[111] Although none of these therapies can transform the personality disorders, all can help alleviate their negative effects. Significant questions remain about implementing these approaches in actual mental health settings and getting patients to enter and remain in them, but there is little doubt that attitudes about the treatability of personality disorders, BPD in particular, are becoming more optimistic.

Conclusion

For the past century and a half, most students of personality have striven to be on the natural science side of the Kantian divide. The major problem they have confronted has been that personality intrinsically involves a component that requires understandings of personal and cultural meanings, which falls on the intuitive side of this division. Although this divide might never be fully bridged, recent trends to acknowledge both biological and environmental factors, construct new forms of measurement, and develop effective therapies might herald genuine progress in defining, explaining, and treating the personality disorders.

NOTES

Chapter 1 · Issues

1. Theophrastus, 2018, 41, 47, 51. Unsurprisingly for his time, all of Theophrastus's characters are male.
2. E.g., Westen, Shedler, and Bradley, 2006.
3. Theophrastus, 2018, 18.
4. See especially Garber, 2020, 322–348.
5. Aristotle, 2009, 23.
6. Aristotle, 2009, 24.
7. Aristotle, 2009, 31.
8. Aristotle, 2009, 52.
9. Aristotle, 2009, 30.
10. Aristotle, 2009, 33–34, 25, 51.
11. Aristotle, 1991, 172–180.
12. Aristotle, 2009, 127.
13. Hippocrates, 2021.
14. *Journal of the American Medical Association*, 1905.
15. Simon, 1978, 215.
16. Herodotus, 1996.
17. Garber, 2020.
18. Quoted in Garber, 2020, 13.
19. Watz, 2011.
20. Susman, 2003, 273–274.
21. Lunbeck, 1994, 68.
22. Mathews, Deary, & Whiteman, 2009.
23. Burckhardt, 1860/1954, 100.
24. Stearns, 1975, 14.
25. Susman, 2003, 279.
26. Abbott, 1988, 283.
27. Kant, 1798/1974; Hughes, 1958; Danziger, 1990, 19–23.
28. Shorter, 1997; Porter, 2002.
29. Zaretsky, 2004, 333.
30. At its heart, psychoanalysis is a science of suspicion: its central principle is that things, including one's own self, are often not what they appear to be (Gay, 1985, 69).
31. Quoted in Gay, 1985, 45–46.
32. E.g., Capshew, 1999; Danziger, 1990.

33. Mead, 1989, xi.
34. Jacoby, 1983, 102.
35. While individuals differ in the degree to which they possess each of the five traits, the traits themselves are seen as invariant across all people and groups.
36. G. W. Allport, 1937, 48.
37. Sacks, 1995, xvii.
38. Sacks, 1985, 110–111.
39. Ehrenberg, 2020, 8.
40. Allport & Allport, 1921, 7.
41. Freud, 1940/1989, 25.
42. Jung, 1921/1971, 467. Jung also used the term "anima" in a different sense to refer to the feminine aspects of personality that contrasted with "animus," which is the masculine side of personality.
43. G. W. Allport, 1937, 48.
44. Mischel & Shoda, 1995.
45. Galton, 1883; 1884.
46. Cloninger, 1986.
47. LeDoux, 2002, 324, 262.
48. Damasio, 1994, 7.
49. Sacks, 1985; 1995.
50. American psychologist William James (1890/1950, 121) set an older age when personality was no longer changeable: "By the age of 30, the character has set like plaster, and will never soften again."
51. Mead, 1942/1971, 25.
52. Geertz, 1984, 126.
53. E.g., Maslow, 1963; Rodgers, 1980.
54. Inkeles, 1961, 173. Some accounts of national character emphasize physical forces such as climate, geographic setting, and air. Others focus on the cultural aspects of the relevant groups.
55. Quoted in Garber, 2020, 14. The characterization of the personality of entire social systems has also been criticized. "Nothing is generally more false and ridiculous than the portraits drawn to represent the characters of different nations," philosopher Claude Adrien Helvetius (1759/2018, 357) bluntly stated.
56. Quoted in Harris, 1968, 395.
57. Spencer, 1873/1933, quoted in Harris, 1968, 400–401.
58. McGoldrick, 1982.
59. Rose, 1996, xviii.
60. E.g., Elder, 1974.
61. E.g., Rosenberg, 2007.
62. Rosenberg, 2007, 13.
63. Kraepelin, 1909–1915.
64. Anthropologist T. M. Luhrmann (2000, 115) observes of the personality disorders, "A patient's symptoms are much more a part of him, much more a part of his intentions, and hard to conceptualize as disease."
65. Oliver Sacks uses this quality for the epigraph to his *An Anthropologist on Mars* (1995): "Ask not what disease the person has, but rather what person the disease has."
66. Prichard, 1835; Kraepelin, 1909–1915.
67. APA, 2013, 20.
68. APA, 2013, 645, italics in original.
69. APA, 2013, 646. The class also contains personality change due to a medical condition and unspecified personality disorder.

70. Fabrega, 1994.

71. APA, 2013, 20. Jerome Wakefield (1992) defines mental disorders as "harmful dysfunctions."

Chapter 2 · Personality Disorders Emerge

1. Gall called the field that he founded "craniology." Galton's successor, Johann Gaspar Spurzheim, coined the term "phrenology."

2. Crocq, 2013, 149.

3. Ehrenberg, 2020, 254.

4. Anderson, 2014.

5. Pastar et al., 2010.

6. At the time, "moral" referred to mental and emotional conditions more generally (Shorter, 1993).

7. Prichard, 1835, 85. American psychiatrist Benjamin Rush anticipated Prichard's work in 1812 when he wrote about cases of "mischief" that stemmed from a "defective organization in those parts of the body which are occupied by the moral faculties of the mind." Quoted in Black, 2013, 22.

8. Many of Prichard's heterogeneous examples of moral insanity did not resemble personality conditions, and many also developed late in life and so did not display the long-standing qualities that mark personality disorders. Therefore, moral insanity had more differences from than resemblances to the later condition of psychopathic personality. See Whitlock, 1982.

9. Koch, 1891.

10. Kraepelin, 1904.

11. Kraepelin, 1921, 118.

12. Kraepelin, 1921, 118, italics in original.

13. Kraepelin, 1921, 130.

14. Kraepelin, 1921, 268, 269.

15. Kretschmer, 1925.

16. Schneider, 1923/1958.

17. Tyrer, Reed, & Crawford, 2015, 719; Tyrer, 2018, 18–19. The current borderline category encompasses both the emotionally unstable and impulsive categories; the *DSM-5* places the abnormal mood and activity type on the bipolar spectrum.

18. Berrios, 1993; Zachar, 2011.

19. Crocq, 2013, 152.

20. *Statistical Manual*, 1918, 39.

21. In the early part of the century some states established specific psychopathic wards in general hospitals that temporarily held allegedly insane cases before their cases were decided (Grob, 1983, 241).

22. Beers, 1908.

23. Danziger, 1990, 164; Abbott, 1988, 23.

24. Meyer, 1938, 486.

25. Freud, 1916–1917/1989, 301. Likewise, fervent crusaders against pornography might have unusually intense sexual drives themselves. Conversely, compulsive seducers of women could unconsciously fear impotence.

26. Freud, 1908/1989b, 294.

27. Freud, 1908/1989b, 294. Freud had been thinking about this perspective earlier in his career. He mentioned "orderly, parsimonious, and obstinate" as interrelated character traits in a letter he wrote to his friend Wilhelm Fliess in 1897.

28. Westen, 1998, 354.

29. Freud, 1908/1989a, 32.

30. Ellis, 1898.
31. Freud, 1914/1989, 545.
32. Freud 1914/1989, 554. Analyst Abraham Brill summarized, "The road to homosexuality always passes over narcissism, that is, love for one's self." Quoted in Lunbeck, 2014, 99.
33. Freud himself underwent four years of painful suffering during his four-year engagement to his future wife, Martha.
34. Freud, 1908/1924.
35. Freud et al. 1954, quoted in Malcolm, 1982, 21.
36. Eksteins, 1989, 21.
37. Gay, 1988, 407.
38. Freud, 1923/1990, 17.
39. A number of commentators (e.g., Jacoby, 1983, 140; Makari, 2008, 464) have pointed out the unfortunate translation of the German *Ech* and *Es* into the awkward "ego" and "id." "I" and "it" would be closer to Freud's usage.
40. Freud, 1933/1965, 73.
41. Freud, 1940/1989, 2.
42. Freud, 1933, 74.
43. Importing a metaphor from Plato's *Republic*, Freud (1933/1965, 77) compared the ego's relation to the id to that of a rider on a horse. The task of the analyst was to appropriate the instinctual energy of the id for the ego's use: "Where id was, there ego shall be," Freud (80) famously proclaimed.
44. Freud, 1940/1989, 62.
45. Freud, 1933/1965, 62.
46. Wrong, 1961, 37.
47. Freud, 1940/1989, 63.
48. Freud, 1933/1965, 78.
49. Freud, 1933/1965, 97.
50. Gay (1985, 123) likens the psychoanalytic view of the mind to a military dictatorship: "inordinately suspicious, addicted to secrecy, insatiable in its demands, armed to the teeth, and not very intelligent."
51. Freud, 1940/1989, 61.
52. Freud (1931/1963, 213) observed, "The hypothesis of these libidinal types throws no fresh light on the genesis of the neuroses. Experience testifies that persons of all these types can live free from neurosis."
53. See especially Zaretsky, 2004.
54. Freud, 1927/1989, 4.
55. Freud, 1930/1961, 91. See also 12, 88.
56. This quote from Freud's "Leonardo da Vinci and a memory of his childhood" (1910/1989) appears as the epigraph for Gay, 1988.
57. Freud, 1919/1963, 214.
58. Freud, 1905/1965, 54.
59. Freud, 1918/1965, 72.
60. Freud, 1931/1963, 212.
61. Lunbeck, 2014, 204.
62. Freud, 1916/1963, 157.
63. Jung, 1921/1971, 500.
64. Letter from Freud to Jones, quoted in Bair, 2003, 286.
65. Watson, 1923.
66. Jung, 1921/1971, 512.

67. See especially Emre, 2018.
68. Danziger, 1990, 19.
69. Capshew, 1999, 4.
70. Quoted in Richardson, 2006, 500.
71. James, 1885/1987, 400.
72. Munsterberg, 1909, 130.
73. Danziger, 1990, 40–42.
74. Watson, 1913, 158.
75. Watson, 1924, 104.
76. Kuklick, 1977, 565.
77. Nicholson, 2002, 8. Historian of psychology Daniel Robinson (1995, 327) observes, "Contemporary psychology then is largely a footnote to the nineteenth century."
78. Roback, 1927, 6.
79. Ward, 2002, 125.
80. Bills, 1938, 385.
81. By the mid-1930s a third of psychologists were employed in applied settings (Capshew, 1999, 29).
82. Paul, 2004.
83. Galton, 1883, 42. Galton was also one of the first scholars to use what came to be called the "lexical method" of defining personality, searching the index of *Roget's Thesaurus* to find a thousand entries that expressed some quality of character.
84. Galton, 1884, 181, 182, 185. Galton's work was strongly influenced by the work of his half cousin, Charles Darwin, who emphasized the advantages of organisms who could best adapt to their environments. For example, Galton postulated that the gregarious instinct of cattle to live in herds was an evolutionary adaptation to predation by carnivorous animals.
85. Zenderland, 1999.
86. Danziger, 1990, 84.
87. In sharp contrast to French statisticians such as Quetelet who extolled the qualities of people who fell in the middle of statistical distributions, Darwin's ideas implied to Galton that people at the positive end of a distribution were the most valuable members of any group while the average person was mediocre. Conversely, he regarded those on the negative tail as deficient and a risk to the health of societies (Bulmer, 2003, 43).
88. Danziger, 1990, 159.
89. Danziger, 1990, 77.
90. Danziger, 1990, 157.
91. Quoted in Kevles, 1968, 567.
92. Woodworth, 1917.
93. Landis, Zubin, & Katz, 1935.
94. Capshew, 1999, 1.
95. Roback, 1932–1933, 215.
96. E.g., Danziger, 1990, 105; Ward, 2002, 127.
97. Danziger, 1990, 159, 163.
98. Poffenberger, 1925, 265–266.
99. E.g., Allport & Allport,1921.
100. G. W. Allport, 1937, 48.
101. G. W. Allport, 1921. See also Allport & Allport, 1921.
102. Freud, 1940/1989, 53.
103. G. W. Allport, 1921.
104. G. W. Allport, 1921.

105. F. H. Allport, 1924, 99, 101.

106. Menninger, 1930/1945, 12–13.

107. E.g., Danziger, 1990; Herman, 1995.

Chapter 3 · *Personality Becomes Social*

1. Hesse, 1919/2013.

2. Traditional forms of art, music, literature, and other fields were also undergoing revolutionary changes during this period.

3. Ellenberger, 1970, 584.

4. Roazen, 1975, 203.

5. Adler, 1927.

6. Makari, 2008, 261.

7. Ellenberger, 1970, 572.

8. Freud, 1914/1959, 338, 339.

9. Freud, 1914/1959, 347.

10. Hughes, 1958, 153.

11. Makari, 2008, 299.

12. See especially Danto, 2007; Gaztambide, 2019.

13. Danto, 2007, 3.

14. Makari, 2008, 378.

15. Abraham, 1925/1942.

16. Abraham, 1916/1948.

17. Alexander, 1929/1946, 1.

18. Alexander, 1929/1946, 50–55.

19. Alexander, 1929/1946, 53–54.

20. Makari, 2008, 382.

21. Alexander, 1935, 278.

22. Makari, 2012, 118.

23. Reich, 1929/1950, 125.

24. P. A. Robinson, 1969, 21.

25. Reich, 1933/1980, 57; Makari, 2008, 395.

26. Reich, 1933/1980, 156.

27. E.g., McWilliams, 1994, 27.

28. Reich, 1962, 72.

29. Sharaf, 1994, 163.

30. Reich, 1927/1986, 4. At the extreme, Reich suggested that the unsatisfactory sex lives of the kaiser and the German aristocracy caused World War I (35).

31. Reich, 1933/1980, 290.

32. Reich, 1927/1986, 198.

33. Reich, 1933/1970, 19.

34. E.g., McWilliams, 1994, 170.

35. Freud, 1908/1989a, 33.

36. Fenichel, 1945/1995, 471.

37. Lunbeck, 2014, 28.

38. Fenichel, 1945/1995, 467.

39. Makari, 2008, 396.

40. Fenichel, 1945/1995, 506, 468.

41. Fenichel, 1945/1995, 506, 526.

42. Letter from Karl Abraham to Sigmund Freud, October 19, 1919. Quoted in Makari, 2008, 369.

43. Quoted in Jacoby, 1983, 63.

44. Horney, 1926. Quoted in Gay, 1988, 520.

45. Horney, 1967, 83.

46. Horney, 1935/1967, 231.

47. Horney, 1937, 239.

48. Horney, 1939, 10.

49. Horney, 1937, 15.

50. Horney, 1937, 17–18.

51. Horney, 1937, 31.

52. Horney, 1937, 2.

53. Horney, 1937, 134–135.

54. Horney, 1937, 20.

55. Horney, 1937, 1.

56. Horney, 1937, 79.

57. Horney, 1937, 158.

58. Leviticus 19:18.

59. Horney, 1937, 177.

60. Horney, 1937, 31. Horney also noted that rigidity only indicated a neurosis when it deviated from cultural patterns.

61. Horney, 1937, 27.

62. J. Paris, 1994, 115.

63. Quoted in Jacoby, 1983, 107.

64. Makari, 2008, 480.

65. Fromm, 1941/1969, 304.

66. Fromm, 1941/1969, 319.

67. Jay, 1973/1996, 92; Friedman, 2013, 35.

68. Friedman, 2013, 37.

69. Fromm, 1941/1969, 239, italics in original.

70. Fromm, 1941/1969, 200–201.

71. Fromm, 1941/1969, 318.

72. Fromm, 1941/1969, 101–102.

73. Fromm, 1947/1990, 69–78.

74. Fromm, 1955/1990, 99.

75. Fromm, 1947/1990, 77.

76. Freud, 1905/1989.

77. Fromm, 1941/1969, 162.

78. Friedman, 2013, 118.

79. Herzog, 2017, 33.

80. Marcuse, 1955/1966, 219.

81. Róheim, 1950, 491.

82. Róheim, 1925.

83. Devereux, 1951; 1978.

84. Kardiner, 1939.

85. Kardiner, 1944.

86. Galton, 1873, 116.

87. Popenoe, 1915, 238.

88. Davenport, 1913, 36.

89. King, 2019, 177.

90. Boas, 1916, 471.

91. Spier, 1959, quoted in Freeman, 1996, 282.

92. Boas, 1916, 476.

93. Malinowski, 1927/2001. The opening sentence of this book notes how "the doctrine of psycho-analysis has had within the last ten years a truly meteoric rise in popular favour."

94. Malinowski, 1927/2001, 1.

95. Malinowski, 1923, 331.

96. Malinowski, 1927/2001, 24.

97. Anthropologist and psychoanalyst Melford Spiro (1993/2010, 39, 162) provided the most extensive critique of Malinowski's theory. Spiro claims Malinowski's evidence is "slim, confusing, and contradictory," and in fact Trobriand boys do develop oedipal hostility toward their fathers and erotic love toward their mothers. He answers the question "Is the Oedipus complex universal?" with "How could it possibly not be?"

98. Benedict, 1934a/1989, 12.

99. Benedict, 1934b, 63.

100. Benedict, 1934a/1989, 278.

101. Mead, 1935/2001, 280.

102. Freeman, 1996, xviii.

103. Mead, 1928/1971, 107.

104. Mead, 1935/2001, 285.

105. King, 2019, 161–162.

106. Mead, 1989, 1.

107. Singer, 1961, 28.

108. Mead, 1935/2001.

109. White, 1942, 190.

110. Dollard, 1937/1988, 17.

111. Dollard, 1937/1988, 256.

Chapter 4 · Personality Flourishes

1. Rieff, 1959, xi.

2. Chapman, 1976.

3. Sullivan, 1953, 110–111.

4. Selective Service System, 1941, 2061.

5. Grob, 1991b, 11.

6. Sullivan, 1941, 208.

7. Grob, 1991b, 10–11; Shephard, 2000, 198–201.

8. Grob, 1991b, 11.

9. Hale, 1995, 204.

10. Grinker & Spiegel, 1945, 11.

11. Quoted in Grob, 1991b, 12.

12. W. C. Menninger, 1947, 578.

13. Malinow, 1981.

14. Grinker & Spiegel, 1945.

15. Swank & Marchand, 1946, 244.

16. Grinker & Spiegel, 1945, 11.

17. Grinker & Spiegel, 1945.

18. Benedict, 1946, 2.

19. Mead, 1942/1971; Gorer & Rickman, 1949.

20. Gorer, 1943.

21. Friedman, 1990, 59.

22. Quoted in Friedman, 1990, 110.

23. Friedman, 1990, 56.

24. K. A. Menninger, 1945, xiv.

25. K. A. Menninger, 1945, 23.

26. K. A. Menninger, 1945, 158.

27. K. A. Menninger, 1945, 35.

28. *Mental Hygiene*, 1946. A slightly reorganized classification appears as "Nomenclature of psychiatric disorders and reactions." War Department, 1946.

29. *Mental Hygiene*, 1946, 466–467, 459.

30. APA, 1952, 13, 34.

31. APA, 1952, 34–35.

32. APA, 1952, 36–37.

33. APA, 1952, 38–39.

34. APA, 1952, 38, 35, 37.

35. APA, 1968, 41.

36. APA, 1952, 34.

37. APA, 1968, 41.

38. Freud, 1927, 283.

39. Freud, 1940/1989, 1.

40. Gay, 1988, 499.

41. Shorter, 1997, 174.

42. Grob, 1994, 196.

43. Zaretsky, 2004, 280–281.

44. Grob, 1994; Hale, 1995.

45. Jacoby, 1983, 142.

46. Herzog, 2017, 216.

47. Broyard, 1993, 45.

48. Makari, 2008, 483.

49. Editors, 1958, vii.

50. Zaretsky, 2004, 204, 278, 279.

51. Hartmann, 1958, 12, 95.

52. Hale, 1995, 238. Other ego psychologists, most notably Anna Freud, focused on the mental health of children, moving the analytic focus away from fathers, the unconscious, sexuality, and fantasies to actual experiences with mothers regarding safety and love. Alongside ego psychology, the school of object relations, which emerged in Great Britain, concentrated on how serious personality disturbances originated in early infancy. It diverged from orthodox analysis in its emphasis on the pre-Oedipal period and on actual, as opposed to fantasized, mother-child relationships during this time of life.

53. Makari, 2012, 123.

54. Wickware, 1947, 98.

55. Hale, 1995, 386–389.

56. Pulver, 1976, 621.

57. Kadushin, 1969, 115.

58. Kadushin, 1969, 116. In general, this study found little relationship between the kind of presenting problems patients reported and the particular diagnosis they received.

59. Marmor, 1975, 42, 43, 61. Another survey of treated patients in New Haven, Connecticut, conducted in 1975 showed smaller numbers. About 10 percent of outpatients and 7 percent of inpatients received a diagnosis of some personality disorder (Redlich & Kellert, 1978, 26).

60. Karl Menninger (1945, 157–158) was among the first to make this observation.

61. Zaretsky, 2004, 325.

62. My discussion is indebted to Lunbeck's (2014) work on narcissism.

63. Wolfe, 1976.

64. Quinn, 1981.
65. Lunbeck, 2014, 50.
66. Malcolm, 1982, 118.
67. Lunbeck, 2012, 211.
68. Lunbeck, 2014, 133.
69. Kohut, 1973, 21.
70. Kohut, 1971.
71. Kohut, 1977, 187.
72. Lunbeck, 2012, 217.
73. Kernberg, 1975.
74. Kernberg, 1975.
75. Kernberg, 1975.
76. Kernberg also wrote extensively about sadomasochistic personality disorders (e.g., 1988), which were not included as a distinct category in the *DSM*.
77. Lunbeck, 2014, 7.
78. Lasch, 1979.
79. Kohut, 1977, 302.
80. Jay, 1973/1996, 39.
81. Horkheimer, 1950, quoted in Herzog, 2017, 177.
82. Horkheimer, 1950, 230.
83. Jay, 1973/1996, 104.
84. Zaretsky, 2004, 236–237.
85. Schlesinger, 1949, 250.
86. Brown, 1950, 178.
87. Adorno et al., 1950, 5, italics in original.
88. Adorno et al., 1950, 971.
89. Adorno et al., 1950/1982, 479.
90. E.g., Christie & Jahoda, 1954; Riesman, Glazer, & Denney, 1950/1969, xxv.
91. Horowitz, 2010, 1006.
92. Riesman, Glazer, & Denney, 1950/1969, xii.
93. Riesman, Glazer, & Denney, 1950/1969, xliv.
94. Riesman, Glazer, & Denney, 1950/1969, 4.
95. Riesman, Glazer, & Denney, 1950/1969, xlix.
96. Riesman, Glazer, & Denney, 1950/1969, xlix.
97. Riesman, Glazer, & Denney, 1950/1969, l.
98. Erikson, 1950/1978, 279.
99. Erikson, 1950/1978, 160.
100. Lunbeck, 2014, 2.
101. Herman, 1995, 5.
102. Capshew, 1999, 1, 30.
103. Cronbach, 1957.
104. Capshew, 1999, 216.
105. Skinner, 1956, 120. Social psychologist John Dollard's apology for using qualitative methods in *Class and Caste in Southern Society* (1937/1988, 16) illustrates the pressure to use statistical techniques. He noted his "bad conscience" for not presenting his findings through quantitative measures that were conventional among psychologists. But "method must conform to material and not vice versa," Dollard proclaimed.
106. Whyte, 1956, 190.
107. Grob, 1994, 192; Herman, 1995, 93.
108. Halliwell, 2013, 115.

109. Ward, 2002, 132.

110. Biographical, life history, and observational studies were virtually absent within psychology at the time.

111. Paul, 2004, 65.

112. Paul, 2004, xii.

113. Hathaway, 1964, 207.

114. Hathaway & McKinley, 1940, 250.

115. Hathaway, 1964, 209.

116. Hathaway (1964, 206) came to realize that many of the items were narrowly culture bound: "It obviously did not occur to us that there were other than the Christian orientation wherein religiosity might be observed."

117. Hathaway, 1964, 205.

118. Hathaway, 1964.

119. Paul, 2004, 53.

120. Hathaway, 1964, 209.

121. Hathaway, 1964, 209.

122. Meehl, 1973, 70.

123. Meehl, 1973, 79.

124. Butcher et al., 1999.

125. Whyte, 1956, 198.

126. Whyte, 1956, 449.

127. Andrew Dobson, "MMPI 2 Clinical Scale—What do the Scores Mean" (blog), *Mindfit Hypnosis*, https://mindfithypnosis.com/mmpi-2-clinical-scale/.

128. Whyte, 1956, 215.

129. See especially Searls, 2017.

130. E.g., Murray, 1938.

131. Searls, 2017.

Chapter 5 · Personality Disorders in the DSM-III

1. Quoted in Decker, 2013, 230.

2. Jeremy Pearce, "Joseph J. Schildkraut, 72, Brain Chemistry Researcher, Dies," *New York Times*, July 8, 2006, http://www.nytimes.com/2006/07/08/us/08schildkraut.html.

3. Harrington, 2019, 198, 165.

4. Szasz, 1961; Laing, 1967; Rosenhan, 1973. Cahalan (2019) indicates that Rosenhan fabricated much of his data.

5. See especially Smith, 1985.

6. Spitzer to Davison, April 15, 1976, DSM Coll.

7. Spitzer's "Research Diagnostic Criteria," which was closely related to the Washington University effort, was a second predecessor of the *DSM-II* (Spitzer, Endicott, & Robins, 1978).

8. Feighner et al., 1972. The diagnoses were the primary affective disorders of depression and mania, secondary affective disorders associated with some other psychiatric or medical diagnosis, schizophrenia, anxiety neurosis, phobic neurosis, hysteria, antisocial personality disorder, alcoholism, drug dependence, mental retardation, homosexuality, transsexuality, organic brain syndrome, and anorexia nervosa, as well as a residual category of undiagnosed disorder.

9. Kendler, Munoz, & Murphy, 2010.

10. Decker, 2013, 195.

11. Quoted in Decker, 2013, 168–169.

12. Quoted in Decker, 2013, 168–169.

13. Goodwin & Guze, 1996, 262.

14. Feighner et al., 1972, 60.

15. Quoted in Decker, 2013, 196. Beck later applied his cognitive behavioral perspective to the personality disorders that emerged in *DSM-III*.

16. Schwartz to Spitzer, no date, DSM Coll.

17. E.g., Cattell, 1965; Eysenck, 1967.

18. Ten percent of diagnoses were of pathological personality, 10 percent of some other character disorder, and 4 percent of immature personality (*NDTI Review*, 1970, 3).

19. Millon, 1981, 63.

20. Kernberg to Spitzer, January 25, 1977, DSM Coll.

21. Gunderson, 1983, 30.

22. Clark, 1995, 482.

23. Spitzer & Wilson, 1969, 425.

24. Nussbaum to Park, April 4, 1979, DSM Coll.

25. Talbott, 1980, 25.

26. Millon, 1983, 809.

27. War Department, 1946.

28. Millon, 1981, 356.

29. APA, 1980, 316.

30. APA, 1980, 307.

31. McGuire & Hall, 1977, 304.

32. Myers, 1980/1995.

33. Susman, 2003, 277.

34. Whyte, 1956, 439.

35. Cain, 2012, 4.

36. APA, 1952, 35–39.

37. APA, 1968, 43. Freud's early writings featured hysteria, and it was a core condition in Schneider's work in the 1920s.

38. My discussion is indebted to Christopher Lane's (2007, 71–103) analysis of the PDAC. I am also grateful to him for sharing the APA files that contain the correspondence related to the group's discussions.

39. Lane, 2007, 78–79, 78, 83.

40. Lane, 2007, 84.

41. APA, 1980, 311.

42. Klein to PDAC, January 11, 1978, DSM Coll.

43. APA, 1980, 324.

44. APA, 1980, 326.

45. Morgan to Glueck, November 27, 1976, DSM Coll.

46. APA, 1980, 313.

47. Quoted in Millon, 1981, 402.

48. APA, 1980, 326.

49. APA, 1980, 313.

50. APA, 1980, 317.

51. Theophrastus, 2018, 47.

52. Prichard, 1835, 85.

53. Kraepelin, 1909–1915.

54. Pickersgill, 2012, 545.

55. McWilliams, 1994, 151.

56. Cleckley, 1941/1976. Shortly after the *DSM-III* was published, psychologist Robert Hare (1983/1991) developed the twenty-item Hare Psychopathy Checklist that operationalized Cleckley's criteria for psychopathy.

57. Bursten, 1972, 320.

58. Cleckley, 1941/1976, 198–199.
59. McWilliams, 1994, 152.
60. APA, 1952, 38.
61. APA, 1952, 38.
62. APA, 1968, 43.
63. See especially Pickersgill, 2012.
64. APA, 1968, 43.
65. APA, 1980, 320–321.
66. Millon, 1981, 181.
67. See also Black, 2013, ch. 8, 191–210.
68. Robins, 1966. Later work confirmed that children who display unruly temperaments are more likely to engage in antisocial behaviors as adults (Westen, 1998, 348).
69. Lion to Spitzer September 30, 1974, quoted in Pickersgill, 2012, 549.
70. Black, 2013, 31.
71. Hare, 1993. Another prominent psychologist, Terrie Moffitt (1993), indicates that only about 5 percent of children who demonstrate behavior problems develop persistent antisocial disorders as adults.
72. Millon, 1981, 182.
73. Quoted in Seabrook, 2008, 71.
74. Kraepelin, 1921, 130, italics in original.
75. Stern, 1938, 467.
76. Stern, 1938, 467–468.
77. McWilliams, 1994, 50.
78. Kernberg, 1975.
79. Hooley, Cole, & Gironde, 2013, 413.
80. Black, 2013, 69.
81. Kaysen's book also insightfully critiqued the *DSM-III* definition of "borderline." She simultaneously accepts its accuracy in describing her earlier condition and sharply criticizes its conflation of nonconformity and mental disorder: "It's what they call people whose lifestyles bother them" (1993, 151). Marsha Linehan, who went on to develop the major treatment for BPD, dialectical behavior therapy, also says she would have satisfied the BPD criteria when she was hospitalized for two years in the early 1960s (2020, 47).
82. Chodoff to Kernberg, June 15, 1976, DSM Coll.
83. Goodwin to Spitzer, January 27, 1977, DSM Coll.
84. Schiff to Spitzer, January 28, 1979, DSM Coll.
85. Millon to Spitzer, June 28, 1978, DSM Coll.
86. Millon, 1981, 331, italics in original.
87. Klein to Spitzer, November 9, 1978, DSM Coll.
88. Klein, 1975; Akiskal et al., 1977.
89. Spitzer to Klein, April 5, 1978, DSM Coll.
90. Spitzer to PDAC, October 10, 1978, DSM Coll.
91. Klein to Spitzer, November 11, 1978, DSM Coll.
92. Kernberg to Spitzer, November 9, 1978, DSM Coll.
93. Lehrman to PDAC, March 22, 1979, DSM Coll.
94. Spitzer to APA members, January 3, 1977, DSM Coll.
95. Spitzer, Endicott, & Gibbon, 1979.
96. APA, 1980, 321.
97. APA, 1980, 322.
98. Skodol, 2013, 36.
99. Hooley, Cole, & Gironde, 2013, 410, 412.

100. Blashfield & Intoccia, 2000.

101. Many experts including Marsha Linehan (2015) and Peter Tyrer (2018, 85) primarily view BPD as a disorder of emotional dysregulation. Millon & Davis (1996, 645–646) also contend that BPD better fits the affective than the personality category.

102. The converse is less likely: 18 percent of those with BPD also qualified for bipolar diagnoses (Elliott & Ragsdale, 2021).

103. Freud, 1931/1950, 249.

104. E.g., McWilliams, 1994, 171.

105. Millon, 1981, 166.

106. APA, 1980, 317.

107. APA, 1980, 305.

108. APA, 1980, 6.

109. APA, 1980, 309, 311, 315, 318, 326, 329.

110. Mill, 1869, 132–133.

111. Friedan, 1963/2001.

112. APA, 1980, 314–315.

113. APA, 1980, 324–325.

114. Loranger, 1990.

115. Google NGram analysis shows that the use of "personality disorder" began to slowly rise from 1940 to 1980, when its usage exploded more than twentyfold by 2012.

116. Pincus et al., 1993.

117. Blashfield & McElroy, 1987, 527.

118. Blashfield, Reynolds, & Stennett, 2013, 611.

119. Blashfield & Intoccia, 2000.

120. Hopwood & Thomas, 2013, 589.

121. Malcolm, 1982, 22.

122. Shorter, 1997, 293–295.

Chapter 6 · Personality Contentions in the DSM-5

1. Whooley, 2019, 180.

2. Mullan & Murray, 1989.

3. Shapiro et al., 1985; Wang et al., 2005; Kessler et al., 2005.

4. APA, 1987, 429.

5. APA, 1994, 647.

6. APA, 1994, 733. The *DSM-IV* also added a diagnosis of depressive personality disorder in an appendix.

7. The following material is drawn from Horwitz, 2021, chapter 5.

8. Caplan, 1995, 87–88.

9. Reich, 1933/1980.

10. Quoted in Figert, 1996, 41.

11. Caplan (1995, 109) dismissed the criteria's explicit exclusion of people who displayed characteristics of SDPD in response to abuse, claiming that clinicians would ignore this qualification.

12. Caplan, 1995, 89.

13. APA, 1987, 370.

14. Millon & Davis, 1996, 474.

15. Klerman, 1983.

16. Mechanic, McAlpine, & Rochefort, 2014, 142.

17. Mojtabai & Olfson, 2008.

18. Mojtabai & Olfson, 2008, 365.

19. Wallerstein, 1991, 430–431.

20. Kupfer, First, & Regier, 2002, 147.

21. Luhrmann's fieldwork indicates that psychiatrists learn diagnostic criteria for Axis I conditions far more thoroughly than for Axis II conditions (2000, 47, 113).

22. Blashfield et al., 2014, 40.

23. Alarcon & Sarabia, 2012.

24. Blashfield & Intoccia, 2000, 472–473.

25. Kendler, 2005, 434–435.

26. A number of factors could account for comorbidity: the presence of one disorder could lead to the presence of another, both conditions could stem from a common underlying factor, or the definitional criteria for both diagnoses could overlap.

27. Samuels & Costa, 2013, 571.

28. Kendell & Jablensky, 2003.

29. Kupfer, First, & Regier, 2002, xviii.

30. Skodol, 2013, 36.

31. APA, 1994, 629.

32. Kupfer, First, & Regier, 2002, 129.

33. Westen & Arkowitz-Weston, 1998, 1769.

34. Kraemer, Shrout, & Rubio-Stipec, 2007, 263.

35. Skodol, 2013, 41.

36. Widiger, 2013, 26.

37. Frances, 1980, 1050.

38. Verheul, 2012, 238.

39. Helzer, 2008, xxv.

40. Regier et al., 2009.

41. Krueger & Tackett, 2003, 109.

42. Rounsaville et al., 2002, 13.

43. Costa & McCrae, 1992.

44. John & Naumann, 2010, 45.

45. McCrae & John, 1992, 194.

46. Costa & McCrae, 1992, 347.

47. Tyrer, 2012, 372–373.

48. Widiger et al., 2013, 101.

49. McCrae, Gaines, & Wellington, 2012, 68.

50. McCrae, Lockenhoff, & Costa, 2005, 269.

51. Torgerson et al., 2000.

52. Merikangas, 2002.

53. Widiger & Clark, 2000, 954.

54. Widiger et al., 2007; McCrae, Lockenhoff, & Costa, 2005.

55. Costa, 2006, 232.

56. See especially Block, 1995; 2010.

57. Krueger et al., 2011, 172.

58. Widiger et al., 2007.

59. Greenberg, 2013, 267.

60. Widiger & Simonsen, 2005.

61. E.g., Cattell, 1965; Cloninger, 2000.

62. Westen et al., 2002, 224.

63. Horowitz et al., 1981, 575.

64. Shedler & Westen, 2004.

65. Westen, Shedler, & Bradley, 2006.

66. Widiger, 2013, 29; Trull, Scheiderer, & Tomko, 2013, 234.

67. Miller, Few, & Widiger, 2013, 130.

68. J. Paris, 2006, 67.

69. Simonsen, 2006, 259.

70. E.g., Morey & Meyer, 2013.

71. Skodol, Bender, & Oldham, 2021, 80.

72. Shea, 2006, 200.

73. Krueger et al., 2008, 97.

74. Kupfer, First, & Regier, 2002.

75. Helzer et al., 2008; Krueger et al., 2008.

76. Livesley, 1998.

77. Zachar, Krueger, & Kendler, 2016, 2.

78. Livesley, 1998; Krueger et al., 2008.

79. Regier et al., 2009, 645.

80. Quoted in Greenberg, 2013, 268.

81. Bernstein et al., 2007. The fact that there were nearly twice as many international as domestic experts represented in this survey (Skodol, 2013, 48) might explain the enthusiasm for replacing the *DSM* categories. Most worked in health care systems that did not require a *DSM* diagnosis to obtain reimbursement.

82. Skodol et al., 2013, 348.

83. Frances, 1993, 110.

84. Zachar, Krueger, & Kendler, 2016, 7.

85. Miller, Few, & Widiger, 2013, 132.

86. Widiger, 2013, 25.

87. Bornstein, 2011, 240.

88. Livesley, 2010, 309.

89. Alarcon & Sarabia, 2012.

90. Luyton & Blatt, 2011; see also Russ et al., 2008.

91. Widiger, 2013, 802.

92. The copyrighted status of existing dimensional systems was a major reason the PPDWG wound up developing its own model instead of using one of the extant measures.

93. The particular 37 traits, which were nominated by PPDWG members, were highly arbitrary (Widiger, 2013, 28).

94. Tyrer, 2012.

95. Clarkin & Huprich, 2011, 196.

96. Greenberg, 2013, 269.

97. Phillips, 2011.

98. Widiger, 2011.

99. Quoted in Greenberg, 2013, 208.

100. Gunderson, 2013, 370.

101. Torgerson, 2013, 202–203.

102. Shedler et al., 2010, 1026, 1027.

103. Gunderson, 2013, 371.

104. Livesley, 2012.

105. Clark, 2013; Krueger, 2013.

106. E.g., Blashfield et al., 2014.

107. Gunderson, 2013.

108. First, 2011.

109. Whooley & Horwitz, 2013.

110. Luyten & Blatt, 2011, 62.

111. These included Peter Tyrer, Giles Newton-Howes, and Roger Mulder (Tyrer, 2018, 35).

112. The alternative *DSM-5* model for personality disorders appears in Section III on emerging measures and models (APA, 2013, 761–782). It contains diagnostic criteria for ASPD, avoidant, BPD, NPD, obsessive-compulsive PD, and schizotypal PD that could be ranked on levels of impairment in identity, self-direction, empathy, and intimacy. It also contains a condition of PD–trait specified that features domains of negative affectivity, detachment, antagonism, disinhibition, and psychoticism that are very similar to the FFM (APA, 2013, 770). In addition, while schizotypal PD was retained in the personality disorders section, it is also, confusingly, placed in the schizophrenic spectrum category. It thus has a unique status as both a form of personality pathology and a milder form of schizophrenia (Kwapil & Barrantes-Vidal, 2013, 437).

113. Zachar, Krueger, & Kendler, 2016, 1.

114. J. Paris, 2013b, 377.

115. Livesley, 2012, 5; Krueger, 2013.

116. Verheul, 2012, 370.

117. First, 2011.

118. Spitzer et al., 2008, 356.

119. Krueger, 2013, 355.

Chapter 7 · *Mental Disorders or Problems in Living?*

1. See especially Rosenberg, 2007.

2. G. W. Allport, 1961, 28.

3. K. A. Menninger, 1945, 158.

4. APA, 1952, 13.

5. APA, 1952, 35.

6. Quoted in Decker, 2013, 168–169.

7. Prichard, 1835.

8. Kraepelin, 1902.

9. Szasz, 1961. For critiques see, e.g., Wakefield, 1992; McHugh, 1999.

10. Whyte, 1956, 204.

11. Lewis, 1953, 119.

12. APA, 2013, 659, 669, 667, 663.

13. Vaillant, 1984, 543.

14. Buss, 2009, 362; Funder, 2001.

15. Wakefield, 2013.

16. Frank & Frank, 1993, 7.

17. Benedict, 1934a/1989.

18. The fact that personality disorders can be identified only through morally loaded criteria does not mean they have no scientific usefulness. Psychologist Peter Zachar (2011) shows how they can be risk factors for, mold the expressions of, and affect the course of various other disorders.

19. Cf. Abbott, 1988, 54.

20. Quoted in Capshew, 1999, 34. In contrast, the profession thoroughly rejected interpretative approaches, such as gestalt, which emphasized how individuals couldn't be isolated from the larger contexts in which they operated.

21. Quoted in Decker, 2013, 196.

22. Although patients with PDs often receive drugs, they are usually aimed at symptoms of other conditions that accompany a PD, not the PD itself (Tyrer, 2018, 120–123).

23. E.g., Rieff, 1966.

24. Westen, 1998, 333.

25. Freud, 1925/1989, 82–83.

26. Meehl, 1973, 79.

27. K. A. Menninger, 1945, 12–13.

28. Westen, 1998, 361.

29. See especially Frank & Frank, 1993.

30. Black, 2013, 88.

31. Widiger, 2013, 28.

32. First et al., 2018.

33. E.g., Spitzer et al., 2008; Shedler et al., 2010.

34. Aristotle, 2009, 31.

35. APA, 2013, 645, italics in original.

36. Trump, 2020, 197.

37. APA, 2013, 645.

38. Sixteenth-century French essayist Michel de Montaigne posed the complexities that this question raises: "We are entirely made up of bits and pieces woven together so diversely and so shapelessly that each one of them pulls its own way at every moment. And there is as much difference between us and ourselves as there is between us and other people." Quoted in Mac-Millan, 2015, 9–10.

39. Skodol, 2021, 111.

40. G. W. Allport, 1937, 48.

41. Carl Jung (1921/1971, 513) likewise observed, "A man of pronounced sanguine temperament will tell you that at bottom he is deeply melancholic; a choleric, that his only fault consists in his having always been too phlegmatic."

42. Freud, 1908/1989a. In dynamic views, holistic concepts such as "authoritarian personality" lose their explanatory power when they are dissembled into separate dimensions such as high conscientiousness, low agreeableness, and low openness to experience (Funder, 2001, 201).

43. Mischel, 1968. A decade later, psychologist Lee Ross (1977) coined the term "fundamental attribution error" to refer to people's mistaken tendencies to attribute human behavior to individual personalities rather than external circumstances.

44. Widiger et al., 2013, 101.

45. Tyrer, 2012, 373.

46. Costa 2006, 196–197.

47. Clark, 2007.

48. Bornstein, 2013.

49. Bender, 2021, 321.

50. Wakefield, 2008, 391.

51. Kendell, 1975, 309.

52. Wakefield, 2022.

53. Shedler et al., 2010.

54. J. Paris, 2013a.

55. Cattell, 1957, 9.

56. Mischel, 1968, 1; Funder, 2001, 199.

57. Funder, 2001, 213.

58. Bornstein, 2011, 242.

59. E.g., Goffman, 1961; 1971.

60. Goffman, 1961, 133.

61. Goffman, 1959, 252–253.

62. G. W. Allport, 1921; Dollard, 1937/1988.

63. Shaw, 1913, 43, quoted in Wilson, 2002, 67–68.

64. Wilson, 2002, 84; see also Westen & Kegley, 2021, 34.

65. G. W. Allport, 1921.

66. Kagan, 2012, 95, 251.

67. Skodal, 2021, 122.

68. Collingwood, 1946, 224.

69. Paul, 2004, 68.

70. Prominent psychiatrist Hagop Akiskal (1996) has revived Hippocratic conceptions of personality. He argues that borderline and avoidant personality disorders are comparable to choleric and phlegmatic temperaments and that manic and depressive conditions involve excesses of sanguine and melancholic temperaments. Like the Hippocratics, Akiskal regards these temperaments as inborn traits that constitute the basic nature of personality.

71. E. g., Tyrer, 2018, 56.

72. Mead, 1949, 280.

73. J. Paris, 2006, 67. One study of 3972 Sardinians that assessed 360,000 alleles is illustrative: it did not find a single significant relationship with any of the "Big Five" personality traits (Terracciano et al., 2010).

74. LeDoux, 2002, 1.

75. Henrich, 2020, xii.

76. Henrich, 2020, 382; see also Kagan, 2012, 23.

77. Henrich, 2020, 21.

78. Kagan, 2012, 276.

79. J. Paris, 2013a.

80. Meyer, 1938; Engel, 1977.

81. Caspi et al., 2002.

82. Similarly, psychiatrist Joel Paris (1994, 82) suggests that social environments characterized by a lack of structure and permissive values are most likely to evoke the impulsiveness of those prone to develop borderline personalities.

83. Fabrega, 1994, 165.

84. J. Paris, 2013a; Funder, 2001.

85. Frances, 2014.

86. NIMH, "About RDoC," https://www.nimh.nih.gov/research/research-funded-by-nimh/rdoc/about-rdoc; Whooley, 2019, 192.

87. Tyrer et al., 2019, 481.

88. First et al., 2021, 47.

89. Bender, Morey, & Skodol, 2011, 332.

90. APA, 2013, 762.

91. APA, 2013, 771.

92. Kotov et al., 2017.

93. Latzman et al., 2021, 1.

94. Krueger et al., 2018, 286, 285.

95. Haeffel et al., 2021.

96. Tyrer, 2018, 105.

97. Bach & First, 2018. https://doi.org/10.1186/s12888-018-1908-3.

98. Tyrer, 2018, 43.

99. APA, 2013, 761.

100. Kotov et al., 2017, 467.

101. Compare Tyrer, Reed, & Crawford, 2015; to Wakefield, 2008.

102. Whyte, 1956, 204.

103. APA, 2013, 761–782.

104. Lunbeck, 2014, 204.

105. APA, 1952, 34–35.

106. Luhrmann, 2000, 115.
107. Tyrer, 2018, 103.
108. Stern, 1938, 468.
109. Linehan, 2015.
110. For CBT, see Beck & Freeman, 1990; for GPM, see Choi-Kain and Hersh, 2021; for stepped care, see J. Paris, 2013c.
111. Tyrer, 2018, 114–119.

Abbott, A. (1988). *The system of the professions*. Chicago: University of Chicago Press.

Abraham, K. (1916/1948). "The first pregenital stage of the libido." Pp. 248–279 in *Selected papers of Karl Abraham M.D.* London: Hogarth Press.

Abraham, K. (1925/1942). *Selected papers of Karl Abraham*. London: Hogarth Press.

Adler, A. (1912/1917). *The neurotic constitution*. New York: Moffat, Yard.

Adler, A. (1927). *Understanding human nature*. Garden City, NY: Garden City Publishing.

Adorno, T. W, Frenkel-Brunswik, E., Levinson, D. J., & Sanford, R. N. (1950). *The authoritarian personality*. New York: W. W. Norton.

Adorno, T. W, Frenkel-Brunswik, E., Levinson, D. J., & Sanford, R. N. (1950/1982). *The authoritarian personality*. Abridged ed. New York: W. W. Norton.

Akiskal, H. S. (1996). "The temperamental foundations of affective disorders." Pp. 3–30 in *Interpersonal factors in the origin and course of affective disorders* (C. Mundt, K. Hahlweg, & P. Fiedler, eds.). London: Gaskell.

Akiskal, H. S., Djenderedjian, A. H., Rosenthal, T. L., & Khani, M. K. (1977). "Cyclothymic disorder: Validating criteria for inclusion in the bipolar affective group." *American Journal of Psychiatry*, 134, 1227–1233.

Alarcon, R. D., & Sarabia, S. (2012). "Debates on the narcissism conundrum: Trait, domain, dimension, type, or disorder?" *Journal of Nervous and Mental Disease*, 200, 16–25.

Alexander, F. (1929/1946). *The psychoanalysis of the total personality: The application of Freud's theory of the ego to the neuroses*. New York: Coolidge Foundation.

Alexander, F. (1935). *The roots of crime*. New York: Alfred A. Knopf.

Allport, F. H. (1924). *Social psychology*. Boston: Houghton Mifflin.

Allport, F. H., & Allport, G. W. (1921). "Personality traits: Their classification and measurement." *Journal of Abnormal Psychology and Social Psychology*, 16, 6–40.

Allport, G. W. (1921). "Personality and character." *Psychological Bulletin*, 18, 441–455.

Allport, G. W. (1927). "Concepts of trait and personality." *Psychological Bulletin*, 24, 284–293.

Allport, G. W. (1937). *Personality: A psychological interpretation*. New York: Henry Holt.

Allport, G. W. (1961). *Pattern and growth in personality*. New York: Holt, Reinhart & Winston.

American Psychiatric Association (APA). (1952). *Diagnostic and statistical manual of mental disorders*. Washington, DC: American Psychiatric Association.

American Psychiatric Association (APA). (1968). *Diagnostic and statistical manual of mental disorders* (2nd ed.). Washington, D.C: American Psychiatric Association.

American Psychiatric Association (APA). (1980). *Diagnostic and statistical manual of mental disorders* (3rd ed.). Washington, DC: American Psychiatric Association.

American Psychiatric Association (APA). (1987). *Diagnostic and statistical manual of mental disorders* (3rd ed. rev.). Washington, DC: American Psychiatric Association.

American Psychiatric Association (APA). (1994). *Diagnostic and statistical manual of mental disorders* (4th ed.). Washington, DC: American Psychiatric Association.

American Psychiatric Association (APA). (2000). *Diagnostic and statistical manual of mental disorders* (4th ed. text rev.). Washington, DC: American Psychiatric Association.

American Psychiatric Association (APA). (2013). *Diagnostic and statistical manual of mental disorders* (5th ed.). Washington, DC: American Psychiatric Association.

Anderson, M. (2014). *After phrenology: Neural reuse and the interactive brain*. Cambridge, MA: MIT Press.

Aristotle. (1991). *The art of rhetoric* (H. Lawson-Tancred, trans.). New York: Penguin.

Aristotle. (2009). *The Nicomachean ethics* (D. Ross, trans.). New York: Oxford World Classics.

Bach, B., & First, M. B. (2018). "Application of the *ICD-11* classification of personality disorders." *BMC Psychiatry*, 18, 351.

Bair, D. (2003). *Jung: A biography*. Boston: Little, Brown.

Beck, A. T., & Freeman, A. (1990). *Cognitive therapy of personality disorders*. New York: Guilford Press.

Beers, C. W. (1908). *A mind that found itself: An autobiography*. New York: Longmans, Green.

Bender, D. S. (2021). "Therapeutic alliance." Pp. 307–334 in *Textbook of personality disorders* (A. E. Skodol & J. M. Oldham, eds.). Washington, DC: American Psychiatric Association.

Bender, D. S., Morey, L. C., & Skodol, A. E. (2011). "Toward a model for assessing level of personality functioning in DSM-5, part I: A review of theory and methods." *Journal of Personality Assessment*, 93, 332–346.

Benedict, R. (1934a/1989). *Patterns of culture*. Boston: Houghton Mifflin.

Benedict, R. (1934b). "Anthropology and the abnormal." *Journal of General Psychology*, 10, 59–80.

Benedict, R. (1946). *The chrysanthemum and the sword*. Boston: Houghton Mifflin.

Bernstein, D. P., Iscan, C., Maser, J., et al. (2007). "Opinions of personality disorders experts regarding the *DSM-IV* personality disorders classification system." *Journal of Personality Disorders*, 21, 536–551.

Berrios, G. E. (1993). "European views on personality disorders: A conceptual history." *Comprehensive Psychiatry*, 34, 14–30.

Bills, A. G. (1938). "Changing views of psychology as a science." *Psychological Review*, 45, 377–394.

Black, D. (1976). *The behavior of law*. New York: Academic Press.

Black, D. W. (2013). *Bad boys, bad men: Confronting anti-social personality disorder*. New York: Oxford University Press.

Blashfield, R. K., & Intoccia, V. (2000). "Growth of the literature on the topic of personality disorders." *American Journal of Psychiatry*, 157, 472–473.

Blashfield, R. K., Keeley, J. W., Flanagan, E. H., & Miles, S. R. (2014). "The cycle of classification: *DSM-I* through *DSM-5*." *Annual Review of Clinical Psychology*, 10, 25–51.

Blashfield, R. K., & McElroy, R. A. (1987). "The 1985 journal literature on the personality disorders." *Comprehensive Psychiatry*, 28, 536–546.

Blashfield, R. K., Reynolds, S. M., & Stennett, B. (2013). "The death of histrionic personality disorder." Pp. 603–627 in *Oxford handbook of personality disorders* (T. A. Widiger, ed.). New York: Oxford University Press.

Block, J. (1995). "A contrarian view of the five-factor approach to personality description." *Psychological Bulletin*, 117, 187–25.

Block, J. (2010). "The five-factor framing of personality and beyond: Some ruminations." *Psychological Inquiry*, 21, 2–25.

Boas, F. (1916). "Eugenics." *Scientific Monthly*, 3, 471–478.

Bornstein, D. P. (2011). "Reconceptualizing personality pathology in *DSM-V*." *Journal of Personality Disorders,* 25, 235–247.

Bornstein, D. P. (2013). "Dependent personality disörder." Pp. 505–526 in *The Oxford Handbook of Personality Disorders* (T. A. Widiger, ed.). New York: Oxford University Press.

Bornstein, D. P., Iscan, C., & Maser, J. (2007). "Opinions of personality disorder experts regarding the *DSM-IV* personality disorders classification system." *Journal of Personality Disorders,* 21, 536–551.

Brown, J. F. (1950). "Review of studies in prejudice." *Annals of the American Academy of Political and Social Science,* 225, July, 178.

Broyard, A. (1993). *Kafka was the rage: A Greenwich Village memoir.* New York: Vintage.

Bulmer, M. (2003). *Frances Galton: Pioneer of heredity and biometry.* Baltimore: Johns Hopkins Press.

Burckhardt, J. (1860/1954). *The civilization of the Renaissance in Italy.* New York: Random House.

Burnham, J. (2012). *After Freud left: A century of psychoanalysis in America.* Chicago: University of Chicago Press.

Bursten, B. (1972). "The manipulative personality." *Archives of General Psychiatry,* 26, 318–321.

Buss, D. M. (2009). "How can evolutionary psychology successfully explain personality and individual differences?" *Perspectives on Psychological Science,* 4, 359–366.

Butcher, J. N., Miller, K. B., Hess, A. K., & Weiner, I. B. (1999). *Personality assessment in personal injury litigation: The handbook of forensic psychology.* New York: John Wiley & Sons.

Cahalan, S. (2019). *The great pretender: The undercover mission that changed our understanding of madness.* New York: Grand Central.

Cain, S. (2012). *Quiet: The power of introverts in a world that can't stop talking.* New York: Crown.

Caplan, P. J. (1995). *They say you're crazy: How the world's most powerful psychiatrists decide who's normal.* Reading, MA: Addison-Wesley.

Capshew, J. (1999). *Psychologists on the march: Science, practice, and professional identity in America, 1929–1969.* New York: Cambridge.

Caspi, A., McClay, J., Moffitt, T. E., Taylor, A., et al. (2002). "Role of genotype in the cycle of violence in maltreated children." *Science,* 297, 851–854.

Cattell, R. B. (1957). *Personality and motivation structure measurement.* New York: World Book.

Cattell, R. B. (1965). *The scientific analysis of personality.* New York: Penguin.

Chapman, A. H. (1976). *Harry Stack Sullivan: The man and his work.* New York: G. P. Putnam.

Choi-Kain, L. W., & Hersh, R. (2021). "Good psychiatric management: Generalist treatments and stepped care for borderline personality disorder." Pp. 407–438 in *Textbook of Personality Disorders* (A. E. Skodol & J. M. Oldham, eds.). Washington, DC: American Psychiatric Association.

Christie, R., & Jahoda M., eds. (1954). *Studies in the scope and method of "The Authoritarian Personality."* New York: Free Press.

Clark, L. A. (1995). "The challenge of alternating perspectives in classification: A discussion of basic issues." Pp. 482–497 in *The "DSM-IV" personality disorders* (J. W. Livesley, ed.). New York: Guilford Press.

Clark, L. A. (2007). "Assessment and diagnosis of personality disorder: Perennial issues and an emerging reconceptualization." *Annual Review of Psychology,* 58, 227–257.

Clark, L. A. (2013). "A critique of Gunderson's views of *DSM-5*." *Personality Disorders: Theory, Research, and Treatment,* 4, 379–380.

Clarkin, J. F., & Huprich, S. K. (2011). "Do *DSM-5* personality disorder proposals meet criteria for clinical utility?" *Journal of Personality Disorders,* 25, 192–205.

Cleckley, H. M. (1941/1976). *The mask of sanity.* St. Louis: Mosby.

Cloninger, C. R. (1986). "A unified biosocial theory of personality and its role in the development of anxiety states." *Psychiatric Development*, 4, 167–226.

Cloninger, C. R. (2000). "Biology of personality dimensions." *Current Opinions in Psychiatry*, 13, 611–616.

Collingwood, R. G. (1946). *The idea of history*. New York: Oxford University Press.

Costa, P. (2006). "Commentary on Trull: Just do it; Replace Axis II with a diagnostic system based on the five-factor model of personality." Pp. 195–198 in *Dimensional models of personality disorders: Refining the research agenda for "DSM-V"* (T. A. Widiger, E. Simonsen, P. J. Sirovatka, & D. A. Regier, eds.). Washington, DC: American Psychiatric Association.

Costa, P. T., & McCrae, R. R. (1992). "The five-factor model of personality and its relevance to personality disorders." *Journal of Personality Disorders*, 6, 343–359.

Costa, P., & Widiger, T. A. (1993). *Personality disorders and the five-factor model of personality*. Washington, DC: American Psychological Association.

Crocq, M.-A. (2013). "Milestones in the history of personality disorders." *Dialogues in Clinical Neuroscience*, 15, 147–153.

Cronbach, L. (1957). "The two disciplines of scientific psychology." *American Psychologist*, 671–684.

Damasio, A. (1994). *Descartes' error: Emotion, reason, and the human brain*. New York: HarperCollins.

Danto, E. A. (2007). *Freud's free clinics: Psychoanalysis and social justice, 1918–1938*. New York: Columbia University Press.

Danziger, K. (1990). *Constructing the subject: Historical origins of psychological research*. New York: Cambridge University Press.

Davenport, C. B. (1913). "Heredity, culpability, praiseworthiness, punishment and reward." *Popular Science Monthly*, 83, 33–39.

Decker, H. S. (2013). *The making of "DSM-III."* New York: Oxford University Press.

Devereux, G. (1951). *Reality and dream: Psychotherapy of a Plains Indian*. New York: International Universities Press.

Devereux, G. (1978). *Ethnopsychoanalysis: Psychoanalysis and Anthropology as complementary frames of reference*. Berkeley: University of California Press.

Dollard, J. (1937/1988). *Caste and class in a Southern town*. Madison: University of Wisconsin Press.

Editors. (1958). "Preface." H. Hartmann, *Ego psychology and the problem of adaptation*. New York: International Universities Press.

Ehrenberg, A. (2020). *The weariness of the self*. Montreal: McGill-Queen's University Press.

Eksteins, M. (1989). *Rites of spring: The Great War and the birth of the modern age*. Toronto: Lester and Orpen.

Elder, G. (1974). *Children of the Great Depression: Social change in life experience*. Chicago: University of Chicago Press.

Ellenberger, H. F. (1970). *The discovery of the unconscious: The history and evolution of dynamic psychiatry*. New York: Basic Books.

Elliott, M., & Ragsdale, J. M. (2021). "Stress exposure and well-being: correlates of meeting criteria for bipolar disorder, borderline personality disorder, or both." *Social Psychiatry and Psychiatric Epidemiology*. https://doi.org/10.1007/s00127-021-02172-z

Ellis, H. (1898). "Autoerotism: A psychological study." *Alienist Neurology*, 19, 260–299.

Emre, M. (2018). *The personality brokers: The strange history of Myers-Briggs and the birth of personality testing*. New York: Doubleday.

Engel, G. L. (1977). "The need for a new medical model: A challenge for biomedicine." *Science*, 196, 129–136.

Erikson, E. H. (1950/1978). *Childhood and society*. New York: W. W. Norton.

Eysenck, H. J. (1967). *The biological basis of personality.* Springfield, IL: Charles C Thomas.

Fabrega, H. (1994). "Personality disorders as medical entities: A cultural interpretation." *Journal of Personality Disorders,* 8, 149–167.

Feighner, J. P., Robins, E., Guze, S. B., Woodruff, R. A., Winokur, G., & Munoz, R. (1972). "Diagnostic criteria for use in psychiatric research." *Archives of General Psychiatry,* 26, 57–63.

Fenichel, O. (1945/1995). *The psychoanalytic theory of neurosis.* 50th anniversary ed. New York: W. W. Norton.

Figert, A. E. (1996). *Women and the ownership of PMS: The structuring of a psychiatric disorder.* New York: Aldine de Gruyter.

First, M. B. (2011). "The problematic *DSM-5* personality disorders proposal: Options for plan B." *Journal of Clinical Psychiatry,* 72, 1341–1343.

First, M. B., Gaebel, W., Maj, M., Stein, D. J., et al. (2021). "An organization- and category-level comparison of diagnostic requirements for mental disorders in *ICD-11* and *DSM-5*." *World Psychiatry,* 20, 34–51.

First, M. B., Rebello, T. J., Keeley, J. W., Bhargava, R., et al. (2018). "Do mental health professionals use diagnostic classifications the way we think they do? A global survey." *World Psychiatry,* 17, 187–195.

Fonacy, P., & Luyten, P. (2013). "Psychodynamic models of personality disorders." Pp. 345–371 in *The Oxford Handbook of Personality Disorders* (T. A. Widiger, ed.). New York: Oxford University Press.

Frances, A. (1980). "The *DSM-III* personality disorders section: A commentary." *American Journal of Psychiatry,* 137, 1050–1054.

Frances, A. (1993). "Dimensional diagnosis of personality: Not whether, but when and which." *Psychological Inquiry,* 4, 110–111.

Frances, A. (2014). "RDoC is necessary, but very oversold." *World Psychiatry,* 13, 47–49.

Frank, J. D., & Frank, J. B. (1993). *Persuasion and healing: A comparative study of psychotherapy* (3rd ed.). Baltimore: Johns Hopkins University Press.

Freeman, D. (1996). *Margaret Mead and the heretic.* New York: Penguin.

Freud, S. (1905/1989). "Three essays on the theory of sexuality." Pp. 239–293 in *The Freud reader* (P. Gay, ed.). New York: W. W. Norton.

Freud, S. (1908/1924). "'Civilized' sexual morality and modern nervousness." Pp. 141–167 in *Collected papers II* (J. Riviere, trans.). London: Hogarth Press.

Freud, S. (1908/1989a). "Character and anal eroticism." Pp. 27–33 in *Character and Culture* (P. Rieff, ed.). New York: Collier Books.

Freud, S. (1908/1989b). "Character and anal eroticism." Pp. 293–297 in *The Freud reader* (P. Gay, ed.). New York: W. W. Norton.

Freud, S. (1910/1989). *Leonardo da Vinci and a memory of his childhood.* New York: W. W. Norton.

Freud, S. (1914/1959). "On the history of the psycho-analytic movement." Pp. 287–359 in *Sigmund Freud: Collected papers,* vol. 1 (J. Riviere, trans.). New York: Basic Books.

Freud, S. (1914/1989). "On narcissism: An introduction." Pp. 545–562 in *The Freud reader* (P. Gay, ed.). New York: W. W. Norton.

Freud, S. (1916/1963). "Some character-types met with in psycho-analytic work." Pp. 157–181 in *Freud: Character and Culture* (P. Rieff, ed.). New York: Collier Books.

Freud, S. (1916–1917/1989). *Introductory lectures on psycho-analysis* (P. Gay, ed.). New York: Liveright.

Freud, S. (1919/1963). "Psychoanalysis and war neuroses." Pp. 215–219 in *Freud: Character and culture* (P. Rieff, ed.). New York: Collier Books.

Freud, S. (1923/1990). *The ego and the id* (J. Strachey, trans.). New York: W. W. Norton.

Freud, S. (1925/1989). *An autobiographical study.* New York: W. W. Norton.

Freud, S. (1927). "Concluding remarks on the question of lay analysis." *International Journal of Psycho-Analysis*, 8, 392–401.

Freud, S. (1927/1989). *The future of an illusion* (J. Strachey, trans.). New York: W. W. Norton.

Freud, S. (1930/1961). *Civilization and its discontents* (J. Strachey, trans.). New York: W. W. Norton.

Freud, S. (1931/1950). "Libidinal types." Pp. 217–220 in *Collected papers*, vol. 5. London: Hogarth.

Freud, S. (1931/1963). "Libidinal types." Pp. 210–214 in *Freud: Character and culture* (P. Rieff, ed.). New York: Collier Books.

Freud, S. (1933/1965). *New introductory lectures on psychoanalysis* (J. Strachey, trans.). New York: W. W. Norton.

Freud, S. (1940/1989). *An outline of psychoanalysis* (J. Strachey, trans.). New York: W. W. Norton.

Freud, S., Bonaparte, M., Freud, A., & Kris, E., eds. (1954). Letter 12 (E. Mosbacher & J. Strachey, trans.). Pp. 73–75 in *The origins of psycho-analysis: Letters to Wilhelm Fliess, drafts and notes: 1887–1902*, ed. S. Freud & M. Bonaparte, A. Freud, & E. Kris, trans. E. Mosbacher & J. Strachey. New York: Basic Books. https://doi.org/10.1037/11538-002.

Friedan, B. (1963/2001). *The feminine mystique*. New York: W. W. Norton.

Friedman, L. J. (1990). *Menninger: The family & the clinic*. Lawrence: University of Kansas Press.

Friedman, L. J. (2013). *The lives of Erich Fromm: Love's prophet*. New York: Columbia University Press.

Fromm, E. (1941/1969). *Escape from freedom*. New York: Avon Books.

Fromm, E. (1955/1990). *The sane society*. New York: Macmillan.

Fromm, E. (1947/1990). *Man for himself: An inquiry into the psychology of ethics*. New York: Henry Holt.

Funder, D. C. (2001). "Personality." *Annual Review of Psychology*, 52, 197–221.

Galton, F. (1873). "Hereditary improvement." *Fraser's Magazine*, 7, 116–130.

Galton, F. (1883). *Inquiries into human faculty*. London: McMillan.

Galton, F. (1884). "The measurement of character." *Fortnightly Review*, 36, 179–185.

Garber, M. (2020). *Character: The history of a cultural obsession*. New York: Farrar, Straus and Giroux.

Gay, P. (1985). *Freud for historians*. New York: Oxford University Press.

Gay, P. (1988). *Freud: A life for our time*. New York: W. W. Norton.

Gaztambide, D. J. (2019). *A people's history of psychoanalysis: From Freud to liberation psychology*. New York: Lexington Books.

Geertz, C. (1984). "From the native's point of view: On the nature of anthropological understanding." *Bulletin of the American Academy of Arts and Sciences*, 28, 26–45.

Goffman, E. (1959). *The presentation of self in everyday life*. Garden City, NY: Anchor Books.

Goffman, E. (1961). *Asylums: Essays on the situation of mental patients and other inmates*. Garden City, NY: Doubleday.

Goffman, E. (1971). *Relations in public: Microstudies of the public order*. New York: Harper.

Goodwin, D. W., & Guze, S. B. (1996). *Psychiatric diagnosis* (5th ed.). New York: Oxford University Press.

Gorer, G. (1943). "Themes in Japanese culture." *Transactions of the New York Academy of Sciences*. Series 2, vol. 5, 106–124.

Gorer, G., & Rickman, J. (1949). *The people of Great Russia*. London: Cresset.

Greenberg, G. (2013). *The book of woe*. New York: Blue Rider Press.

Grinker, R. R., & Spiegel, J. P. (1945). *Men under stress*. Philadelphia: Blakiston.

Grob, G. N. (1983). *Mental illness and American society, 1875–1940*. Princeton, NJ: Princeton University Press.

Grob, G. N. (1991a). "Origins of *DSM-I*: Appearances and reality." *American Journal of Psychiatry*, 148, 421–431.

Grob, G. N. (1991b). *From asylum to community: Mental health policy in modern America*. Princeton, NJ: Princeton University Press.

Grob, G. N. (1994). *The mad among us: A history of the care of America's mentally ill*. New York: Free Press.

Gunderson, J. G. (1983). "*DSM-III* diagnoses of personality disorders." Pp. 20–39 in *Current perspectives on personality disorders* (J. Frosch, ed.). Washington, DC: American Psychiatric Association.

Gunderson, J. G. (2013). "Seeking clarity for future revisions of the personality disorders in *DSM-5*." *Personality Disorders: Theory, Research, and Treatment*, 4, 368–376.

Haeffel, G. J., Jeronimus, B. F., Fisher, A. J., Kaiser, B. N., Weaver, L. J., Vargas, I., & Goodson, J. T. (2021). "HiTop is not an improvement over the *DSM*." *Clinical Psychological Science*. www.researchgate.net/publication/356834904_HiTOP_is_Not_an_Improvement_Over_the_DSM.

Hale, N. (1995). The rise and crisis of psychoanalysis in the United States. New York: Oxford University Press.

Halliwell, M. (2013). *Therapeutic revolutions: Medicine, psychiatry, and American culture, 1945–1970*. New Brunswick, NJ: Rutgers University Press.

Hare, R. (1983/1991). The Hare psychopathy checklist-revised. North Tonawanda, NY: Multi-Health Systems.

Hare, R. D. (1993). *Without conscience: The disturbing world of the psychopaths among us*. New York: Pocket Books.

Harrington, A. (2019). *Mind fixers: Psychiatry's troubled search for the biology of mental illness*. New York: W. W. Norton.

Harris, M. (1968). *The rise of anthropological theory*. New York: Thomas Y. Crowell.

Hartmann, H. (1958). *Ego psychology and the problem of adaptation*. New York: International Universities Press.

Hathaway, S. R. (1964). "MMPI: Professional use by professional people." *American Psychologist*, 19, 204–210.

Hathaway, S. R., & McKinley, J. C. (1940). "A multiphasic personality schedule (Minnesota): I. Construction of the schedule." *Journal of Psychology*, 10, 249–254.

Helvetius, C. A. (1759/2018). *De l'espirit*. Farmington Hills, MI: Gale Ecco.

Helzer, J. E. (2008). "Preface." Pp. xxv–xxvii in *Dimensional approaches in diagnostic classification: Refining the research agenda for DSM-V* (J. E. Helzer et al., eds.). Washington, DC: American Psychiatric Association.

Helzer, J. E., Kraemer, H. C., Krueger, R. F., Wittchen, H.-U., Sirovatka, P. J., & Regier, D. A., eds. (2008). *Dimensional approaches in diagnostic classification: Refining the research agenda for "DSM-V."* Washington, DC: American Psychiatric Association.

Henrich, J. (2020). *The WEIRDest people in the world: How the West became psychologically peculiar and particularly prosperous*. New York: Farrar, Straus and Giroux.

Herman, E. (1995). *The romance of American psychology*. Berkeley: University of California Press.

Herodotus. (1996). *The histories, revised* (J. M. Marincola, ed.). New York: Penguin.

Herzog, D. (2017). *Cold War Freud: Psychoanalysis in an age of catastrophes*. New York: Cambridge University Press.

Hesse, H. (1919/2013). *Demian: The story of Emil Sinclair's youth*. New York: Penguin Classics.

Hippocrates of Cos. (2021). *The sacred disease* (W. H. S. Jones, trans.). Cambridge: Loeb Classical Library. www.loebclassics.com/view/hippocrates_cos-sacred_disease/1923/pb_LCL148.175.xml?readMode=recto.

Hooley, J. M., Cole, S. H., & Gironde, S. (2013). "Borderline personality disorder." Pp. 409–436 in *The Oxford handbook of personality disorders* (T. A. Widiger, ed.). New York: Oxford University Press.

Hopwood, C. J., & Thomas, K. M. (2013). "Paranoid and schizoid personality disorders." Pp. 582–602 in *The Oxford handbook of personality disorders* (T. A. Widiger, ed.). New York: Oxford University Press.

Horkheimer, M. (1950). "The lessons of fascism." Pp. 209–242 in *Tensions that cause wars* (H. Cantril, ed.). Urbana: University of Illinois Press.

Horney, K. (1926). "The flight from womanhood: The masculinity-complex in women as viewed by men and women." *International Journal of Psycho-analysis*, 7, 324–339.

Horney, K. (1935/1967). "The problem of feminine masochism." Pp. 214–233 in *Feminine Psychology*. New York: W. W. Norton.

Horney, K. (1937). *The neurotic personality of our time*. New York: W. W. Norton.

Horney, K. (1939). *New ways in psychoanalysis*. New York: W. W. Norton.

Horney, K. (1967). *Feminine psychology* (H. Kelman, ed.). New York: W. W. Norton.

Horowitz, D. (2010). "David Riesman: From law to social criticism." *Buffalo Law Review*, 58, 1005–1010.

Horowitz, L. M., Post, D. L., French, R. D., Wallis, K. D., & Siegelman, E. Y. (1981). "The prototype as a construct in abnormal psychology." *Journal of Abnormal Psychology*, 90, 575–585.

Horwitz, A. V. (2021). *"DSM": A history of psychiatry's bible*. Baltimore: Johns Hopkins University Press.

Hughes, H. S. (1958). *Consciousness and society: The reorientation of European social thought 1890–1930*. New York: Vintage.

Inkeles, A. (1961). "National character and modern political systems." Pp. 172–208 in *Psychological anthropology* (F. L. K. Hsu, ed.). Homewood, IL: Dorsey Press.

Jacoby, R. (1983). *The repression of psychoanalysis: Otto Fenichel and the political Freudians*. New York: Basic Books.

James, W. (1885/1987). *Essays, comments, and reviews*. Cambridge, MA: Harvard University Press.

James, W. (1890/1950). *The principles of psychology*. New York: Dover.

Jay, M. (1973/1996). *The dialectical imagination: A history of the Frankfurt Institute of Social Research, 1923–1950*. Berkeley: University of California Press.

John, O. P., & Naumann, L. P. (2010). "Surviving two critiques by Block? The resilient Big Five have emerged as the paradigm for personality trait psychology." *Psychological Inquiry*, 21, 44–49.

Journal of the American Medical Association. (1905). August 12. "Editorial," 468.

Jung, C. G. (1921/1971). *Psychological types*. Princeton, NJ: Princeton University Press.

Kadushin, C. (1969). *Why people go to psychiatrists*. New York: Atherton Press.

Kagan, J. (2012). *Psychology's ghosts: The crisis in the profession and the way back*. New Haven, CT: Yale University Press.

Kant, I. (1798/1974). *Anthropology from a pragmatic point of view* (M. J. Gregor, trans.). The Hague: Martinus Nijhoff.

Kardiner, A. (1939). *The individual and his society*. New York: Columbia University Press.

Kardiner, A. (1944). "Some personality determinants in Alorese culture." Pp. 176–190 in *The people of Alor* (C. DuBois, ed.). Minneapolis: University of Minnesota Press.

Kaysen, S. (1993). *Girl, interrupted*. New York: Vintage.

Kendell, R. E. (1975). "The concept of disease and its implications for psychiatry." *British Journal of Psychiatry*, 127, 305–315.

Kendell, R. E., & Jablensky, A. (2003). "Distinguishing between the validity and utility of psychiatric diagnoses." *American Journal of Psychiatry*, 160, 4–12.

Kendler, K. (2005). "Toward a philosophical structure for psychiatry." *American Journal of Psychiatry*, 162, 433–440.

Kendler, K. S., Munoz, R. A., & Murphy, G. (2010). "The development of the Feighner Criteria: A historical perspective." *American Journal of Psychiatry*, 167, 134–142.

Kernberg, O. (1975). *Borderline conditions and pathological narcissism.* New York: Aronson.

Kernberg, O. (1988). "Clinical dimensions of masochism." *Journal of the American Psychoanalytic Association*, 36, 1005–1029.

Kessler, R. C., Demler, O., Frank, R. G., Olfson, M., Pincus, H. A., Walters, E. E., et al. (2005). "Prevalence and treatment of mental disorders, 1990–2003." *New England Journal of Medicine*, 352, 2515–2523.

Kevles, D. J. (1968). "Testing the army's intelligence: Psychologists and the military in World War I." *Journal of American History*, 55, 565–581.

King, C. (2019). *Gods of the upper air.* New York: Doubleday.

Klein, D. F. (1975). "Psychopharmacology and the borderline patient." Pp. 75–92 in *Borderline states in psychiatry* (J. E. Mack, ed.). New York: Grune and Stratton.

Klerman, G. (1983). "The significance of *DSM-III* in American psychiatry." Pp. 3–25 in *International perspectives on "DSM-III"* (R. L. Spitzer, J. B. Williams, & A. E. Skodol, eds.). Washington, DC: American Psychiatric Press.

Koch, J. L. A. (1891). *Die psychopathischen Minderwertigkeiten* [A short textbook of psychiatry]. Ravensburg: Maier.

Kohut, H. (1971). *The analysis of self.* New York: International Universities Press.

Kohut, H. (1973). "Psychoanalysis in a troubled world." *Annual of Psychoanalysis*, 1, 3–25.

Kohut, H. (1977). *The restoration of the self.* New York: International Universities Press.

Kotov, R., Krueger, R. F., Watson, D., Achenbach, T. M., et al. (2017). "The hierarchical taxonomy of psychopathology (HiTOP): A dimensional alternative to traditional nosologies." *Journal of Abnormal Psychology*, 126, 454–477.

Kraemer, H. C., Shrout, P. E., & Rubio-Stipec, M. (2007). "Developing the *Diagnostic and Statistical Manual V*: What will 'statistical' mean in *DSM-V*?" *Social Psychiatry and Psychiatric Epidemiology*, 42, 259–267.

Kraepelin E. (1902). *Clinical psychiatry.* New York: Macmillan.

Kraepelin E. (1904). *Psychiatrie: Ein Lehrbuch* (7th ed.). Leipzig: Barth.

Kraepelin, E. (1909–1915). *Psychiatrie: Ein Lehrbuch* (8th ed.). Leipzig: Barth.

Kraepelin, E. (1921). *Manic-depressive insanity and paranoia* (R. M. Barclay, trans.). Edinburgh: E. & S. Livingstone.

Kretschmer, E. (1925). *Körperbau und Character.* Berlin: Springer Verlag.

Krueger, R. F. (2013). "Personality disorders are the vanguard of the post-*DSM-5.0* era." *Personality Disorders: Theory, Research, and Treatment*, 4, 355–362.

Krueger, R. F., Eaton, N. R., Clark, L. A., et al. (2011). "Deriving an empirical structure for personality pathology for *DSM-5*." *Journal of Personality Disorders*, 25, 170–191.

Krueger, R. F., Kotov, R., Watson, D., & Forbes, M. K. (2018). "Progress in achieving quantitative classification of psychopathology." *World Psychiatry*, 17, 282–293.

Krueger, R. F., Skodol, A. E., Livesley, W. J., Shrout, P. H., & Huang, Y. (2008). "Synthesizing dimensional and categorical approaches to personality disorders." Pp. 85–99 in *Dimensional approaches in diagnostic classification: Refining the research agenda for DSM-V* (J. E. Helzer, H. C. Kraemer, R. F. Krueger, H.-U. Wittchen, P. J. Sirovatka, & D. A. Regier, eds.). Washington, DC: American Psychiatric Association.

Krueger, R. F., & Tackett, J. L. (2003). "Personality and psychopathology: Working toward the bigger picture." *Journal of Personality Disorders*, 17, 109–128.

Kuklick, B. (1977). *The rise of American philosophy.* New Haven, CT: Yale University Press.

Kupfer, D. J., First, M. F., & Regier, D. A. (2002). *A research agenda for "DSM-V."* Washington, DC: American Psychiatric Association.

Kwapil, T. R., & Barrantes-Vidal, N. (2013). "Schizotypal personality disorder: An integrative review." Pp. 437–477 in *The Oxford Handbook of Personality Disorders* (T. A. Widiger, ed.). New York: Oxford University Press.

Laing, R. D. (1967). *The politics of experience and the bird of paradise.* New York: Pantheon.

Landis, C., Zubin, J., & Katz, S. E. (1935). "Empirical evaluation of three personality adjustment inventories." *Journal of Educational Psychology*, 26, 321–330.

Lane, C. (2007). *Shyness: How normal behavior became a sickness.* New Haven, CT: Yale University Press.

Lasch, C. (1979). *The culture of narcissism: American life in an age of diminishing expectations.* New York: W. W. Norton.

Latzman, R. D., Krueger, R. F., DeYoung, C. G., & Michelini, G. (2021). "Connecting quantitatively derived personality—psychopathology models and neuroscience." *Personality Neuroscience*, 4, 1–8.

LeDoux, J. (2002). *Synaptic self: How our brains become who we are.* New York: Penguin.

Lewis, A. (1953). "Health as a social concept." *British Journal of Sociology*, 2, 109–124.

Linehan, M. (2015). *DBT skills training manual* (2nd ed.). New York: Guilford Press.

Linehan, M. (2020). *Building a life worth living.* New York: Random House.

Livesley, W. J. (1998). "Suggestions for a framework for an empirically based classification of personality disorder." *Canadian Journal of Psychiatry*, 43, 137–147.

Livesley, W. J. (2010). "Confusion and incoherence in the classification of personality disorder." *Psychological Injury and Law*, 3, 304–313.

Livesley, W. J. (2012). "Disorder in the proposed *DSM-5* classification of personality disorder." *Clinical Psychology and Psychotherapy*, 19, 364–368.

Loranger, A. W. (1990). "The impact of *DSM-III* on diagnostic practice in a university hospital." *Archives of General Psychiatry*, 47, 672–675.

Luhrmann, T. M. (2000). *Of two minds: The growing disorder in American psychiatry.* New York: Alfred A. Knopf.

Lunbeck, E. (1994). *The psychiatric persuasion.* Princeton, NJ: Princeton University Press.

Lunbeck, E. (2012). "Heinz Kohut's Americanization of Freud." Pp. 209–231 in *After Freud left: A century of psychoanalysis in America.* (J. Burnham, ed.). Chicago: University of Chicago Press.

Lunbeck, E. (2014). *The Americanization of narcissism.* Cambridge, MA: Harvard University Press.

Luyten, P., & Blatt, S. J. (2011). "Integrating theory-driven and empirically-derived models of personality development and psychopathology: A proposal for *DSM-V.*" *Clinical Psychology Review*, 31, 52–68.

MacMillan, M. (2015). *History's people: Personalities and the past.* Toronto: House of Anansi Press.

Makari, G. (2008). *Revolution in mind: The creation of psychoanalysis.* New York: Harper.

Makari, G. (2012). "*Mitteleuropa* on the Hudson: On the struggle for American psychoanalysis after the *Anschluß.*" Pp. 111–123 in *After Freud left: A century of psychoanalysis in America* (J. Burnham, ed.). Chicago: University of Chicago Press.

Malcolm, J. (1982). *Psychoanalysis: The impossible profession.* New York: Vintage.

Malinow, K. (1981). "Passive-aggressive personality." Pp. 121–132 in *Personality disorders* (J. Lion, ed.). Baltimore: Williams & Wilkins.

Malinowski, B. (1923). "Psycho-analysis and anthropology." *Psyche*, 4, 293–322.

Malinowski, B. (1927/2001). *Sex and repression in savage society.* New York: Routledge.

Marcuse, H. (1955/1966). *Eros and civilization: A philosophical inquiry into Freud.* Boston: Beacon Press.

References   209

Marmor, J. (1975). *Psychiatrists and their patients: A national study of private office practice*. Washington, DC: American Psychiatric Association.

Maslow, A. (1963). *Toward a psychology of being*. New York: Wiley.

Matthews, G., Deary, I. J., & Whiteman, M.C. (2009). *Personality traits*. New York: Cambridge University Press.

McCrae, R. R., Gaines, J. F., & Wellington, M. A. (2012). "The five factor model in fact and fiction." Pp. 70–91 in *Handbook of psychology, personality and social psychology*, 2nd ed., vol. 5. (I. B. Weiner, H. A. Tennen, & J. M. Suls, eds.). Hoboken: Wiley.

McCrae, R. R., & John, O. P. (1992). "An introduction to the five factor model and its applications." *Journal of Personality*, 60, 175–215.

McCrae, R. R., Lockenhoff, C. E., & Costa, P. A. (2005). "A step toward *DSM-V*: Cataloguing personality-related problems in living." *European Journal of Psychiatry*, 19, 269–286.

McGoldrick, M. (1982). "Irish families." Pp. 310–339 in *Ethnicity and Family Therapy*. (M. McGoldrick, J. K. Pearce, & J. Giardano, eds.). New York: Guilford Press.

McGuire, W., & Hall, R. F. C. (1977). *C. G. Jung speaking: Interviews and encounters*. Princeton, NJ: Princeton University Press.

McHugh, P. R. (1999). "How psychiatry lost its way." *Commentary*, December, 32–38.

McWilliams, N. (1994). *Psychoanalytic diagnosis: Understanding personality structure in the clinical process*. New York: Guilford Press.

Mead, M. (1928/1971). *Coming of age in Samoa*. New York: Harper Perennial.

Mead, M. (1935/2001). *Sex and temperament in three primitive societies*. New York: Harper Perennial.

Mead, M. (1942/1971). *And keep your powder dry: An anthropologist looks at America* (expanded ed.). New York: William Morrow.

Mead, M. (1949). *Male and female: A study of the sexes in a changing world*. New York: William Morrow.

Mead, M. (1989). "Preface." In R. Benedict, *Patterns of culture*. Boston: Houghton Mifflin.

Mechanic, D., McAlpine, D., & Rochefort, D. (2014). *Mental health and social policy* (6th ed.). New York: Pearson.

Meehl, P. E. (1973). *Psychodiagnosis: Collected papers*. New York: W. W. Norton.

Menninger, K. A. (1930/1945). *The human mind* (3rd ed.). New York: Alfred A. Knopf.

Menninger, W. C. (1947). "Psychiatric experience in the war, 1941–1946." *American Journal of Psychiatry*, 103, 577–586.

Mental Hygiene. (1946). "Revised psychiatric nomenclature adopted by the army." 30, 456–476.

Merikangas, K. (2002). "Genetic epidemiology: bringing genetics to the population—the NAPE Lecture 2001." *Acta Psychiatrica Scandinavica*, 105, 3–13.

Meyer, A. (1938). "The relation of psychiatry to psychology," in *The Collected Papers of Adolf Meyer* (Eunice Winters, ed.), 4 vols. Baltimore: Johns Hopkins University Press.

Mill, J. S. (1869). *The subjection of women*. London: Longman, Green, Reader & Dyer.

Miller, J. D., Few, L. R., & Widiger, T. A. (2013). "Assessment of personality disorders and related traits: Bridging *DSM-IV-TR* and *DSM-5*. Pp. 108–140 in *The Oxford handbook of personality disorders* (T. A. Widiger, ed.). New York: Oxford University Press.

Millon, T. (1981). *Disorders of personality: "DSM-III," Axis II*. New York: John Wiley & Sons.

Millon, T. (1983). "The *DSM-III*: An insider's perspective." *American Psychologist*, 38, 804–814.

Millon, T., & Davis, R. (1996). *Disorders of personality: "DSM-IV" and beyond*. New York: John Wiley & Sons.

Mischel, W. (1968). *Personality and assessment*. New York: Wiley.

Mischel, W., & Shoda, Y. (1995). "A cognitive-affective system theory of personality: Reconceptualizing situations, dispositions, dynamics, and invariance in personality structure." *Psychological Review*, 102, 246–268.

Moffitt, T. (1993). Adolescence-limited and life-course-persistent antisocial behavior: A developmental taxonomy. *Psychological Review*, 100, 674–701.

Mojtabai, R., & Olfson, M. A. (2008). "National patterns in antidepressant treatment by psychiatrists and general medical providers: Results from the National Comorbidity Survey Replication." *Journal of Clinical Psychiatry*, 69, 1064–1074.

Morey, L. C., & Meyer, J. K. (2013). "Course of personality disorder." Pp. 275–295 in *The Oxford handbook of personality disorders* (T. A. Widiger, ed.). New York: Oxford University Press.

Mullan, M. J., & Murray, R. M. (1989). "The impact of molecular genetics on our understanding of the psychoses." *British Journal of Psychiatry*, 154, 591–595.

Münsterberg, H. (1909). *Psychotherapy*. New York: Moffat Yard.

Murray, H. A. (1938). *Explorations in personality*. New York: Oxford University Press.

Myers, I. B. (1980/1995). *Gifts differing: Understanding personality types*. Palo Alto, CA: Davies-Black.

NDTI Review. (1970). "The psychiatrist in private practice." March 2, 1–5.

Nicholson, I. A. M. (2003). *Inventing personality: Gordon Allport and the science of selfhood*. Washington, DC: American Psychological Association.

Paris, B. J. (1994). *Karen Horney: A psychoanalyst's search for self-understanding*. New Haven, CT: Yale University Press.

Paris, J. (1994). *Borderline personality disorder: A multidimensional approach*. Washington, DC: American Psychiatric Association.

Paris, J. (2006). "Neurobiological dimensional models: A review of three models." Pp. 61–72 in *Dimensional models of personality disorders: Refining the research agenda for "DSM-V"* (T. A. Widiger, E. Simonsen, P. J. Sirovatka, & D. A. Regier, eds.). Washington, DC: American Psychiatric Association.

Paris, J. (2013a). "Pathology of personality disorder: An integrative conceptualization. Pp. 399–406 in *The Oxford handbook of personality disorders* (T. A. Widiger, ed.). New York: Oxford University Press.

Paris, J. (2013b). "Anatomy of a debacle: Commentary on 'seeking clarity for future revisions of the personality disorders in *DSM-5*.'" *Personality Disorders*, 4, 377–378.

Paris, J. (2013c). "Stepped care: An alternative to routine extended treatment for patients with borderline personality disorder." *Psychiatric Services*, 64, 1035–1037.

Parsons, T. (1951). *The social system*. New York: Free Press.

Pastar Z., Petrov B., Krizaj A., & Jukic V. (2010). "Diagnoses of personality disorders between 1879 and 1929 in the largest Croatian psychiatric hospital." *Croatia Medical Journal*, 15, 461–467.

Paul, A. M. (2004). *The cult of personality testing*. New York: Free Press.

Phillips, J. (2011). "The great *DSM-5* personality bazaar." *Psychiatric Times* www.psychiatrictimes.com/view/great-dsm-5-personality-bazaar.

Pickersgill, M. (2012). "Standardising antisocial personality disorder: The social shaping of a psychiatric technology." *Sociology of Health and Illness*, 34, 544–559.

Pincus, H. A., Henderson, B., Blackwood, D., & Dial, T. (1993). "Trends in research in two general psychiatric journals in 1969–1990: Research on research." *American Journal of Psychiatry*, 150, 135–142.

Poffenberger, A. T. (1925). "School achievement and success in life." *Journal of Applied Psychology*, 9, 22–28.

Popenoe, P. (1915). "Nature or nurture." *Journal of Heredity*, 6, 238.

Porter, R. (2002). *Madness: A brief history*. New York: Oxford University Press.

Prichard, J. C. (1835). *A treatise on insanity and other disorders affecting the mind*. London: Sherwood, Gilbert and Piper.

Pulver, S. E. (1976). "Survey of psychoanalytic practice 1976." *Journal of the American Psychoanalytic Association*, 26, 615–631.

Quinn, S. (1981). "Oedipus vs. Narcissus." *New York Times*, June 30, 120.

Redlich, F., & Kellert, S. R. (1978). "Trends in American mental health." *American Journal of Psychiatry*, 135, 22–28.

Regier, D. A., Narrow, W. E., Kuhl, E. A., & Kupfer, D. (2009). "The conceptual development of DSM-V." *American Journal of Psychiatry*, 166, 645–650.

Reich, W. (1927/1986). *The function of the orgasm* (V. R. Carfagno, trans.). New York: Macmillan.

Reich, W. (1929/1950). "The genital character and the neurotic character." Pp. 124–144 in *The psychoanalytic reader* (R. Fliess, ed.). New York: International Universities Press.

Reich, W. (1933/1980). *Character analysis* (V. R. Carfagno, trans.). New York: Macmillan.

Reich, W. (1962). *The Sexual Revolution*. New York: Noonday Press.

Richardson, R. D. (2006). *William James: In the maelstrom of American modernism*. New York: Houghton Mifflin.

Rieff, P. (1959). *Freud: The mind of a moralist*. Chicago: University of Chicago Press.

Rieff, P. (1966). *The triumph of the therapeutic*. Chicago: University of Chicago Press.

Riesman, D., Glazer, N., & Denney, R. (1950/1969). *The lonely crowd*. New Haven, CT: Yale University Press.

Roazen, P. (1971). *Freud and his followers*. New York: Da Capo Press.

Roback, A. A. (1927). *The psychology of character*. New York: Harcourt, Brace.

Roback, A. A. (1932–1933). "Personality tests: Whither?" *Character and Personality*, 1, 214–224.

Robins, L. N. (1966). *Deviant children grown up*. Baltimore: Williams & Wilkins.

Robinson, D. N. (1995). *An intellectual history of psychology* (3rd ed.). Madison: University of Wisconsin Press.

Robinson, P. A. (1969). *The Freudian left*. New York: Harper & Row.

Rodgers, C. R. (1980). *A way of being*. Boston: Houghton-Mifflin.

Roheim, G. (1925). *Australian totemism: A psychoanalytical study in anthropology*. London: Allen & Unwin.

Roheim, G. (1950). *Psychoanalysis and anthropology*. New York: International University Press.

Rose, N. (1996). *Inventing ourselves: Psychology, power, and personhood*. New York: Cambridge University Press.

Rosenberg, C. (2007). *Our present complaint: American medicine now and then*. Baltimore: Johns Hopkins University Press.

Rosenhan, D. (1973). "On being sane in insane places." *Science*, 179, 250–258.

Ross, L. (1977). "The intuitive psychologist and his shortcomings: Distortions in the attribution process." *Advances in Experimental Social Psychology*, 10, 173–220.

Rounsaville, B. J., Alarcón, R. D., Andrews, G., Jackson, J. S., Kendell, R. E., & Kendler, K. (2002). "Basic nomenclature issues for DSM-V." Pp. 1–29 in *A research agenda for "DSM-V"* (D. J. Kupfer, M. B. First, & D. A. Regier, eds.). Washington, DC: American Psychiatric Association.

Russ, E., Shedler, J., Bradley, R., & Westen, D. (2008). "Refining the construct of narcissistic personality disorder." *American Journal of Psychiatry*, 165, 1473–1481.

Sacks, O. (1985). *The man who mistook his wife for a hat*. New York: Summit Books.

Sacks, O. (1995). *An anthropologist on Mars*. New York: Alfred A. Knopf.

Samuels, J., & Costa, P. T. (2013). "Obsessive-compulsive personality disorder." Pp. 582–602 in *The Oxford handbook of personality disorders* (T. A. Widiger, ed.). New York: Oxford University Press.

Schlesinger, A. M., Jr. (1949). *The vital center: The politics of freedom*. Boston: Houghton Mifflin.

Schneider, K. (1923/1958). *Psychopathic personalities* (M. W. Hamilton, trans.). London: Cassell.

Seabrook, J. (2008). "Suffering souls: The search for the roots of psychopathy." *New Yorker*, November 10, 64–73.

Searls, D. (2017). *The inkblots: Hermann Rorschach, his iconic test, and the power of seeing*. New York: Crown.

Selective Service System, Medical Circular No. 1. (1941). "Minimum psychiatric inspection." *Journal of the American Medical Association*, 116, 2059–2066.

Shapiro, S., Skinner, E. A., Kramer, M., Steinwachs, D. M., & Regier, D. A. (1985). "Measuring need for mental health services in a general population." *Medical Care*, 23, 1033–1043.

Sharaf, M. (1994). *Fury on earth: A biography of Wilhelm Reich*. Boston: Da Capo Press.

Shea, M. T. (2006). "What to do with the old distinctions?" Pp. 163–167 in *Dimensional models of personality disorders: Refining the research agenda for "DSM-V"* (T. A. Widiger, E. Simonsen, P. J. Sirovatka, & D. A. Regier, eds). Washington, DC: American Psychiatric Association.

Shedler, J., Beck, A., Fonagy, P. Gabbard, G. O., Gunderson, J., Kernberg, O., Michels, R., & Westen, D. (2010). "Personality disorders in *DSM-5*." *American Journal of Psychiatry*, 167, 1026–1028.

Shedler, J., & Westen D. (2004). "Refining *DSM-IV* personality disorder diagnosis: Integrating science and practice." *American Journal of Psychiatry*, 161, 1350–1365.

Shephard, B. (2000). *A war of nerves*. Cambridge, MA: Harvard University Press.

Shorter, E. (1993). *From the mind into the body: The cultural origins of psychosomatic symptoms*. New York: Free Press.

Shorter, E. (1997). *A history of psychiatry: From the era of the asylum to the age of Prozac*. New York: Wiley.

Simon, B. (1978). *Mind and madness in Ancient Greece*. Ithaca, NY: Cornell University Press.

Simonsen, E. (2006). "Focusing on the clinician's need for a better model." Pp. 219–226 in *Dimensional models of personality disorders: Refining the research agenda for "DSM-V"* (T. A. Widiger, E. Simonsen, P. J. Sirovatka & D. A. Regier, eds.). Washington, DC: American Psychiatric Association.

Singer, M. (1961). "A survey of culture and personality theory and research." Pp. 9–90 in *Studying personality cross-culturally* (B. Kaplan, ed.). Evanston, IL: Row, Peterson.

Skinner, B. F. (1956). "A case history of scientific method." *American Psychologist*, 11, 221–233.

Skodol, A. E. (2013). "Diagnosis and *DSM-5*: Work in progress." Pp. 35–57 in *The Oxford handbook of personality disorders* (T. A. Widiger, ed.). New York: Oxford University Press.

Skodol, A. E. (2021). "Manifestations, assessments, diagnosis, and differential diagnosis." Pp. 105–140 in *Textbook of personality disorders* (A. E. Skodol & J. M. Oldham, eds.). Washington, DC: American Psychiatric Association.

Skodol, A. E., Bender, D. S., & Oldham, J. M. (2021). Pp. 65–104 in *Textbook of personality disorders* (A .E. Skodol & J. M. Oldham, eds.). Washington, DC: American Psychiatric Association.

Skodol, A. E., Morey, L. C., Bender, D. S., & Oldham, J. M. (2013). "The ironic fate of the personality disorders in DSM-5." *Personality disorders: Theory, research, and treatment*, 4, 342–349.

Smith, M. B. (1985). *Small comfort: A history of the minor tranquillizers*. New York: Praeger.

Spencer, H. (1873/1933). *Descriptive Sociology*. New York: D. Appleton.

Spiro, M. E. (1993/2010). *Oedipus in the Trobriands*. New Brunswick: Transaction.

Spitzer, R. L., Endicott, J., & Gibbon, M. (1979). "Crossing the border into borderline personality and borderline schizophrenia." *Archives of General Psychiatry*, 36, 973–983.

Spitzer, R. L., Endicott, J., & Robins, E. (1978). "Research diagnostic criteria: rationale and reliability." *Archives of General Psychiatry*, 35, 773–82.

Spitzer, R. L., First, M. B., Shedler, J., Westen, D., & Skodol, A. E. (2008). "Clinical utility of five dimensional systems for personality diagnosis: A 'consumer preference' study." *Journal of Nervous and Mental Disorders*, 196, 356–374.

Spitzer, R. L., & Wilson, P. T. (1969). "*DSM-II* revisited: A reply." *International Journal of Psychiatry*, 7, 421–426.

Statistical Manual for the Use of Institutions for the Insane. (1918). New York: National Committee for Mental Hygiene.

Stearns, P. (1975). *European society in upheaval: Social history since 1750.* New York: MacMillan.

Stern, A. (1938). "Psychoanalytic investigation of and therapy in the border line group of neuroses. *Psychoanalytic Quarterly*, 7, 467–489.

Sullivan, H. S. (1941). "Psychiatry and the national defense." *Psychiatry*, 4, 201–217.

Sullivan, H. S. (1953). *The interpersonal theory of psychiatry.* New York: W. W. Norton.

Susman, W. I. (2003). *Culture as history.* Washington, DC: Smithsonian Institution Press.

Swank, R., & Marchand, W. (1946). "Combat neuroses: Development of combat exhaustion." *Archives of Neurology and Psychiatry*, 55, 236–247.

Szasz, T. (1961). *The myth of mental illness: Foundations of a theory of personal conduct.* New York: Harper & Row.

Talbott, J. A. (1980). "An in-depth look at *DSM-III*: An interview with Robert Spitzer." *Hospital and Community Psychiatry*, 31, 25–32.

Terracciano, A., Sanna, S., Uda, M., Deiana, B., et al. (2010). "Genome-wide association scan for five major dimensions of personality." *Molecular Psychiatry*, 15, 647–656.

Theophrastus. (2018). *Characters: An ancient take on bad behaviors* (J. Romm, ed.). New York: Callaway.

Torgerson, S. (2013). "Epidemiology." Pp. 186–205 in *The Oxford handbook of personality disorders* (T. A. Widiger, ed.). New York: Oxford University Press.

Torgerson, S., Lygren, S., Oien, P. A., Skre, I., Onstad, S., Edvardsen, J., Tambs, K., Kringlen, E. A., et al. (2000). "A twin study of personality disorders." *Comprehensive Psychiatry*, 41, 416–425.

Trull, T. J., Scheiderer, E. M., & Tomko, R. L. (2013). "Axis II comorbidity." Pp. 219–236 in *The Oxford handbook of personality disorders* (T. A. Widiger, ed.). New York: Oxford University Press.

Trump, M. L. (2020). *Too much and never enough.* New York: Simon & Schuster.

Tyrer, P. (2012). "Diagnostic and Statistical Manual of Mental Disorders: A classification of personality disorders that has had its day." *Clinical Psychology and Psychotherapy*, 19, 372–374.

Tyrer, P. (2018). *Taming the beast within: Shredding the stereotypes of personality disorder.* London: Shedler Press.

Tyrer, P., Mulder, R., Kim, Y.-R., & Crawford, M. J. (2019). "The development of the ICD-11 classification of personality disorders: An amalgam of science, pragmatism, and politics." *Annual Review of Clinical Psychology*, 15, 481–502.

Tyrer, P., Reed, G. M., & Crawford, M. J. (2015). "Classification, assessment, prevalence, and effect of personality disorder." *Lancet*, 385, 717–726.

Vaillant, G. E. (1984). "The disadvantages of *DSM-III* outweigh the advantages." *American Journal of Psychiatry*, 141, 542–545.

Verheul, R. (2012). "Personality disorder proposal for *DSM-5*: A heroic and innovative but nevertheless fundamentally flawed attempt to improve *DSM-IV*." *Clinical Psychology and Psychotherapy*, 19, 369–371.

Wakefield, J. C. (1992). "The concept of mental disorder: On the boundary between biological facts and social values." *American Psychologist*, 47, 373–388.

Wakefield, J. C. (2008). "The perils of dimensionalization: Challenges in distinguishing negative traits from personality disorder." *Psychiatric Clinics of North America*, 31, 379–393.

Wakefield, J. C. (2013). "DSM-5: An overview of major changes and controversies." *Clinical Social Work Journal*, 41, 139–154.

Wakefield, J. C. (2022). "Klerman's 'credo' reconsidered: Neo-Kraepelinianism, Spitzer's views, and what we can learn from the past." *World Psychiatry*, 21, 4–25.

Wallerstein, R. S. 1991. "The future of psychotherapy." *Bulletin of the Menninger Clinic*, 55, 421–443.

Wang, P. S., Lane, M., Olfson, M., Pincus, H. A., Wells, K. B., & Kessler, R. C. (2005). "Twelve-month use of mental health services in the United States." *Archives of General Psychiatry*, 62, 629–640.

Ward, S. C. (2002). *Modernizing the mind: Psychological knowledge and the remaking of society.* Westport, CT: Praeger.

War Department. (1946). "Nomenclature of psychiatric disorders and reactions." Technical Bulletin, *Medical 203. Journal of Clinical Psychology*, 2, 289–296.

Watson, J. B. (1913). "Psychology as the behaviorist views it." *Psychological Review*, 20, 158–177.

Watson, J. B. (1923). "Jung as Psychologist." *New Republic*, November 7.

Watson, J. B. (1924). *Behaviorism.* Chicago: People's Institute.

Watz, M. (2011). "An historical analysis of character education." *Journal of Inquiry & Action in Education*, 4, 34–53.

Westen, D. (1998). "The scientific legacy of Sigmund Freud: Toward a psychodynamically informed psychological science." *Psychological Bulletin*, 124 (3), 333–371.

Westen, D., & Arkowitz-Weston, L. (1998). "Limitations of Axis II in diagnosing pathology in clinical practice." *American Journal of Psychiatry*, 155, 1767–1771.

Westen, D., Heim, A., Morrison, K., et al. (2002). "Simplifying diagnosis using a prototype-matching approach: Implications for the next edition of the *DSM*." Pp. 221–250 in *Rethinking the "DSM": A psychological perspective* (L. E. Beutler & M. L. Malik, eds). Washington, DC: American Psychological Association.

Westen, D., & Kegley, A. R. (2021). "Theories of personality and personality disorders." Pp. 13–46 in *Textbook of personality disorders* (A. E. Skodol & J. M. Oldham, eds.). Washington, DC: American Psychiatric Association.

Westen D., Shedler, J., & Bradley R. (2006). "A prototype approach to personality disorder diagnosis." *American Journal of Psychiatry*, 163, 846–856.

White, L. (1942). *The Pueblo of Santa Ana, New Mexico.* Memoir 60. Menasha, WI: American Anthropological Association.

Whitlock, W. A. (1982). "A note on moral insanity and psychopathic disorders." *Bulletin of the Royal College of Psychiatrists*, 6, 57–59.

Whooley, O. (2019). *On the heels of ignorance: Psychiatry and the politics of not knowing.* Chicago: University of Chicago Press.

Whooley, O., & Horwitz, A. V. (2013). "The paradox of professional success: Grand ambition, furious resistance, and the derailment of the *DSM-5* revision." Pp. 75–94 in *Making the "DSM-5": Concepts and controversies* (J. Paris & J. Phillips, eds). New York: Springer.

Whyte, W. H. (1956). *The organization man.* New York: Simon & Schuster.

Wickware, F. S. (1947). "Psychoanalysis." *Life*, February 3, 1947, 98.

Widiger, T. A. (2011). "The DSM-5 dimensional model of personality disorder: Rationale and empirical support." *Journal of Personality Disorders*, 25, 222–234.

Widiger, T. A. (2013). "Historical developments and current issues." Pp. 13–34 in *The Oxford handbook of personality disorders* (T. A. Widiger, ed.). New York: Oxford University Press.

Widiger, T. A., & Clark, L. A. (2000). "Toward *DSM-V* and the classification of psychopathology." *Psychological Bulletin*, 126, 946–963.

Widiger, T. A., Samuel, D. B., Mullins-Sweatt, S., Gorre, W. L., & Crego, C. (2013). "An integration of normal and abnormal personality structure: The five-factor model." Pp. 82–107 in

The Oxford handbook of personality disorders (T. A. Widiger, ed.). New York: Oxford University Press.

Widiger, T. A., & Simonsen, E. (2005). "Alternative dimensional models of personality disorder: Finding a common ground." *Journal of Personality Disorders*, 19, 110–130.

Widiger, T. A., Simonsen, E., Sirovatka, P. J., & Regier, D. A., eds. (2007). *Dimensional models of personality disorder*. Washington, DC: American Psychiatric Press.

Wilson, T. (2002). *Strangers to ourselves: Discovering the adaptive unconscious*. Cambridge, MA: Belknap Press.

Wolfe, T. (1976). "The 'me' decade and the third great awakening." *New York Magazine*, August 23, 126–167.

Woodworth, R. S. (1917). *Personal data sheet*. Chicago: C. H. Stoelting.

Wrong, D. (1961). "The oversocialized conception of man in modern sociology." *American Sociological Review*, 26, 183–193.

Zachar, P. (2011). "The clinical nature of personality disorders: Answering the neo-Szaszian critique." *Philosophy, Psychiatry, & Psychology*, 8(3), 191–202.

Zachar, P., Krueger, R. F., & Kendler, K. S. (2016). "Personality disorder in DSM-5: An oral history." *Psychological Medicine*, 46, 1–10.

Zanarini, M. C., Frankenburg, F., Reich, D. B., & Fitzmaurice, G. (2010). "Time to attainment of recovery from borderline personality disorder and stability of recovery: A 10-year prospective follow-up study." *American Journal of Psychiatry*, 167, 663–667.

Zaretsky, E. (2004). *Secrets of the soul: A social and cultural history of psychoanalysis*. New York: Alfred A. Knopf.

Zenderland, L. (1999). *Measuring minds: Henry Herbert Goddard and the origins of American intelligence testing*. New York: Cambridge University Press.

mood disorders, 14, 21, 116, 118, 120

moral insanity, 20–21, 113. *See also* antisocial personality disorder; psychopathy

morality and character, 5, 6. *See also* value judgments in defining personality disorders

Morgan, James A., 112

mothers: and borderline personality disorder, 84; as center of family, 55; and ego psychology, 187n52; and narcissistic disorders, 83

multiaxial system of *DSM*, 107–9, 123, 128, 133–35, 142, 151, 156. *See also* dimensional models

Münsterberg, Hugo, 33

Murray, Henry, 97

Myers-Briggs Type Indicator (MBTI), 32, 110

narcissism: in Adler, 47; and borderline personality disorder, 116–17, 119; Freud on, 26, 29, 30, 84, 120–21; and homosexuality, 26; and psychoanalysis post–World War II, 82, 83, 84–85, 121; in Stern, 116–17; and success, 16

narcissistic personality disorder: in *DSM-II*, 77, 112; in *DSM-III*, 108, 109, 120–21; in *DSM-5*, 146–47, 149, 150, 158, 195n112; overlap with antisocial personality disorder, 146; precursors to, in Schneider, 22; and research volume, 124, 133, 146; and value judgments, 158

National Institute of Mental Health (NIMH), 100, 136, 151, 173

national personality or character, 9, 12–13, 73–74, 89

natural selection, 63

natural vs. cultural world debate, 11–14, 169–71

Nazism, 48, 60–61, 70, 170

neo-Freudian school, 9, 45–46, 53–61, 64, 85, 170

neurochemical systems: lack of findings on, 133, 134, 142, 170–71; and natural vs. cultural world debate, 11–12, 170–71; rise of research studies in, 133, 134

neurosis: in Freud, 18, 24, 26–29; in Menninger, 75; in neo-Freudians, 55–57; in PEN model, 138; in Reich, 50

Neurotic Constitution, The (Adler), 46

Neurotic Personality of Our Time, The (Horney), 56

neurotic type in Menninger, 75

New Introductory Lectures on Psychoanalysis (Freud), 28

New Ways in Psychoanalysis (Horney), 58

Nicomachean Ethics (Aristotle), 2

nidotherapy, 178

NIMH (National Institute of Mental Health), 100, 136, 151, 173

normality and personality tests, 38, 41–42, 92, 95–96

normal personality vs. personality disorders, challenge of differentiating: in culture and personality school, 56, 57, 65–66, 67; and dimensional approaches, 165–66; in *DSM-III*, 103, 105, 116, 124–25; in *DSM-5*, 16, 147, 150; in *DSM-5* Section III, 174–75, 176; and five-factor model, 138; in *ICD*, 174; in neo-Freudians, 56, 57; overview of, viii, 16–17, 155–58, 162–63; in psychoanalysis, 29–30, 49, 51, 52–53, 56, 57; and psychology's focus on normality, 34–36

NOS (personality disorder not otherwise specified), 109, 134–35, 144, 145, 150, 180n69

Nussbaum, Kurt, 107–8, 109

object relations, school of, 187n52

obsessive-compulsive disorders: in *DSM-III*, 108, 133; in *DSM-IV*, 149; in *DSM-5*, 16, 146, 149, 195n112; in the military, 73; precursors to, in Freud, 25; precursors to, in Schneider, 22; and research volume, 133

Oedipus complex, 27, 54, 55, 59, 65, 85

"On Narcissism" (Freud), 26

oral character type and stage, 25, 42, 48, 89

orderliness, 25

Organization Man (Whyte), 95, 96

orgone accumulators, 52

outer-directed personality, 85

paranoia: in culture and personality school, 65–66, 158; in *Medical 203*, 76

paranoid personality disorder: in *DSM-I*, 76, 125; in *DSM-II*, 109, 125; in *DSM-III*, 109, 122, 125; in *DSM-5*, 15–16, 149; and inflexibility, 164; precursors to, in Kraepelin and Schneider, 21–22; and research volume, 133

paranoid personality type in *Medical 203*, 76

Paris, Joel, 142, 167, 197n82

parsimony, 25

passive-aggressive personality disorder: in *DSM-I*, 76–77, 110; in *DSM-II*, 77, 109, 110; in *DSM-III*, 109, 122; in *DSM-IV*, 128; in *DSM-5*, 149; increase in diagnoses, 81; and research volume, 133

pathos, 3

Patterns of Culture (Benedict), 65–66

Paul, Annie Murphy, 93

reliability: and *DSM-III*, 101, 116, 125, 127; and
 DSM-5, 142; projective tests, 97
repression: in Freud, 29, 45, 51, 55, 82; in Jung, 31;
 in Reich, 51
research: future trends in, 172–73; growth of, 98;
 homogeneity of samples, 92, 169, 171; psychology's focus on, 8, 18, 32–37, 159; and social
 sciences post–World War II, 85–90; and
 Washington University, 102
Research Domain Criteria, 151, 173
researchers vs. clinicians: and challenges in de-
 fining personality disorders, 154, 161–62; and
 dimensional models, 173, 177; and *DSM-III*,
 98–99, 102–3, 105–8, 120, 123–24, 131–33; and
 DSM-5, 145–53, 161, 162; and multiaxial ap-
 proach, 108
Rieff, Philip, 70
Riesman, David, 87–89, 161
rigidity. *See* inflexibility
Roback, A. A., 39
Robins, Lee, 106, 115–16
Rockland, Lawrence, 118
Róheim, Géza, 62
Rorschach, Hermann, 96
Rorschach test, 96
Rose, Nikolas, 14
Rosenhan, David, 99
Ross, Lee, 196n43
Rush, Benjamin, 181n7
Russia, national character of, 74

Sacks, Oliver, 10, 12
sadistic personality disorder, 130, 131
sadomasochistic personalities: and authoritarian-
 ism, 60–61, 86; in Kernberg, 188n76; masochistic
 personality disorder, 129–30; sadistic personality
 disorder, 130, 131
Schildkraut, Joseph, 99
schizoid personality disorder: in *DSM-I*, 76, 110;
 in *DSM-II*, 109, 110, 111; in *DSM-III*, 109, 111–12,
 122; in *DSM-5*, 15–16, 149; increase in diagnoses
 post–World War II, 81; and inflexibility, 164;
 precursors to, in Kretschmer and Schneider, 22
schizoid personality type in *Medical 203*, 76
schizoid temperament in Kretschmer, 22
schizoid type in Menninger, 75
schizophrenia, 14, 112, 119, 195n112
schizothymic temperament in Kretschmer, 22

schizotypal personality disorder: in *DSM-III*, 109,
 111, 112; in *DSM-5*, 15–16, 146, 149, 195n112; and
 inflexibility, 164; and research volume, 124, 133;
 and temperament in Kretschmer, 22
Schneider, Kurt, 22
school of object relations, 187n52
Scientific Review Committee, 151
scoring: and dimensional models, 166; and MMPI,
 92, 94, 95–96; personality tests, 41–42
Selective Service Commission, 71–72
self, unity of, 29
self-assessment: vs. assessment by others, 169;
 Freud on, 41; and future trends in dimensional
 models, 175; and personality tests, 38, 40, 41, 91;
 and stability vs. situational debate, 168–69
self-defeating personality disorder, 130–31
self-esteem: and borderline personality disorder,
 117; and narcissistic personality disorder, 147;
 self-esteem movement, 83
self-psychology, 82–83
self-realization, 57
separation anxiety, 62
Sex and Temperament in Three Primitive Societies
 (Mead), 66
sexism, 54, 58
sexuality: in Adler, 47; and culture, 56, 65, 66;
 as foundational in psychoanalysis, 25–26; in
 Horney, 58; in *Medical 203*, 76; in neo-Freudians,
 58; in Reich, 51–52; sexual autonomy of women,
 55, 56; in tripartite theory, 27–29
sexually deviant personality disorder, 77
sexually deviant personality type, in *Medical 203*, 76
shell shock, 37
Shorter, Edward, 78
Siever, Larry, 144
Simonsen, Erik, 140
Skinner, B. F., 90, 170
Skodol, Andrew, 144, 169
Smiles, Samuel, 5
social aspects: anthropology's focus on culture and
 social aspects of personality, 46, 61–68, 161, 170;
 changing norms and interest in, 45–46; in ego
 psychology, 53, 80; and Frankfurt School, 85–86;
 and Freud on need for repression of individualism, 29, 45, 51, 55, 82; and future trends in
 dimensional models, 176; and future trends in
 research, 172–73; of identity, 89; and narcissism,
 85, 121; and natural vs. cultural world debate

121–23, 125, 157; in *DSM-5*, 157–58; in early
psychiatry, 21; and future trends in dimensional
models, 176; in historical approaches, 2–4; in
Kraepelin, 15, 21, 156–57; in *Medical 203*, 76; and
psychology's rejection of character concept, 34;
and psychopathic/antisocial personalities, 21,
104; as ubiquitous, vii, 15, 156–58; and women,
123
Verheul, Roel, 152
veterans, 71, 73
virtue, 2–3

Wallerstein, Robert, 132
Washington University, 102, 118
Watson, John, 32, 33–34, 170
WEIRD personalities, 171
West, the (civilization): psychoanalysis's focus on,
65; and WEIRD personalities, 171
Westen, Drew, 140
White, Leslie, 67
Whyte, William, 90–91, 95, 96, 110, 157, 176

Widiger, Thomas, 139, 144, 148
Wilson, Timothy, 168–69
women: and borderline personality disorder, 117;
and cultural/social norms, 45, 46, 54–58; and
masochistic personality disorder, 129–30; and
mood disorders in Kraepelin, 116; oppression
of and personality disorders, 122–23; and rise
of personality as term, 5–6
Woodworth, Robert, 38
World Health Organization, 107
World War I, 26–27, 37, 184n30
World War II, 70, 78–79
Wrong, Dennis, 28
Wundt, Wilhelm, 32–33, 159

Yerkes, Robert, 38
youth: and counterculture, 82, 89–90; and mental
hygiene movement, 23–24

Zachar, Peter, 195n18, 196n18
Zaretsky, Eli, 82

OTHER BOOKS BY THE AUTHOR
FROM HOPKINS PRESS

Anxiety
A Short History
Allan V. Horwitz

"Horwitz's touch is light and ironical and his scholarship impeccable . . . It is a book to be savored by disease buffs."
—Edward Shorter, *Bulletin of the History of Medicine*

PTSD
A Short History
Allan V. Horwitz

"In the context of sociocultural forces and timeless controversies, Horwitz brings to light the 'construction' and 'contentious history' of PTSD."
—Gerald M. Rosen, University of Washington (emeritus)

DSM
A History of Psychiatry's Bible
Allan V. Horwitz

"*DSM: A History of Psychiatry's Bible* is the first comprehensive account of American psychiatry's growing obsession with diagnosis, and the massive flaws that have undermined this project."
—Andrew Scull, author of *Madness in Civilization: A Cultural History of Insanity from the Bible to Freud*